Han Suyin has written a poignant love-story set against the background of a China ravaged by the merciless four-year war with Japan.

"An extremely valuable piece of work, and with considerable literary merit" *Time and Tide*

Also by Han Suyin in Panther Books

Han Suyin

Destination Chungking

Panther

Granada Publishing Limited
Published in 1973 by Panther Books Ltd
Frogmore, St Albans, Herts AL2 2NF
Reprinted 1976

First published in Great Britain by
Jonathan Cape Ltd 1942
Made and printed in Great Britain by
C. Nicholls & Company Ltd
The Philips Park Press, Manchester
Set in Intertype Plantin

Contents

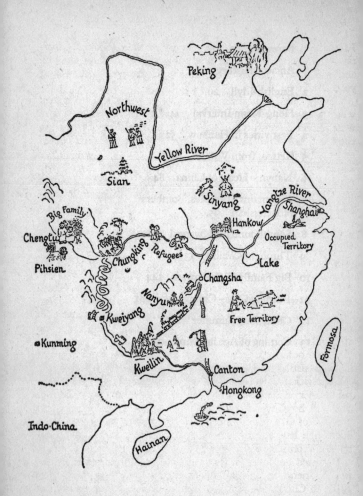

FOREWORD

I have been asked to write a new foreword to my book, *Destination Chungking,* which was first published in England in 1942, and which, my publisher informs me, is to be reissued, eleven years later.

Casting back mind and body to eleven years ago, to myself when young in Chungking at war, I recall the world as it then was, a solid one; words of assured meaning; ends self-evident, right and honourable; doubt a grievous offence against oneself and others; virtue, and faith, carrying one through hunger, pain and trouble. One was sure to live to laugh again, to enjoy life in spite of present trouble and the ever-recurring theme of bombing which accompanied each sunny day; everything was surely going to come right in the end.

I did not have the intention to write anything. I worked, an apprentice midwife, in a small midwifery hospital run by Marian Manly, an American missionary, in Chengtu in the province of Szechwan. Pao my husband was away in the north-west, and during his absence I stayed with Marian in her hospital.

Marian's father and mother had been missionaries in China. Her sister was a missionary. She herself, a missionary doctor, had spent most of her life in China. She had designed and built this small hospital, and there she trained Chinese midwives who after graduation went out into the countryside, and settled in the small outlying towns, doing the most needed work of all in China, assisting other women in their childbirth toil.

I sat with her one night over a charcoal fire glowing in a copper brazier in her room, and we spoke of books we had read. She said how often she had wanted to gather the human experience of her years of love and compassion in China into a book. She had already written many short stories and poems, but not a complete book.

I showed her jottings, fragments written, in moments of idleness, to friends in England who wanted to know how things were going in China. She scanned them and said: "There's a lot of good material in this; it could be worked into a story. Why not make a book of it?"

I was frightened. My English learnt in Peking when I was only ten years old, and mostly acquired through reading, not through conversation, would never be sufficient to write a book.

But Marian was fired with a great enthusiasm, and it was her enthusiasm which carried us through the writing of *Destination Chungking*.

As I said in the previous foreword, *Destination Chungking* was written piecemeal; in the evening by oil light in what was left of the room after the day's bombing; in the afternoon returning from a night- and morning-long case; in intervals of respite between cooking, cleaning, and peering at the sky for more enemy airplanes. Wedged in with the family cooking pot and my daughter I carried to the shelter of the hill dugout the manuscript of *Destination Chungking*.

Very nearly through most of the writing Marian and I were divided by distance; I with Pao in Chungking, or following him round Free China; she stuck to her hospital in Chengtu. Yet our collaboration was uninterrupted and devoted, and although it is trite to say it, it is true that without Marian's corrections, criticism, and often recasting of whole chapters, *Destination Chungking* would not have seen the light.

Whenever I had finished a chapter, I sent it off by air mail to Marian. Back and forth over Chungking flew the manuscript, from author to co-author, typed on flimsy translucent Chinese silk paper, the lightest to pack tight into airmail envelopes.

Then one day a publisher accepted it.

But the authorship of the book could not, at the time, be publicly acknowledged, and for an odd reason. I had become, if only temporarily, through my husband, a member of my country's diplomatic corps. Ladies of the diplomatic corps do not write books. The set in which I lived considered writing an unwomanly occupation, destructive of one's moral character, like acting. Even that enormously vital and fascinating autobiography, *Huilan Koo*, by Madame Wellington Koo, wife of the present Ambassador of Nationalist China to Washington, was abruptly and undeservedly withdrawn from circulation. I was lucky to acquire one copy before its extinction. *Destination Chungking* suffered no such fate, but I remained, for many years, diffident about it.

That is the story behind *Destination Chungking*.

Apart from this new introduction, I have made no essential alterations in the original text, apart from a few corrections of errors in grammar and spelling.

HAN SUYIN

February 1953

8

CHAPTER ONE

ANCIENT HISTORY

Ever since the day Pao pulled off the red strings wound tight around my three stiff little pigtails, and sent me howling to my mother, we have not been able to do without each other. Most of the time there lay an unfinished quarrel between us and, neither willing to let it rest, we stubbornly sought each other for a chance to renew it. Now in our life together the contrary pull of our will and thought continues still, to spice with excitement the deep accord of our marriage.

As children we shared the same games along the banks of the canal, beneath the willow-trees, the dusty, grey-green willows of Peking – always the war games of Pao's choice. When we grew older and taller we were by ancient Chinese custom separated. I must not run and shout in the street like a little vagabond. I must keep within gates, learn prim, modest ways, the deportment of a lady. Pao, at the age of twelve, must enter upon the serious studies which were to prepare him for his destined place in life as a fit representative of his family. We were no longer permitted to see each other; it was not seemly for growing boys and girls to play together like children. We shed rebellious tears; we composed pre-suicide verses, concealed them under our tear-wet pillows; slept soundly over our tragedies . . . forgot, almost. . . .

Pao's home and mine were in the same street in Peking, a half-street that ambled leisurely along the bank of a canal in the Forbidden City: on the one side blank, secret walls and roofed gateways flanked by curled and grinning carved stone lions; on the other side the willows and the water. Pao's house was very important, much the richest and most noble in our street. Great gates opened upon a vista through courtyard after courtyard, spacious, imposing. Pillared pavilions supported wide roofs that swept in stately curves against the sky. Gold leaf and lacquer and deep-cut carving made splendid the doors and pillars. My home at the far end of the short street was quite modest by comparison – a single courtyard surrounded by small, unpretentious rooms.

This great house of Pao's family was in a continual stir of magnificent activity, fascinating to all the children in our street.

We would gather about the gateway, watching, listening. It was a pageant for our benefit and we missed none of it. In the morning we came running to see the departure of Pao's father for the yamen, where the government offices were. The mounted bodyguard would be drawn up at the gates, waiting. The lord of the house would issue forth, take his place in his carriage, and drive away, with the solemn clatter of many hoofs accompanying him.

Later in the forenoon came merchants. It might be a slender, smart young clerk, carrying some small and valuable parcel. It might be the proprietor of a shop himself, plump and prosperous, idly wafting his fan, followed by apprentices loaded with bundles and boxes. For the women of this household preferred not to soil their satin shoes, running about the streets. They lived for the most part secluded within their own inner courtyards, and when they wished to purchase anything – whether silks, or thin porcelain bowls and cups, or ear-rings of silver-gilt set with jade or coral – a selection was brought for their choice. They were seldom seen in the thronged markets of Peking – Lung Fu Ssü, Tung An Shih – where one could buy a monkey or the latest American novel, or flower-pots, Japanese shirts, canned pineapples, microscopes, and paper frogs, so various were the wares.

At noon in the winter we watched the "doing of good works". Files of the poor and beggars would come on the hour as though summoned. They would stand at the gates with their cracked bowls and pots, waiting for the gift of food each day distributed. The stewards of the household then came out, carrying huge crocks of *jow,* the soft-cooked rice, steaming in the frosty air. They would ladle out the *jow* into the bowls held out to them by gaunt and dirty hands, and the beggars would warm their hands on the bowls as they sucked up the scalding hot rice.

Most dazzling of all the glories of Pao's house, to the watching children, were feast nights, when guests came riding to the gates in rickshaws and four-wheeled open carriages, all tinkling with bells on the harness, with footmen attending before and behind. We edged into the outer courtyards, as close as we might come to the centre of festivity in the high court beyond. Here we could see and hear and even smell of things sumptuous, as gorgeously robed ladies passed us almost close enough to touch, smelling of flowers and sandalwood and musk; and hurrying servants crossed and recrossed the courtyard bearing great bowls and platters that left on the air a trail of exquisite savour to make the mouth water.

Creeping still closer we would watch, enchanted, the actors

brought to entertain the company, the best in Peking (and that meant the best in China!). Emperors and heroes of long-ago dynasties came to life in their song and pantomime, to the brazen music of gongs and cymbals, the intricate beat of drums, the shrill quaver of stringed instruments. We knew by heart each play and legend; we hailed by name the characters as they appeared, recognizing Tsao-Tsao by his treacherous, skull-white face and loyal Kung by his green robe and scarlet complexion, and the clowns with a tiny white patch over the bridge of the nose. Before a word was spoken we knew what scene was to be played. We were endlessly fascinated by the gold-encrusted robes, the helmets plumed with yard-long pheasant feathers. And even to us, children though we were, there was significance and beauty in the stylized acting. There was excitement and meaning in the dance combat with spears and swords whirling, gowns and pheasant feathers whirling, drums and cymbals clashing, lights glancing gold and violet and crimson over the rich embroidered robes. . . .

Pao was a part of all this splendour, yet one of us. He escaped the walled-in grandeur of the great house to run and play in the street with us, in the utter, unself-conscious democracy of childhood which never is recaptured by deliberate effort in later years. He was our acknowledged leader, not by any imposed standards of rank and wealth, but by natural right. All our games were games of war and fighting. Pao was our general; he organized us into an army and we held pitched battles with the boys in the next street. I strove loyally to be worthy of Pao's approbation as a good henchman, but fell short in many respects. Being a girl, I could not match the boys in running or fighting. But when called upon to be "wounded" I excelled in dramatic fervour, with loud cries of agony so convincing that passers-by would pause to ask what ailed me.

As far back as our short memories went the children of our generation knew frequent war, chaos, fighting. None of us but had a first-hand acquaintance with civil war. Even in our quiet street, where willows bowed lazily to their reflection in the sluggish canal, war was a recurrent alarm. The armies of rival war lords fought back and forth for control of the north and for Peking with its rich revenues. Sometimes the conqueror was welcomed, if he had a reputation as a lenient ruler who did not over-tax and who restrained his soldiers and kept them in order. Flags were hung out at every door – the original five-striped flag, red, white, blue, yellow, black, that preceded the present bright-sun

11

flag. Fire-crackers sputtered with sharp explosions and blue smoke. Gay *pai-lou,* triumphal arches, spanned the streets as the fickle city rejoiced in a new lord and decked herself to greet him. But again, when the winning war lord was known to have no ideal or incentive except the desire for loot, for power; when it was his custom to turn loose his lawless, hungry troops for three days' plunder unchecked, then all our courtyard gates were closed and the city lay silent, cowering, sullenly afraid. Through slits in the gates we children watched the newly victorious soldiers marching through our street in ranks, or roving in disorganized bands, looking for loot. Sometimes, with a tingling delight in adventure, we slipped out, unnoticed. Who would harm us? We were only children. Martial law kept our elders within doors. We explored a world disordered, brought home horrific rumours of riot and executions. We learned of war.

The war lords were a curious phenomenon born of the uncertain times when no strong central government existed to keep law and order throughout the length and breadth of China. The Manchu Dynasty was overthrown but as yet no unifying power had been established to take its place. In ancient Chinese history you may read how, when dynasties fell into decay, this huge, unwieldy nation broke up into warring states, into small, divided kingdoms, each with its own master; how these made alliances, fought, conquered, united, until finally a new dynasty emerged and the country was again one nation. The war lords of our own time were an anachronism transposed from such a chapter of our history. Half-legendary figures – here a petty magistrate of the old regime; there an ambitious, uneducated minor officer; or a bandit with his army of desperadoes; or a shrewd old classical scholar; or a thoughtful peasant rising into leadership by force of will; or a renegade revolutionist bought by foreign capital; or a high councillor of the abolished empire. Power was for anyone who could seize it. It was his to use as he would, and his as long as he could hold it against the encroachment of his rivals.

It is not strange that in a time of governmental impotence such opportunists set up each his own sphere of dominion and fought, each with his neighbour, to extend his sovereignty. What is strange and a matter for admiration and wonder is that, throughout the era of the war lords, China still considered herself one nation – *was* one nation, undivided in spirit. Her people were united as a people. Except in time of active fighting in some limited area, people passed freely from one region to another, and education spread, and gradually the idea of a Republic of China penetrated past all barriers and through all classes of society. So strong was this inner consciousness of "one people under heaven", as the old Chinese proverb states it, that even the most despotic of the war lords paid their respects to it. Some kind of national government persisted for diplomatic and educational purposes. No war lord ever seceded from China. Each still considered his private kingdom as a section of one nation, to be reunited politically in good time (preferably under himself as emperor or the equivalent). And regardless of the rivalries of her petty masters, China – the people – remained unperturbed by any sectional hatred, consciously one race, one people, under a government temporarily somewhat disjointed.

Pao and I and the others of our generation are the children of this chaotic period. We were born in the midst of the war. War clouded our childhood. Ever since we could comprehend the speech of our elders we have heard talk of war, of fighting. Our own lives were all entangled with history in the making; our selves, our families, were involved in its tragic events. Later there were a few brief years of seeming peace, lived in the intensity of youth's awareness, when we grasped avidly for all experiences of beauty and joy, in the knowledge of imminent invasion – then the lightning storm of a new and more terrible war. We do not know what it is not to fear catastrophe.

My family came to Peking first as refugees. Our ancestral home was in far-distant Szechwan Province, beyond the mountains in the west, on the borders of Tibet. I had never seen Szechwan. I was born in Honan. When I was five or six years old we had our home in the town of Sinyang, where my father held a post on the railway as engineer. We lived in a fine house provided by the railway administration, with a big garden and sheds for animals. We kept chickens, pigs, and one or two cows. I had a lamb given to me which I loved like a sister. It was a tiny, limp-eared, knob-kneed creature about as big as a rabbit, wrapped in a fuzz of off-white wool. It followed me about crying "Ma-a-a." We could not be parted. I was troubled that my lamb should live in the shed with other mere animals. I brought it up to the house, into the parlour where my mother was entertaining guests.

"Take that little beast down to the stables before it does anything."

"But it's cold, Mother. It is going to be night-time and my lamb will be cold."

"Lambs don't get cold. Do you think you are going to take it to bed with you? Go away with it at once."

I knew it was useless to argue further. Grimly I prepared to obey to the letter. I went about collecting old sweaters and padded garments in which to swathe my treasure, and exiled myself to the stable with the lamb. We lay down together, wrapped in a torn quilt, and fell asleep. Late in the evening the servants found me and carried me, still sleeping, to my bed. In the morning my lamb greeted me alive and frisking.

In the garden also lived a friendly tame hedgehog. I set out food for it each day and called it by name. It learned to recognize my voice and come hurrying like a plump, overgrown caterpillar, making little squeaking noises.

In Sinyang we were almost rich. Therefore when the tide of civil war shifted the borders of some war lord's territory and his troops passed through Sinyang upon campaigns which involved more marching and display of numbers than actual fighting, our home might be requisitioned as headquarters for the higher officers. Our household shared the policy of appeasement with which towns and cities greeted their conquerors: Welcome them, feed them, and send them on their way in amiable mood.

We had our preferences in the matter of war lords. They were by no means of one stamp. Once when Sinyang had fallen bloodlessly to a new master, the commander and his bodyguards were our guests for supper. His tents were pitched in our garden. His soldiers were billeted in almost every house in town, but they were quite orderly and paid for what they took. The commander was an enormous man – fully seven feet tall and broad in proportion – or so it seemed to one small girl at that first encounter. My estimate has required only slight revision upon a second view in recent years. A huge, flat-featured face; the eyes small, almost concealed in the thick folds of the eyelids; the nose broad, nostrils spreading; the heavy lips parted to show large, strong white teeth. He wore a grey cotton-padded uniform, not overclean, with no insignia of rank. On his large feet he wore home-made black cotton shoes.

We spread the table for him. We served him *mien*, skeins of wheat-flour noodles, and *chiao-tze,* small meat dumplings. In a loud, booming voice he recited scripture blessings over the simple, abundant meal, for at that time he was a Christian; then fell to, with the great appetite which went with his great body. This was Feng Yu-hsiang, the peasant war lord, noted for his lack of personal ostentation, the discipline of his troops, and his

14

genuine interest in the welfare of the people he governed. Even the children knew of his just reputation and had no fear of his soldiers. We passed sweets to his bodyguards and they thanked us politely. They were all big men. They wore high leather boots with spurs and carried great broad-bladed knives in scarlet sheaths, slung behind their shoulders, but we were not afraid – fascinated, rather. His soldiers came and went among us, and when next day they left we were sorry, although their visit had cost us all our hens and a pig and a young calf. Even good soldiers must eat.

But the fortunes of war shifted and less than a year later Feng's army was withdrawn from our district. In the vacuum so created, an area under no higher control, lawless minor war lords no better than bandit chiefs wandered and marauded. Their troops – wild, undisciplined, shabby, hungry, unpaid – were kept loyal only by unlimited chance for loot. For three or four months, then, we lived in this uneasy interregnum, hearing rumours of raids and petty wars in neighbouring counties, waiting for the bandit armies to sweep down upon Sinyang like a plague of locusts.

On an afternoon in late autumn we were in the garden, where the sunlight still had warmth and power and chrysanthemums were a splendour of colour and sweet-bitter perfume. My mother, I remember, sat in the pavilion, making embroidery with small, close stitches of gay silks. We, my sisters and I, played near her. All sounds were drowsy, diffused in the hovering music of summer insects having their last festival before the frost.

There must have been some warning clink of metal or rustle of bushes forced apart for, abruptly, our eyes were drawn one way, watching, where over the silver and gold flower hedge a horrifying head peered in at us. Under a square, dirty grey soldier's cap a grinning face with a hole for a nose. . . . Beside him a second, then a third, equally dirty, almost equally repulsive, appeared. My mother rose to her feet in one swift motion. Her eyes never wavered from their fixed gaze, but her hands reached left and right to gather us to her. The soldiers laughed; they levelled their guns at us. They made jocose threats. I felt my mother's hand tremble only a little, pressing my head against her. None of us cried out.

Then, with no word spoken, my mother sat down in her place, took up her embroidery hoop from the ground where it had fallen, and with firm, skilled fingers began again setting the little stitches evenly in the pattern. The rabble soldiers still jeered raucously and called out filthy names. The swift silver needle
15

stabbed the fabric through; the shining thread whipped after. My mother's calm absorption obliterated the ruffians. They were not there; they ceased to exist. My sisters and I, reassured against our momentary terror, returned to our play. Behind the flower hedge the soldiers lingered for a little while uncertainly, then went away.

They were the first. There would be others, many more, come to Sinyang to plunder, to spoil, perhaps to kill. My mother rose up again quickly and called us to the house. My father came home from his office, agitated. "They've come —"

"Yes. We saw them."

At dark we left our home, going across the fields to take refuge with a friend, an Italian engineer my father knew. A foreigner's house might be respected. We carried only such things as could be quickly tied in bundles to provide us with warm clothing, for winter would be coming. Just before we started my mother knelt beside me and unhooked from my ears the wires of my ear-rings. She took off my sisters' ear-rings and her own as well. It was not that the bits of silver and gold were of any great value. But if we met marauding soldiers on our way they would snatch at the bangles, in their haste ripping them out, tearing through the flesh.

When I understood we were going away and why, I would have run back to fetch my lamb, now a half-grown sheep, but they would not let me. Crying bitterly, I was led away.

The Italian engineer gave us shelter during the days the terror lasted. When the bandit war lord had passed on with his troops, we went home again to find our house stripped clean of everything worth stealing, strewn with litter and wreckage. The door leaned aslant with a broken hinge; the window-panes were cracked and shattered. The rooms seemed shrunken, unfamiliar in their bareness.

But I had little concern for the house. I ran through to the garden, to the stables, calling my lamb by name. Surely it would come, gambolling awkwardly, to meet me. But when I had searched everywhere and found no trace of any living thing, I sat down in the doorway and buried my head in my arms, weeping heartbroken for my loss. There was an odd little squeak and rustle in the dead leaves drifted at the door. It was my hedgehog, nosing about for the dinner I had not brought him. I could have stroked him; I could have picked him up and hugged him! I ran to find food for him and was a little comforted.

We camped in our desolate house for a few days until it was

decided we should move to Peking. Here in Sinyang was no prospect of security. In the raw dawn of the last morning we were wakened and dressed and dragged off, still dazed with sleep, to board the train. I cried again – life was a series of bereavements; I had been given no chance for farewell to my hedgehog. The train carried us off to Peking. Pao's path and mine crossed.

Pao was born in the spring, in the month when swallows return to the north, and the child name given him was Yen – "swallow". It is apt, for his mind has the arrowing swiftness, the control and sureness, of a swallow's flight. He was born into a family which has for centuries held proudly to the traditional Confucian code of honour and morality. From his family have come scholars who have preferred a life of retirement to the emptiness of official pomp, men learned yet simple, who loved the quietude of the country and wrote exquisite verse for their friends to enjoy. Of his name, also, there have been righteous magistrates, so honest that they died in poverty, but were remembered and mourned for years in the districts they had governed. There have been soldiers, loyal to a leader or to an ideal, who refused to sell their swords for profit. Pao, also, is a true son of the family. He is so straight and pure and single-minded that sometimes I am afraid for him, afraid for what the world, which hates and envies his kind, may do to him.

From his father, whom he worshipped, Pao learned tales out of Chinese history: of Kungmin, the peerless strategist; of Wen Tien-hsiang; of Kung, who became the God of War; of Yueh Fei, the great patriot of the Sung Dynasty, who drove back the Golden Tartars and was done to death by court intrigue; of heroes who united the warring Three Kingdoms; of heroes who fought barbarian invasion in the north. . . . The code of the Confucian gentleman was impressed upon him. He learned by heart the classic phrases of the analects and in their difficult and formal language was instructed in the necessity for uprightness, the essence of loyalty. All this before he was ten years old. Listening, as a child will, to conversations of his elders not intended for his understanding, he heard talk of revolution, of ideals, of right and honour and freedom. The battles of ancient heroes rematerialized for him in modern guise, with his father in a leading role.

His father was a revolutionist. No penniless, irresponsible anarchist, but a disciplined soldier and a scholar who in his youth

17

had joined the secret party, the Kuomintang, plotting the over-throw of the corrupt Manchu Empire and the establishment of a Republic of China. To those ideals he devoted his life and never swerved in his loyalty. Others, growing discouraged by reverses in the sixteen years it took to bring the revolution to a successful conclusion, veered from one side to the other, making private deals with the war lords to their own profit, betraying their cause. He, on the other hand, drained the family fortune to hasten the establishment of just and equitable government, asking no repayment.

He fought in that first battle of the revolution, the tenth day of the tenth month, 1911, when Wuhan was taken. His name is enrolled among the names of patriots whose victory we celebrate each year upon that day. The revolution made swift headway under its leader, a quiet, middle-aged doctor of medicine, Sun Yat-sen. The Manchu Dynasty was ended, a republic was formed and a president elected. Refusing the honour for himself, Sun Yat-sen gave place to Yuan Shih-kai, an astute politician whose ideas, however, were not geared to the times. Yuan Shih-kai, perjuring his oath as president, set about to proclaim himself emperor. The coup did not come off. Opportunely, Yuan Shih-kai fell ill and died. But the unstable new republic fell into confusion and division and the day of the war lords dawned.

Against this chaos the forces of the revolution fought on for many years. Pao's father relinquished official position, wealth, and personal advantage to follow the uncertain fortunes of the southern republican movement. The armies of the revolution were ill-clad, poorly equipped, and very seldom paid, in contrast to the private armies of the war lords which waxed fat on loot. The officers shared the lot of their men. Pao's father refused luxury his soldiers could not have. What money he could collect by sacrifice of property went to feed and equip his troops. He himself knew actual hunger, cold, danger, wounds, defeat. Once in the winter when he had fought for three days without food he was wounded and given up for dead. He recovered, though his health was never again the same. Yet he continued fighting. His spirit was indomitable.

After years of intermittent struggle with little to show in the way of victories, the revolution at last found a leader (a successor to Sun Yat-sen, who had died), organized an army, provided itself with an adequate cadre of well-trained officers, and in two years – 1926 to 1928 – spread from Canton, its stronghold, marched northward and westward, until one government was established throughout the country. The war lords were crushed. One by one their cities were taken from them. They fled or submitted. The best of them had a change of heart and entered the revolutionists' ranks, bringing with them their armies and equipment. In spite of heavy odds against it in the beginning, that triumphal epic movement knew only victory. It led to the unification of all China.

It was due to the genius of one man, a slim, unassuming young Chinese officer, that the revolution was at last accomplished after sixteen years of struggle in the dark. It was willed by a will as stern as the Great Wall, as irresistible as the flood of China's rivers. For the Northern Expedition of 1928 was planned and led by the man in whose hands the fate of our four hundred millions still is laid – Chiang Kai-shek.

The vicissitudes of his father's career were reflected in the life of Pao's family in Peking. After that year when we first came as refugees to the street by the canal, the glories of the great house in our neighbourhood declined. Its lavish hospitality and free largess, the glitter and splendour of its feasts, its dawn-to-midnight bustle of activity, gradually faded into stillness. The carriages with their gay balloons and stamping ponies ceased coming. The servants were few. The huge gates stood half-closed. The wind whirled dust in the courtyards.

Bit by bit the properties from which the family revenues had been derived were sold to feed the soldiers of the revolution – that long, tragic struggle which was at last waking to new strength, pushing forward, threatening the entrenched power of the war lords. The war lords recognized this. They knew that their regime was over if once the uprising of the oppressed people became general through all the land. Therefore any whisper of sympathy with the southern armies of the revolution was met with harsh and thorough suppression. Many of the friends who in former days had visited the great house in our street and partaken of its hospitality dropped away, ashamed and afraid to have their names linked with that of a revolutionist. Of the many interrelated households who formed the "Big Family" various units moved away. It was no longer safe for Pao's father to return to his home. He moved his immediate family to Hupeh Province. Pao, only, was left in Peking to continue his studies. In the great house of many courtyards, where half the rooms were closed, untenanted, where voices echoed hollow in the huge, empty pavilions, Pao remained, one small boy of twelve, alone except for the vague guardianship of an elderly uncle.

I knew little of this phase of Pao's life. We never saw each other for we had now reached an age when we were no longer considered children. For Pao, in a sense, childhood had actually ended. It must have been at this time that his round, boyish face first learned the expression of maturity, of the concentrated, controlled feeling he still assumes to mask any strong emotion. We call it his *hsiung* expression – eyes very wide and fixed, lips tightly compressed, the muscle at the angle of the jaw hard, all the lines of his face deep-cut and rigid. The only translation for *hsiung* is "fierce", but it means more than that. Determined. Intense.

A small, serious schoolboy in uniform, studying geography, mathematics, classics – but history was his passion. History, which was his father's business, the history of the future. When he was fourteen he joined the revolutionary party.

There was a revolutionary party in Peking. Though it was certain death to be known as a member, thousands risked their lives to keep the cause of freedom alive under the reign of despotism. Not only did the war lords keep the country in a turmoil with their fighting and drain all wealth into their own coffers, but they were constantly intriguing with foreign capital to finance their wars in return for liens on China's resources. They had sold China into virtual slavery to Japan, consenting (though they had not the authority to speak for our country; to the infamous Twenty-one Demands, receiving in return arms and money with which to fight each other or, more especially, the revolutionists in the south. When Japan raves of broken promises, it is to these treaties she refers – concessions bought from traitors who had neither the right nor the power to deliver what they promised, and revoked when China became united and of one mind.

Against this treachery in the north the secret revolution within fought with courage and persistence. For all the watchfulness of the street patrols, slogans were chalked on walls, posters were put up (no one knew when or by whom) appealing to the people: "Down with the war lords! Kill those who have sold your country! Down with all imperialism! Resist!" Secret newspapers were circulated (death to be found in possession of one) revealing the betrayal of the republic. The issue was kept before the people by one means or another.

Revolutionists were recruited in the schools – only the young were wakeful enough to care that their future and the freedom of their country were being sold away from them. Older men, in general, were complacent towards the war-lord regime, indifferent as long as their private fortunes were unmolested. Peking University, Chung Hwa University, were hot-beds of radicalism. With a sprinkling of older men, editors and writers for the most part, the revolution was a movement of schoolboys and young students. To Pao it seems quite natural that at fourteen he should have been a leader of his class at school in printing secret newspapers and circulating them among his fellow students.

The government – that is, the war lords – feared and hated this movement among the students. The universities and middle schools were regularly searched for revolutionists and all activities were rigorously dealt with. This was no particularly drastic suppression, but in China everything turns ruthless and bloody once suppression starts. Underlings, perhaps with a sadistic streak, zealous to prove efficient in the performance of their duty, would receive general orders from their superiors – to put down certain tendencies. The interpretation and execution were their own affair.

There was a place near the Tu-ti Miao, the Temple of the Earth Gods, where every week on sunny afternoons people would go to watch the executions. I myself remember seeing three mule carts jolting toward the Tu-ti Miao, and standing in them men and boys, naked to the waist, condemned revolutionists going to their death. Around them thronged an excited crowd, going to see them die as one goes to see a circus. Is that cruelty in my race? I do not know. It *is* indifference to suffering and death. The young revolutionists were as indifferent, seemingly. They laughed their hardy laughter and harangued their audience to the final moment. Converts were won that way, sometimes.

This was all open to the sunlight. There were whispers of things more sinister – torture, burial alive. Between one hour and the next men disappeared and were never seen or heard of again. They were secretly assassinated and their bodies disposed of. This was what one faced, entering the party. Yet the movement never lacked for ardent young recruits, burning to perform high deeds. Many paid with their lives, but the revolution was at last accomplished, the sooner for their sacrifice.

One evening at dusk when the air was filled with the calling of the crows, Pao stepped over the high threshold of the gate into the grey street – and never returned. He walked out of the house casually with a geometry book under his arm, as he had done each evening, to study with a few class-mates, preparing

21

for examinations. Or such was the explanation he gave his uncle.

This time he went by a circuitous route through narrow byways to the West City. This district, though within the city walls, is sparsely built up. The streets are like roads, wandering among trees and fields. Here Pao came to the rendezvous of the young revolutionists, a small temple set back from the road, half hidden under the shadow of widespreading trees.

Lonely, quiet within its encircling red walls, its single courtyard was paved with broken flagstones. Before the low, wide flight of steps rising to the hall of the gods stood a huge incense burner of cast bronze, like an enormous cauldron on three legs, and on either side the great round drum and the massive bronze bell with no tongue. At the hour for morning and evening worship the old priest-caretaker who lived alone in the temple struck upon the bell with a wooden rod, pounded on the drum with a padded pole, burned a sacrifice in the incense burner, lighted small candles in the shrine before the images. These loomed dimly in the shadows with their faint and distant smile, paint and gold leaf flaking from their robes.

In the space behind the shrine Pao and his fellow students had their meeting-place. They came together each evening to receive forbidden information on the programme of the revolution. The slight clank of their hand press was muffled by the enclosing trees and walls. There were few houses within close earshot. The priest-caretaker had been bribed; it was nothing to him what went on in the world of politics. They had been using this place as a rendezvous for months. They were quite safe. . . .

Dusk deepened. The crows streamed in clamorous flocks toward the temple groves of the West City, croaked and conversed in their guttural speech, alighted in the trees at the gate, rose to circle discontentedly, and finally, as darkness closed in, settled to roost and were silent. The old priest's voice droned on in monotone to the click of his small wooden hand drum, as he chanted the sutras before the shrine. In the recess behind the seat of the gods dim lamplight brought into relief the boys' tense, earnest young faces and flung monstrous shadows upon the walls of the room. The press revolved with a subdued mechanical clanking, turning out sheet after sheet of forbidden print, dangerous words of liberty. They were safe. . . .

Outside the red walls government soldiers, quietly surrounded the place. Some enemy, some traitor, had lodged information against the group. The soldiers carried no firearms. They had only red-sheathed, broad heavy knives, two feet long. They had

22

their orders to be quick, thorough, and silent, to accomplish what they were sent to do without causing outcry. Noise might call forth inconvenient inquiry, for many of the lads were of good family.

With the cordon drawn around the temple, soldiers burst in at the gate. There was the merest fraction of a moment's warning – an excited gabble among the crows, the crash of the gates flung open. They rushed in upon the defenceless boys. The press with its damning evidence was in their hands. But Pao in that instant was over the outer wall and dodging fleetly through the shadowy trees. He evaded the cordon posted to catch all who attempted escape in this way – he knew the paths in the dark – and was quickly beyond pursuit. A few others of his friends also made their escape. Those who were arrested were made to kneel in the courtyard and were beheaded on the spot. Firewood was piled in the huge incense burner. The heads and bodies were collected and systematically burned to ashes. Of those rash children, all under twenty, who paid the price of their radical allegiance, not a trace was left. It was not until years later that their fate was known.

Pao quickly put distance between himself and the place. The remainder of the night he spent wandering and hiding, evading the challenge of the night-watch at lighted street corners. He dared not return home; his name would be known; they would find him there. He could not go back to school. There everyone knew who had been his companions and friends. When they failed to appear there would be questioning. No place where he was known would be safe shelter for him. A boy of fourteen, he had no one to depend on but himself. His uncle could not help him. His father was far away in the south. He was alone.

When daylight came he lost himself among the crowds waiting for the big, iron-studded gates of the city to be unbarred for the day. In the rush he passed the guards unnoticed. Probably it was too soon for the alarm to have been given. He was outside Peking – free – his total resources ten dollars – about five shillings – which he happened to have in his pocket. He set off on foot for Tientsin, about sixty miles distant. He walked until he met a train of mule carts, loaded high, moving eastward. Pao was a Peking boy, with a quick native wit and a fund of stories gained from reading and the theatre. He could talk anybody into giving him what he wished. He was good company, and the mule drivers were happy to let him ride atop their loads. Along the way his ready tongue won him welcome in farm-houses, where they gave him food and lodging for the night. In seven days he reached Tientsin, where he took deck passage for Shanghai. There at last he made connections with relatives. It is in just such words Pao tells of that journey when he will speak of it at all. Stoic, factual, with no mention of fear or weariness, of grief for his comrades, of horror, loneliness, or bewilderment. He refuses to see in the exploit anything exceptional. But all these years after I feel an ache at the throat when I think of that young, self-reliant boy turning his back upon the massive grey gates and walls of Peking, walking into exile without one backward look.

For both of us Peking is home as no place else will ever be. We are exiled and disinherited until we may return. Beneath all tragedy there was an essential peace there, a deep substratum of unshakable harmony. There was beauty, the more poignant for its stately sadness. Our feet trod dust so rich in history, so weary with centuries of battle, so old with glory, that we were made wise and self-contained beyond our years.

The beauty of Peking is not merely a pleasing pattern to the eye. There is a new word needed for this beauty, such power and dignity it has and such vast serenity. The sky over Peking is of a fiery blue, so intense yet fragile a colour it must surely break in pieces like thin porcelain if voices in the street are raised above a murmur. But the people of Peking are a placid folk, and the soft Peking tongue has a blurred, gentle quality, and the sound of wheeled traffic is muffled in dust, and the street cries are musical and mournful, so that the sky's thin, curving shell remains unshattered. The Western Hills on the horizon are blue, grey, purple, as the sunlight shifts with the hour; in the evening, dark against the blinding sunset, they are edged with burning. Grey roofs of the million homes, gold glazed roofs of the great palaces, spread wide eaves like a gesture of benediction. Grey walls with the strength of cliffs guard the city, the defences of a past century futile now against new weapons of a new invasion as ruthless as, and more efficient than, our ancient threat of barbarian encroachment in the north.

For me the break did not come so abruptly as for Pao. There were years of school and university in Peking, beyond my childhood there. I grew into youth in that interval of peace when our country was united and all her factions at last in fair accord. To be young was to be patriotic, to love China with a fierce fervour of pride. The future was all promise and expectation. It is true,

24

if we paused to think soberly, there was a shiver of apprehension in the knowledge that Japan waited like a cat, watchful for her opportunity, poised to spring. But the crisis might never come. China was so rapidly growing in strength for defence. If we could but win that race against time!

There was new freedom for our generation. We escaped the restraint of conservative homes to find release and stimulus in the university. The campus was beautiful with its cropped grass and waving trees, its small river with islands, its pagoda tower, its buildings after the style of ancient palaces. Learned men from foreign countries as well as the best minds of China were our teachers. Books in our own tongue and books from all the world were in the libraries for us. In those immense stone halls, silent save for the rustle of many books, we discovered the thrill of new knowledge. We would discuss eagerly among ourselves philosophy, political science, religion – all was new, exciting; nothing was difficult for us. We were learning to fashion a new world free of ancient feuds and prejudices, and the feat seemed easy of accomplishment, we were so young and confident.

Traditional barriers of constraint between boy and girl melted away in an atmosphere of easy comradeship. We shared classes and discussion. We would gather in the evenings in the raftered hall of some old Peking mansion, a hundred of us, two hundred or more, so spacious were the rooms; the girls in flowered dresses, slim, sheath-fitted *shan*, with flowers in their hair. There would be music and dancing in the Western style, boy and girl together. In groups we picnicked on the smooth grass by the river that wound through the campus. We read Li Po's poems under the willows in the blazing autumn moonlight (the moon is so brilliant in Peking) by the banks of the Peihai Lakes. We took pleasure-boats, poled along lazily on the canals under the camel-backed bridges, thrusting among lotus flowers upheld like lanterns, swaying, above their flat green leaves. There would be the distant faint whisper of a lute, or the thin music of the four-stringed *chin*, or a strain from an ancient love song. . . .

With all the new there was a solid heritage we had from older generations who had learned the art of comfort and good living. Nowhere else were the leisure and zest for enjoyment brought to such perfection. There is a litany repeated reverently by those banished from their Peking homes by the exigencies of war – the list of Peking restaurants, Tung Hsin Lou, Ho Pe Fu, the West City restaurants, the Han, Tartar, and Mohammedan restaurants. Restaurants of the Han race – where one sat down to course after course of lordly dishes, food to be tasted nowhere else in the world. The delicate soups; the rich, dark sauces; the savoury meats; fish cooked with a tang of ginger; duck browned and crisp and served with rare condiments – a symphony of subtle flavours that elevated the sense of taste to its due place among the nobler aesthetic perceptions. Restaurants of the northern Tartars – where they roasted sheep whole over glowing wood fires in the courtyards, after the custom of their tribes on the bleak plains of Mongolia. Icicles hanging a foot long from the eaves of the curving roofs, the red warmth of the fire, the smell of wood-smoke, the sizzling brown-red meat so bursting with goodness it dripped rich juice to spatter and hiss among the red coals. One ate until it was not possible to eat more, and sallied forth well fortified within against the bitter cold.

The old Moon Calendar was studded with feast days, each one an excuse, if excuse were needed, to invite guests to enjoy the special dishes of the season, or to go oneself from house to house, from friend to friend, eating, always eating. The Dragon Feast and the rice cakes; the Moon Feast and the moon-cakes; the New Year, a month of fire-crackers and feasting, and with *mien* and sugar dumplings and spring cakes thin as tissue paper, and the first green vegetables of the year. All over China the gourmets heave deep sighs of nostalgia as they survey their depleted bulk and mourn for the good things to eat in the days of plenty in Peking.

Even during the years when successive war lords ruled Peking the essential peace and good living of the city were scarcely disturbed. Relatively few of her citizens took their politics as seriously as the revolutionists. There would be a brief interval of confusion, as the last war lord was ousted by the next, but when the dust settled everything would be much as it was before. Peking was the willing prize for any conqueror, whether Chang Tso-lin, Wu Pei-fu, or Feng Yu-hsiang. She accepted a change of government with equanimity, with celebrations, with flags and lanterns and *pai-lou* spangled with flowers, for the contending armies were, after all, Chinese, and these civil wars were no more than brawls within the family.

Peking is no longer ours. Where we walked heavier boots tread, in dust that is only meaningless dust, not the drifted ash of history. Short-statured yellow strangers (our northern Chinese are tall) swagger about the streets, arrogant. Children are pushed rudely from their path, to stumble and fall in the gutter. Women who in the crowd unintentionally brush against them are slapped

26

across the face. These strangers are very proud, resenting any slight. They are very brave. But when it is dusk and the sun drops down behind the Western Hills they hurry to barracks with their heads between their shoulders and dare not venture out while the night is dark. Our universities have been converted into barracks for their troops, or into prisons for our youth, where boy and girl students are held for questioning and torture. Dangerous thoughts and dreams of freedom are more rigidly proscribed than in the time of the war lords, and more mercilessly punished.

Peking is no longer ours. Our children will never see the moon reflected in the Peihai Lakes, or the lotus flowers on the canals. They will not watch the slow procession of camels loaded with coal, striding across the bare northern plains and past the huge grey city walls. They will never know the beauty of old palaces and temples of Peking, unless we win back the north for them! China must regain her ancient Capital of the North. We are exiled and disinherited; our lives are incomplete unless we see Peking again before we die.

When we remember Peking it is with hollow loneliness at the heart. Our two homes – the house of Pao's Big Family with its scores of rooms and my small house at the far end of the street – stand silent and deserted. The old gatekeeper hobbles outside his lodge seeking the wintry sunlight. His is the only moving shadow in the empty courts. When shall we return, and the courtyards be gay again in the evening with the shouts of children playing? In the distance the cry of a vendor is a long wail of mourning. The little gong of the blind is sad in the silent night. On frosty mornings the beggars are found dead in the streets. . . .

We remember Peking when she bore the proud name of Capital of the North. There we have both wandered among the massive palaces of the Imperial City – red-walled, yellow-tiled – along the marble terraces with their marble balustrades, carved with dragon and phoenix – thousands of tons of white marble carried by elephants a thousand miles across China from the quarries of the Burma border. That tells the magnificence of the emperors five hundred years ago! Blood and sweat built the Imperial City, forced labour and taxes ground from the poor. Many young moderns of my race see in it only a monument to tyranny.

Yes . . . but stand in the sunlight silent before its vast dignity. All is proportioned with such just and balanced sureness: the still courtyards, level as water; the ground plan true with the compass and the sun, east, south, west, north; the mounting terraces, foundation to majestic pavilions with their red walls – a

27

red more burning and golden than scarlet – with their tall arched doorways and their golden roofs sweeping downward in curves of sheer power. It is the imagination of China! By oppression and tyranny the blocks of marble were laid, the roof beams hewn. Yes. But the essential design – the inevitable, exact proportions, the soul-releasing magnitude – is the outgrowth of all China. It dwarfs the individual man; it is the expression of a nation; no emperor could have lived worthy of this setting. No one architect could have conceived these stately dimensions and this splendour of strong, simple colour. This stability, this centred peace, this harmony with earth and sky – this is the final statement on concrete beauty of the Chinese philosophy of life.

CHAPTER TWO

ENGLISH IDYLL

What we loved best about England was the grass – the short, clean, incredibly green grass with its underlying tough, springy turf, three hundred years in growing. After the yellow, dust-storm barrenness of our North China plains, after the bitter, windy winters, the dazzling, burning summers, this greenness of England was a thing for wonder and delight. That first summer in Kent, in the country, when Pao and I met each other again in a foreign land, we remember now for the loveliness of an England yet inviolate under a gentle sun and still gentler rain. The air had the fragrance of honey, and the sunlight, honey-golden, was never too hot. Its crystal clearness held a hidden keen freshness, like a sharp sword under its smoothness.

We were of the world's elect – we had everything then. Pao was twenty-two; I was younger still. We were free as few Chinese young people are ever free. We had the privilege of travel and study abroad. In this new air we could forget concerns too heavy for our years and the troubled, tragic events of our earlier youth. Even more recent bereavements seemed distant and less bitter. We were fortune's favoured children, not least in the luck – or was it destiny? – that brought us together again by diverse paths to meet so strangely in a foreign country.

When Pao fled Peking he rejoined his family in Hankow. At seventeen he was sent to the Central Military Academy in Nanking to become a soldier. This school had been created by the leaders of the revolution to train up young officers of a new type – well-educated, disciplined, loyal. These young men selected to become the nucleus of China's new armies were to be of a different stamp from the ignorant, self-seeking war lords and their henchmen. There were to restore peace and order, retake the north-eastern provinces lost to Japan, eradicate foreign imperialism, whether of encroaching armies or the subtler invasion of powerful capital – in short, they were to rebuild China, a nation sovereign and united.

The head of the Central Military Academy was Marshal Chiang Kai-shek, already distinguished as the leader who had brought the revolution to a victorious close. Each Sunday morning for four uninterrupted hours he would lecture to the three thousands cadets, drawn up in ranks before him on the drill grounds. Bareheaded under the intense sun of Nanking, Marshal Chiang expounded; rigid at attention the cadets listened. Though he talked of history, of politics, of military tactics, the emphasis of his teaching was ethical. Theirs, he said, was an immense responsibility. Among their number would be found China's future leader. Therefore more important than learning and technique was the development of character. He used the term *tso jen* – "to be man" – defining all the pride and dignity inherent in the word. No one who heard him could ever forget.

The proud climax of Pao's course at the Central Military Academy came when he was one of three chosen out of three thousand cadets to be sent abroad for further study. Marshal Pai Chung-hsi, head of the Military Training Department, was sponsor for a very few outstanding Chinese students each year sent by special arrangement with foreign governments to study military science with their own young officers. Pao was to go to Sandhurst, to the Royal Military College and the College of Artillery, classical training schools for British officers. He would be a student, but also a representative of his country, his race, in a foreign land.

Close upon this triumph, however, came the blow of a grave bereavement. His father died. Pao's feeling for his father is something no one but a Chinese can truly comprehend, so much beyond affection and common dutifulness is involved. It had in it an almost religious intensity, for this father-son relationship is one of the four made sacred by Confucian ethic. His father had been Pao's hero from earliest childhood; his ideals were Pao's north star.

Pao was called from the basket-ball field to receive the telegram. It said simply, "My son, I am ill." When he read this he knew that his father was going to die. For no lesser reason would that stoic soldier have mentioned the matter. Pao turned upon his heel, hurried to his small bare cell in the student barracks, and shut the door to be alone. He could not disgrace his father by public display of feeling.

Next day he took ship for Hankow. When he reached the city, when he came into the street where his family had their home, his heart stood still. There were white lanterns hanging at the gateway – white, the colour for death. He had come too late. He stepped over the threshold. There was the keening of women's voices, and the rhythmic wailing of mourners. They were calling upon his father's spirit by name, entreating him to return. Pao walked through the courtyard, his face very set and *hsiung*, to the upper room where the huge black coffin, made from thick halved timbers, lay already sealed. His mother knelt beside it, weeping aloud, crying upon the dead. Pao, the eldest son, stood straight and rigid in his uniform and said in a loud voice, "Let no one weep here, or I go!"

When they had carried the coffin out of the city for burial, Pao walked among the mourners with his head unbowed. There was none of the customary loud lamentation along the way. At the grave they made the sacrifices due to the dead, burning silver-paper money and paper images of all things needful to his spirit, setting off fire-crackers, chanting prayers, and making music with wind instruments and gongs for the comfort of the departing soul. Pao's mother, in her ravelled, coarse white garments of widowhood, and with a white cloth bound about her head, stood by the heaped fresh earth, shaken with silent grief. The assembled relatives all kept silence, not daring to utter the funeral wailing, because the eldest son and chief mourner forbade, and himself stood, stiffly erect, his face like carven stone. . . .

When Pao left home for England he was unmarried and unpromised. This was unusual for the son of a family proud in tradition, to whom the continuity of the line was everything. He was young; he was leaving home for a period of years. If custom and the wishes of his mother had prevailed, Pao would already have knelt at the ancestral altar with a girl of his parents' choice. When he went abroad his wife would have remained in the home in filial attendance upon his mother. If all went well she would have given a son to the family within the allotted period of months. Strange to return, after years of the social freedom of the West, with mind subtly changed by contact with another civilization – to come back to a wife who is a stranger and to a solemn-eyed child shy of the father he has never seen!

Pao's mother greatly desired a daughter-in-law. As early as his sixteenth birthday she began looking about among families of their acquaintance for a bride for him. But Pao was not one to brook coercion. When he was told a fiancée had already been selected, the negotiations almost completed, Pao ran away from home and was gone for two months. His mother gave him a year or two to outgrow this schoolboy reluctance, then resumed her quest of the perfect daughter-in-law. But he was no more amenable the second time. His mother, with what she doubtless considered daring unconventionality, offered to arrange a meeting with the girl she had chosen. "She is very beautiful," she promised. "You will see for yourself."

Pao answered, "Mother, how can I marry a girl I know not, I love not? Live with her intimately, day after day for all my life, share with a stranger my thoughts and hopes? I do not care so much whether she is pretty; I must know her heart and that I cannot know in one brief interview. I must choose a wife who will uphold the honour of our house, who will give me children to be proud of. There must be respect and understanding between us. I shall not wish, later when I have achieved some success, to put aside the wife I was married to in my youth and take a new, a younger and more clever wife, as many men do. Nor, should I dislike the wife my family gave me, could I console myself with concubines. Marriage should be indissoluble – a contract to be entered into once, neither by the man nor by the woman to be repeated in a lifetime. It is the sacred giving of one's word. Therefore, with knowledge of the responsibilities, I must choose for myself. It is a thing no one can do for me."

His mother was astounded; these were the dangerous modern views of the new generation. But Pao is and has always been a traditionalist. It was no aping of Western ways that influenced him, but a considered and thoughtful reappraisal of Chinese ideals of family life. He was independent enough to think for himself, to choose what good should be conserved, what fault should be remedied. His mother did not yet understand his position. This was nothing but a transient phase, she thought; let a few years pass and this youthful rebellion would be forgotten. A third time before he left home she urged betrothal, having made certain inquiries by letter of a family with a marriageable daughter. But Pao was more stubborn than ever. He refused even to listen to the name of the young lady. This third choice of Pao's mother for a daughter-in-law was myself. . . . Pao sailed for England, heart-whole and free from any family-made agreement.

Of the engagement which did not take place I knew little at the time. I knew only that my uncle (who had become my guardian upon the death of my parents a year or two earlier) was entertaining various offers for my hand. But I did not believe in marriage of any kind. In the university I had tasted freedom; I was launched upon a scientific course and was determined to

32

devote my life to a career. If I had followed my own natural bent, I should have tried for a degree in literature. But, with all my generation, I burned to serve my country and saw no utility or power in empty words. Science was our god, a beneficent god to make of China a rich and happy nation. With test-tube and microscope and dynamo we would bring wealth and comfort to all the millions of the poor, eradicate misery and disease. Therefore I laid aside the books I loved, the poetry and plays and novels, and spent my days in the laboratory and my evenings poring over formulae and diagrams.

But I was never made for abstract research. I had to use this science as a tool for some practical end. Suddenly in a chance visit to the hospital, calling upon a friend who had a new baby, I discovered the use for my biology and chemistry. Midwifery . . . I remember the *chieh-sen-po*, "the old woman who meets the birth", with her long black finger-nails and her huskily whispered charms against all the devils that threaten mother and baby. Ineffective, often, for I remembered white lanterns at the gate and a long black coffin carried forth, or a tiny rough box or small bundle wrapped in old matting taken away to be buried. And here all was shining, exquisite cleanness, and a compassionate easing of pain and a watchfulness against danger, with all the resources of science to safeguard the new life and the mother in her stress. This was my calling.

I brushed aside my uncle's matrimonial plans for me and prevailed upon him to send me to England for advanced training in obstetrics. Days of lectures in the class-room; days in the laboratory, watching the changing colours in test-tubes held against the light of the window. Outside the rain, the eternal English rain; the shining wet pavements; the umbrellas jostling in the street. Days in the clinic, listening to the heart tones of the unborn; under my touch sensing its life and movement. Days in the delivery-room, bent over a groaning and agonized woman; the harsh smell of ether, the sweetish odour of chloroform, the strong, sharp reek of lysol and alcohol; the breathless moments before the emergence of the new life; the suspense of that interval before the first gasping cry of the newborn; the utter joy of achievement when all was safely accomplished. Days in the wards and nurseries, watching the greedy pleasure of babies at the breast, the rapt delight in the faces of the mothers – everywhere white cleanness and the smell of flowers. There was also the tragic side – the sudden terror of haemorrhage or the ghastly convulsions and coma of eclampsia, death darkening the threshold of life. But how seldom! Not as in my country, where women longing for children yet approach their hour with dread and misgiving, where two or three in a hundred are doomed to die in childbirth; and where of the babies born a half will not live until their first birthday. When I held in my hands these blue-eyed babies, bald-headed or with a wisp of blond down, I thought of our dark-haired Chinese babies with their slit-shaped black eyes so wise-looking, and I wished for them and their mothers this same care and defence against death. With my knowledge of the beauty and terror of birth, I grew in the daily realization of the worth of life, the irreplaceable value of each new life thus brought into being through love and pain.

Something happened to my thinking about this time. I have to tell this, because when I first wrote this book I did not wish it to be taken as propaganda to enlist war aid for our cause or stir up hatred against our enemies. I became a pacifist. In spite of my ardent love of country, my indignation at the encroachments of Japan, already entrenched in Manchuria, and my passion for freedom, I became convinced that war is utterly evil, never justifiable. I came to this belief through a strange liberation and enlargement of spirit from reading Jeans and Eddington, the great philosophical scientists. I probably did not understand one-half of what I read, but as I read of worlds beyond worlds and star suns, gold and white and coloured fire, I realized what an infinitesimal dark dust speck in the great winds of the universe was our small planet, Earth. I escaped in fancy to other habitable worlds, peopled by radiant, kindly beings of more than human wisdom, living at peace in their shining crystal cities, beautiful with fountains and strange, glowing flowers.

But if, in all the universe, there is no habitable world but earth, what then? No place else where life exists, no other home for humankind where it may develop in beauty and dignity? I was checked in my flight, brought back to earth. I began to search for a pattern of life, an ideal loveliness man might attain. I read history for the answer – Greek, Roman, Egyptian, Chinese, European – looking for a time and place which offered the perfect pattern. There were many hints of a Golden Age – we had it in our own legends of the Emperors Shen and Wu who reigned four thousand years ago – but always it was a lost Golden Age, its records blurred by antiquity. When history crystallized into definite dates and events it became a lamentable recital of crimes, of wars, of aggressions, of beautiful cities and great civilizations

destroyed without reason. In China no less than in other nations
– though through all Chinese history there runs a saving vision,
the contempts of the solitary sage for power and riches won by
force. Or, again, where the high aloofness of a Buddha or the
profound compassion of a Jesus has influenced, though ever so
faintly, the course of the world's history, there are dissenters
from the chorus of glorification of waste, tragedy, and ruthlessness which is war. With this minority I took my stand, and found
myself one of a group who called themselves pacifists.

The pattern for peace did not exist, except in the mind. All
Golden Ages of antiquity were myth. We of this generation, we
of the future, must shape in actual living the new design of peace
and co-operation between one nation and another. We must re-
nounce war, even in self-defence. For any war may mask behind
that name, leading to revenge and hatred. At this time I
discovered the Bible, and this was the word that summed up all,
the sentence I read over and over again, that brought tears to my
eyes, so beautiful it was – "Blessed are the meek, for they shall
inherit the earth. . . ."

The clarity and sureness of conviction I held then is lost . . . I
have learned that war is not the ultimate evil, that there is de-
gradation beyond the horror of killing. A time was to come when
I should realize, little by little, what the domination of evil does
to an invaded country, when I was to hear of the opium dens
and houses of prostitution in Peking, my home – protected, pro-
moted by Japan for the debauching of our youth. Then I could
no longer hold to my belief in absolute pacifism. With grief but
without hate, like millions of other peace-loving Chinese, I have
consented in my heart to a war of resistance against this corruption and enslavement.

But it was while I was still in the vehement all-or-nothing
phase of pacifism that I met Pao again. We were guests together
in a group of British and foreign students enjoying the hospitality of a country house in Kent. My room-mate, a Chinese girl,
introduced us: "Miss Han, Mr. Tang." We bowed; the names
meant nothing; there are thousands of Tangs and millions of
Hans in China. In casual talk we did not discover we were already
known to each other. Nor did I know, for Pao was not in uniform, that he had come to England on a government appointment to study military science. From some remark he dropped, I
assumed he was studying engineering. I was not enlightened until
a day or two later when we were among those attending a lecture
on China. The speaker, a clergyman who was a confirmed

pacifist, expanded on the theme, "Love your enemies." His kind eyes beaming behind his glasses, he exhorted us to love the Japanese.

Now there is a point here which needs to be made clear: we have no racial hatred for the Japanese, such as I have observed in Europe between nations at odds. Even now, after three years of war, of massacre, of unspeakable treatment we have suffered at the hands of the invaders, we still do not hate the Japanese. True, our soldiers rush upon the enemy with the cry, "*Sha!*" "Kill!" Our slogans urge, "Resist!" But we do not retaliate. We discriminate between the oppressed, misguided people and their venal overlords. We have never felt it necessary to loathe the Japanese people, even though we have suffered so much at their hands. True, we call them "small devils", but we do not kill our prisoners as they have done. We expect to win this war, but we do not intend to invade in turn, occupy Japan and cripple her economically. We hope when peace comes – a peace not dictated by an arrogant victor, but a just treaty agreed upon in mutual respect – that Japan and China will bury all bitterness and, with no desire for revenge, begin to see things the same way.

So to the Chinese students present, schooled as we were in humiliation by Japan's aggressions of many years, the estimable clergyman's views were the babblings of a well-intentioned amateur. Pao listened with scowling brows, refuting in his mind the theories of the speaker. I listened, agreeing in principle but unsatisfied, wishing for a more profound analysis than these charming generalities. When the lecture was over, Pao and I strolled together in conversation.

Pao said, "We may love our enemies, but we must fight them first!"

I could not accept this assumption of inevitability of war with Japan. Hotly I protested against all use of violence. Pao answered (cynically, I thought), "Then all the good people will be killed off and evil will flourish unchecked."

I flared in reply, "What I hate most is this worship of force! If you kill in turn, how are you better than your enemies? I would rather die than defend my ideal by violence. I hate this pride in the martial virtues; all this glorification of murder! They dress it up in gaudy uniforms and decorate it with flags and call it patriotism and valour and national honour! I think it is loathsome and stupid; whoever admires it is unable to think clearly!"

Pao gave me one black look, swung round, and walked away without a word.

36

I was startled and angry and mortified. "Your friend Mr. Tang is very rude," I told my room-mate.

"How?"

I related the incident. She laughed at my discomfiture. "But didn't you know he was sent by the Chinese government to study artillery at Sandhurst? Your ideas would be fire to his gunpowder! He is very proud, very patriotic, and very young. He is a soldier and the son of a soldier." She named Pao's father.

Light dawned on me. "Is he of *that* Tang family!" I exclaimed. "Why, I know him! We lived in the same street in Peking, played together when we were children. . . ."

When we met again Pao preserved a stony silence, barely bowing to me with frigid politeness. But I could see behind the mask of the stern young soldier the face of the small boy who had been my prince and captain when we played war in the dusk under the willows in the quiet by-street in Peking. "Don't you know me, Tang Yen?" I said, using his child-name. "Don't you remember the canal in the Forbidden City and the battles we fought along its banks? I wasn't a pacifist then."

All that summer – the summer of 1937 – we met at intervals, usually in the company of others, seldom alone. There are never a great many Chinese students in England; they naturally drift together, so Pao and I were sure to see something of each other. We quarrelled at every encounter, and on every subject. In any discussion of more than casual moment our ideas struck sparks. I wrote of my contacts in my letters home, mentioning Pao's name among others without special emphasis. My uncle replied in stilted, formal phrases: "This gentleman's honoured mother approached us some three years ago in view of a possible connection between our families, involving yourself and her son. Since the contract did not take place, it is better now that you avoid him entirely. It would not be proper for you to know each other."

The joke was too good to keep. Pao had already told me of his mother's three-time-thwarted attempts to negotiate a marriage for him. At the first opportunity I drew him out again upon the subject of engagements. Pao expounded with great earnestness; I listened demurely, then murmured, "Do you know the name of your third rejected fiancée? It is Han Suyin."

Pao stared at me in startled horror. "Good heavens! Yourself!"

I felt my cheeks burn with a hot blush. "Yes, but do not think anything of it," I stammered. "I, also, would have been unwilling." I talked on rapidly against my mounting embarrassment. "It is of no personal significance. I did not know, myself, of the inquiry until my uncle wrote me recently. But at that time I had already decided I would never marry. So the whole thing is of no consequence."

Pao looked relieved. "I do not believe in marriage either," he said. Then, gravely but with a devastating frankness, "We are really fortunate that this engagement came to nothing. We should never have suited each other; we cannot agree on anything. I think you are wise in your decision, for you must know your temper is really quite difficult."

"It is very much like your own!" I retorted.

"That is what I said," answered Pao.

I lived that summer in a world that has since crashed in flames, China was far away in time and distance. I lived in the peace and quiet of an England where no invader had set foot since the Norman William, where no threat of conquest had seriously disturbed her serenity since the time of the Spanish Armada. It was a pleasant land of rose gardens and green lawns, of abundant food, of rosy children, calm, beautiful girls, and gracious ladies hospitably pouring tea in their drawing-rooms. I had friends, interesting work, leisure for play. It was an interval of happy tranquillity, the more dear and lovely in retrospect because it now belongs to an irretrievable past.

In July there was brief mention in the news of a skirmish on the outskirts of Peking. There had been an interchange of shots between Chinese soldiers and Japanese who were manoeuvring without warrant. By the terms of an outdated treaty various foreign governments were permitted to maintain garrisons in the north to keep open the road from Peking to the sea. The Japanese had stretched this to justify the posting of thousands of troops in the northern provinces. This was not the first time their army of occupation had clashed with the rightful inhabitants of the country.

To me it was merely another incident. I must have been blind that I did not know the signs of gathering fury in the East. I must have been lulled and made unperceptive in the atmosphere of peace about me. I had forgotten the tense insecurity of China. But Pao knew at once that war, long expected, had come. He applied at the Chinese Embassy in London for permission to return home without delay. The Embassy cabled the Military

Training Department for advice, and the reply came back from Marshal Pai Chiang-hsi: "Complete training before return to China."

Following the outbreak of hostilities, there were weeks of indeterminate negotiation, an exchange of protests, an effort to localize the disturbance. But it became increasingly evident that, unless China was prepared to grovel and abase herself and make concessions, Japan would force action. Then, in August, with the flimsy excuse of an incident that occurred *after* Japanese warships had already left their base *en route* for Shanghai, havoc broke loose. The war was on!

China was headline news. We in England followed events with breathless excitement. As weeks passed and the defence of Shanghai still held, we became wild with hope. Our country, ill-prepared, so recently emerged from the chaos of civil war, for three months held Shanghai against the attacks of one of the world's greatest navies and an army equipped with every modern device for destruction. The best of our troops were flung against the Japanese forces in desperate, splendid sacrifice, which is no longer considered good strategy, and China put all her strength into one magnificent act of resistance that gave pause to the invader and won the world's respect.

Pao chafed against the order that kept him in England, inactive, while on the battlefields around Chapei his friends and companions of the Central Military Academy were mown down by the score. Every letter from home brought lists of their names. He became morose and silent; I grew to know his grim, *hsiung* look that signified his inner brooding. We were together in a London cinema when a news-reel flashed on the screen the black, rolling smoke clouds over the grey roofs of burning Chapei, the northern section of Shanghai, beyond the International Settlement. The scene shifted; we saw the shattered brick walls of the South Station in Nantao, the Native City, and the formless heaps which were the mutilated dead. Again, we watched a road choked with refugees. We saw our people, lean and clothed in rags, driven from their homes and from the green and yellow fields which were their sustenance. A thin, stooped farmer, his load swinging from the two ends of a shoulder-pole; a small girl-child, alone, barelegged, hair unkempt, dragging her matting roll of bedding – they passed across the screen, staring at us with patient eyes. We could not endure more. Pao muttered, "Let's get out of here!" We tramped the streets a long time in the winter fog of London, silent with our thoughts.

The war had gone on for a year. Shanghai was lost, then Nanking was lost and the world assumed China would capitulate. Instead, we retreated, still fighting; we harried enemy communications with guerilla warfare; we drew upon our vast resources of man power and our reserves of morale; we entered upon the second phase of the war – endurance, outlasting the enemy. With the victory of Taierchwang in the spring, hope revived afresh; it was proved Chinese could defeat Japanese in spite of the disparity in armaments. With good courage we faced the second year of war.

Letters from Peking were few and uninformative; Japanese censorship was strict. Life continued in some fashion, but hedged about and restricted on every side. There was no career, no future possible for ambitious youth. All universities but two were closed and those two under constant surveillance, their students suspect, in danger of arrest. Of my friends and classmates, many migrated to Free China; others, chafing under the soul-destroying repression of the Japanese regime, fled to join the guerillas. From these who had left Peking we had letters telling of a life that was not life – deadening existence for those others remaining, for whom physical escape was impossible. I read of one and another of those friends seeking escape in opium dreams or the release of tension in sensual excesses. Everywhere flourished openly the houses of prostitution and opium dens, under Japanese auspices. First the monotony, the despair, all the strong currents of life dammed and stagnant; then perversion and decay of all decency.

When I read of these things and understood the pervasive evil of alien rule whose only aim is exploitation, I could not be a pacifist. We must resist as one resists disease – building up barriers against its further encroachment; fighting the poison that drains our strength; restoring, reclaiming for health and function, areas already infected. I could not stand apart, coolly indifferent. I had to be *in* the struggle, a part of China's resistance. I had to return to China. Even if there were nothing of significance I could do, I had to *be* there to share the suffering and the hazards. I was Chinese. . . .

So when Pao told me he had his sailing fixed for September – his course was finished and he could go – I said, "I am going back too." We knew each other very well by this time. We had discovered that, although we could always be angry in hot argument, we still sought each other again for stimulus and excitement and a certain deep understanding. It was a rainy evening in August. Pao had called for me at my boarding-house in South Kensington; we were going to a show. Both of us loved the theatre. But a word had been said that precipitated crisis. We went down the stairs and into the street, silent. We walked on and on, into the heart of London. We needed the soothing of rain to help us to bear our thoughts. Cars rushed past, their headlights flaring upon the wet asphalt, their wheel tracks instantly erased by the rain. Street lights were moons with an aura of fog. We walked on, hands in coat pockets, staring straight before us.

"Han Suyin," Pao said at last, in a choked voice, "you must not return to China. You have been thinking a lot of fine things about love of country and dying for ideals. But it is not like that, noble and beautiful. War is a terrible thing. You have said yourself it is filthy and wasteful and cruel. You cannot endure even to look at the picture of it in a newspaper or on the screen. You must remain abroad, enjoy plays and music and interesting books. What can you do in China, one girl, alone? What can you do that is worth giving up life for death?"

"Tang Pao," I said, "you are not a good friend of mine! You should not persuade me against this choice. I, also, am a Chinese. How shall I live in ease and cheerfulness in a foreign country when my people suffer trouble and distress?"

We were talking Chinese. Brushing shoulders with passers-by, we were alone together, isolated by speech in our own language.

"But what is it has changed you?" cried Pao. "You who were so bitter against all war – now you will put on a uniform and shoulder a rifle and recruit a girls' battalion!"

"I am not going back to fight," I answered, "I do not know whether I am going back to nurse the wounded. What is the good of saving wounded soldiers and sending them back to face the bombs and cannon again? I think I could even be indifferent to the conquest of China by Japan, if Japan had a civilization superior to our own to give us. In a hundred years we should have absorbed them. But Japan will not give us anything of good. She has no distinctive culture; in the beginning she borrowed her culture from China and now she borrows from the West. Japan can teach us only evil. She will use us; she will destroy our youth, all those who should be our leaders of the future. She will make us a nation of peasants and coolies, a tool for her use. Against this aggression China is right to resist. I am young and I want to be there, to be a part of this resistance."

Pao walked on in silence. Then he turned abruptly to me.

"You are a very stubborn girl!" he said. "You will not be understood; you will not be thanked. For those who work for China there is only bitterness, hard drudgery, perhaps an empty glory after death. Even Sun Yat-sen found it so."

"I know this. But it is my country. I must return."

"But who will take care of you, Han Suyin? War is not for women. I think of my mother – she is in conquered territory; she cannot escape. My old mother and my little brother, no one looks after them. And you – what family have you except in far-away Szechwan?"

"I do not need anyone," I said. "I am a woman, but I am an adult person also. I will be responsible for myself."

"If you must go back," Pao said, "I would like to be with you. Might we take passage on the same ship? I would like to take care of you. Han Suyin, let us be friends for ever!"

"But I need no one!" I answered. "Tang Pao, you think disdainfully of women when you wish only to protect us!"

"Han Suyin, your temper is awful! You cannot consider any question impersonally. You cannot argue without spitting fire! Will you not be kind to me a little?" He quoted from a poem of Li Po's: "'In the wind and the rain, what pleasure to be ship companions! To the evening moon we lift our wine-cups, petitioning for life!' ... Suyin, if I do not protect you too much, if it is only that I wish to be with you ... would you marry me? It might not be for very long. I shall probably be killed quite soon." And Pao tried to look tragic.

"I'd rather you were not!" I said.

Pao's face cheered. "Then you wish it will be many years? For life? One never knows how long that is. Han Suyin, shall we be married?"

The street lamp glistened on passing umbrellas, on the rubber raincoat of the policeman at the corner, on the shining cars, the wet pavement. The rain drizzled down, more mist than rain. We stood and stared at each other, hands in our coat pockets. Without a kiss, without touching of hands, we exchanged our promises. Perhaps, being Chinese, we bowed a slight, formal bow to each other. We felt very solemn. Pao and I were engaged. We were both a little startled that it had happened. We had been prejudiced against marriage, for we thought it would hamper our work for China. But under the rain-haloed light on a London street corner we realized that without each other our work would be hollow and meaningless.

Though we had become engaged without consulting our families, we felt that it would be best to wait for their sanction before we were married. All our tradition was against a hasty wedding. Also I had a feeling, perhaps sentimental, that I wanted to be home in China to begin this new life with Pao.

In two or three weeks we were eastward bound on a small French steamer with uncommonly bad food. For the first few days, however, this was of no importance to me. I was desperately seasick. On the third day, when I lay spent and pale on a deck chair, Pao found nothing better to do than feed me with very small, very hard, very green apples saved from his lunch. For pride's sake I swallowed them, with dire consequences. . . .

Behind us Europe swirled into the current of a mill-race rushing toward war. Hitler had taken Austria and was reaching toward the Sudetenland. Czechoslovakia and Poland saw their new and hard-won freedom threatened. In England our friends were being fitted with gas masks. We were happy to be homeward bound while ships might still move freely on the seas.

CHAPTER THREE

HONG-KONG INTERVAL

In Hong-Kong harbour great drifts of grey, dirty clouds crept over the sea and sky. The air was still and sultry, the water a dull sheen reflecting the heavily brooding sky. North-westward the hills of the mainland rose steeply abrupt from the sea – the hills of China! Hong-Kong, like a huge ant-hill with its narrow streets and slatternly tenements, sprawled along the base of the mountain whose peak went up into the clouds.

It was the thirtieth of September and my birthday. I was twenty-one. There seemed to be a special significance to that. I was of age. I had returned to China, no longer a dreamy girl, but a woman ready and willing for my part in my country's ordeal.

September 1938 – the world has cause to remember that date. The day before our landing the Munich pact had been agreed upon. Headlines of newspapers sold on the dock flashed the report. "Peace in our time" for Europe ... so brief, uneasy, and shabby a peace! There was a moment of pause at the onset of our war when China could have bought a similar respite, at the price of her northern provinces and a large share of her freedom. But we knew what the word of an aggressor is worth.

Our ship nosed into dock on the Kowloon side, across the bay from the island city of Hong-Kong. This was continental China, territory leased to Britain, but China nevertheless. From Kowloon westward ran the railroad, piercing the range of barren, rocky hills that hemmed the harbour, a slender double band of steel, the road to Canton, to Hankow, the life-line for supplies of war. Disembarking, we stood upon the Chinese mainland. Our wish sped inland. We turned from the hills and the railroad with reluctance, to take the ferry for Hong-Kong.

Our wish sped inland. ... We are home, yet not home. China is about us, the teeming turmoil of Chinese life: brown, familiar faces; the graceful long gowns of men and women; shop signs in our lovely calligraphy. Refugees – the first we have seen. British rule makes here a circle of immunity. This is neutral ground; this is safety. But we are not seeking safety. We have returned to accept a part in China at war. Hong-Kong is for us only a station by the way.

We snatch at the newspapers with fear and eagerness. News from Hankow, word of the fighting at the front. Hankow our goal, the war-time capital, with the enemy closing in upon the High Command, and upon him, the Generalissimo. *He* is there, Chiang Kai-shek, not shirking danger; and the armies of China with him, holding back that strangling loop of the Japanese forces. There is a decisive battle in progress, and we not there to share it! We *must* reach Hankow – as though our strength might turn the scale! We smile at our own youthful foolishness. But we must go on. For no purpose, then, but the sober reason that our work waits for us there, the thing we have come back to do. We must reach Hankow, and quickly – or it may be too late. The way may not be open. . . .

The way was already beset with difficulties. Canton, the gateway to Free China, was being visited by bombing squadrons daily. It was difficult to realize this, safe in Hong-Kong. And almost daily the Japanese attacked the railway, swooping down to bomb trains, bridges, villages, along the way. Labour gangs, maintained all along the line, repaired all but the most serious breaks in a few hours, and kept trains moving. But the Canton terminus had been so badly wrecked that no trains had left the city now for a month. Munitions and other essential supplies were sent to points from which they could be forwarded by rail. But the passenger service was so irregular and hazardous that few chose to take the risk, and there was little demand for it.

Other means of transportation which we investigated offered no better hope. Bus lines had been discontinued, for the routes were all but impassable. Plane tickets were not to be had. The Eurasia and China National Airways were on an irregular and reduced schedule, since one of the C.N.A.C. planes had been shot down recently and all the passengers killed. In spite of that disaster, every seat was booked for weeks ahead.

With a sinking of the heart we stared at the barrier of silent hills. In such an impasse, we turned to that first and last resort of every Chinese in difficulties – our friends and relatives. Our friends, our uncles and cousins, the friends of our friends, the relatives of our friends and the friends of our relatives, will turn up at intervals all through this narrative. Pao's friends spread all over China; they run into the hundreds. So it may be as well to explain here the curious institution of friendship as it is understood in China.

Nowhere else in the world are personal relationships so important and so binding. This may be right; it may be wrong –

but it is there, a fact. Kinship and friendship are the double foundation stone of the Chinese social structure – friendship through every kind of casual association, kinship spun out to the most remote degree.

The Big Family is the unit in China. Here the clan lives together in one household, under close-crowded roofs, in the many communicating courtyards centring about the High Hall where the tablets of the ancestors are reverenced. The Big Family can never be so scattered by migration, war, or business necessities, but that the sons and daughters to the third generation born in exile will still refer to the ancestral dwelling as home and may return to its welcome after a hundred years. Thus, my home is in Pihsien, a town in Szechwan, although I was born in Honan, lived in Peking, and might never have seen Szechwan but for the war that drove me westward.

Under the wide roofs of the Big Family there are always guests. They may be distant connections – an "uncle" perhaps, who is the thrice-removed half-cousin of your second stepmother. They may be "dry brothers and sisters", the children of other families who have bowed to the ancestral tablets of your household, presented gifts, and by these ceremonies placed themselves under the protection of the house; they are thenceforth entitled to the privileges of blood kin. They may be friends, or strangers who come bearing letters of introduction from your friends. They are all assured of hospitality for as long as they may need it.

Friends are acquired almost as automatically as relatives and the tie is as close. If you have joined a club, entered a trade, studied abroad, held office, all those associated with you in those enterprises are *per se* your friends. Especially binding is the relationship between those who have attended the same school; they call each other brother. All who have ever been cadets at the Central Military Academy are Pao's sworn brothers. He may never have met them before, but the fact of their having frequented the same buildings, drilled on the same parade grounds, makes them of one fellowship.

The code of friendship is exacting. You must never fail your friend. Even though he be a confirmed cad, you lend him money, encourage him with good advice, help him to find work and a fresh chance. If he beats his wife and she comes running to your wife with complaints, you do not criticize or condemn, but play the mediator to smooth out his domestic difficulties. For almost every situation friendship holds the solution. If you need a sym-

46

pathetic ear for your woes, a discount on some purchase, a guest to share a banquet, a source of loans, a recommendation for a job or influence to secure political advancement, an introduction to a young lady you hope to marry, a ticket for train, bus, plane, or ship when none is available, you look to your friends. In a case at law you may not rely upon the justice of your cause, but you must seek out a friend who is the cousin by marriage of a man who knows the judge; then you may rest content that your plea will be favourably received. A Chinese war lord, once, who had driven his rival into a tight place forbore to deliver the final blow that would have crushed him, belatedly remembering that they were in the nature of things friends, since they had in youth been at the same school. This is the complex and far-reaching system of friendship, responsible for much of the good as well as some of the evil of our social organization.

We came to Hong-Kong as strangers in a strange city, and friends cropped up as if by magic everywhere. They hailed us on the streets, friends we had not seen for years. They insisted on giving us big dinners, though we could not but see how over-taxed were their reduced resources. They all gave us of their time and hospitality without stint. Fortunes of war had brought them to Hong-Kong, some as refugees, some in government employ, posted here at the port of entry for Free China. We had seen them last in Peking or Tientsin. We had known the graciousness of their lovely, spacious homes and shared their life of leisurely, mellow enjoyment. We met them again, dispossessed of their lands, all their material wealth gone, living crowded together in tiny rooms in Hong-Kong, yet preserving still that inner buoyancy and mature philosophy of our race to make the best of their meagre circumstances.

Our guardian and rescuing angel in particular was a certain Fu Hsing-sen, one of Pao's friend's relatives, a stout and hearty gentleman, once head of a flourishing export and import business. His fortunes wrecked by the war, everything sacrificed for his country, he was now in Hong-Kong on secret-service duty. With his wife and five young sons he lived in a little two-roomed apartment high on the slopes of the Mountain. He welcomed us as though we were his returning prodigal children, took charge of our six large trunks, regretted that limited space made it impossible for him to have us as guests in his house, and guided us to a good hotel within our means.

Armed with introductions provided by Fu Hsing-sen, we called upon his friends who might be able to help us on our way.

We went anxiously from office to office, from friend to friend, following up each thread of hope, always graciously received, sympathetically heard. We sipped innumerable bowls of tea, nibbled sweets, met charming people, but we got no further with our quest. In the course of our wanderings we encountered others who, like ourselves, were bent on reaching Hankow at all costs. We made common cause with them, gathering recruits as we went. We investigated the practicability of hiring a bus and driving through with our company of adventurers. But that hope flickered out. It would be difficult and dangerous, if at all possible, for roads and bridges had been bombed. And with no allowance for wreck or breakdown, it would take at least two weeks.

Everywhere we were promised help with the utmost sincerity, but nothing crystallized into definite action. At the end of the day, exhausted with fruitless search, we arrived four hours late at the Golden Dragon Restaurant for dinner with Fu Hsing-sen and his family. The five little boys must have been quite faint with hunger, but they betrayed no sign when their father dismissed our apologies with an airy wave of the hand and the customary polite phrase, "But it is early, quite early."

Although during that long day we took no time off for rest or recreation, I could not resist this last chance for shopping. In the stores of Hong-Kong there was displayed merchandise from all the world – and we were about to plunge into the interior, cut off by war from all this profusion of lovely things to buy. The Wing On department store, elegant with its rococo towers and wide plate-glass windows, offered the beautiful embroidered *lingerie* hand-made by the women of Swatow and Ningpo. Pao stood uneasily by while I selected a few pieces; it was probably the first time he had ever gone shopping with a girl. I consulted his tastes in choosing, but he was completely unhelpful. He fingered the filmy *crêpe de Chine* and murmured, "Won't you be cold in this stuff? It doesn't look very durable, either.' Then he wandered off and became engrossed in a display of watches. When I rejoined him he was inspecting a tiny platinum watch on a linked bracelet. "Is this the one you would choose?" he asked. It was indeed a beauty, the handsomest in the show-case. He locked it on my wrist. "For your birthday," he said.

It was my betrothal gift as well, for we had been too excited, leaving England, to remember the customary exchange of presents. If we had been affianced by family arrangement, in the correct, time-honoured Chinese way, gifts as many and as rich as our respective clans could afford – rolls of heavy silk, gold

48

rings, embroidered hangings, vases, lacquer ware – would have been carried in procession through the streets on gaily painted trays, two bearers to each tray, with flute and cymbals going before, making the music of announcement. But there was something far more real than all such ceremonial ostentation in Pao's bestowal of his gift, his fingers fastening the clasp upon my wrist.

In three days of running about Hong-Kong we grew very familiar with that odd city – a grey old Victorian business centre with its stolid and dusty brick buildings sprouting galleries and arcades in concession to the tropics, grafted upon a maze of Chinese streets, gaudy and cluttered, with their flimsy two- and three-storied structures, shoulder to shoulder for miles. Rickshaws with carriage wheels raced recklessly with honking motorcars, and jerky little tramcars trundled along their tracks, and everywhere the small brown southern Chinese crowded the streets and wharves. There was a babel of many tongues against the background of staccato Cantonese. All the dialects of the southern coast – Ningpo, Hingwha, Foochow – with the slower, gentler northern mandarin, and all the languages of Europe, were blended in the composite voice of Hong-Kong. The city was thronged with new arrivals: rich Chinese fleeing to neutral territory to preserve their wealth; refugees who had escaped with no more than their lives; Chinese government officials conducting the intricate business of credits and communications; spies of all nationalities; men with something to sell; men looking for something to buy. War in China, somewhere behind those brown hills on the Kowloon side, was reflected in the tempo of Hong-Kong, like the pounding throb of an engine forced beyond its capacity load.

This was China, no matter how different this pressure and urgency from the stately rhythm of the Peking we had known. With our return to China (though as yet we were only at the threshold) with our re-absorption into the life we belonged to, our sojourn in England became an unreal memory, indistinct in outline as a morning dream that fades on waking. Those years were as though cancelled. We were nearer in thought and feeling to our earlier youth in the north. Surely it was not longer ago than yesterday that we walked by the canal, under the grey-green willows bent a little with the sun's heavy heat. We were again eager and impatient as those children, too early thrust into maturity but buoyant with courage and ideals, sure of the world's

49

essential goodness and the glory of our country, which needed only us and our generation to set all right that yet needed mending.

Three days we wasted in Hong-Kong, no nearer solution of our problem. There seemed no chink or defect in the barricade of circumstances which withheld us from continuing our journey toward Hankow. Release came without warning, a good omen of the luck that is with us whenever we do things together. Fu Hsing-sen's voice over the telephone: "I have heard there will be a train leaving for Canton at four this afternoon, going through to Hankow – probably the last." We thanked him hurriedly. We ran to the station, not daring to believe. We had followed so many disappointing clues; this would prove a false rumour; we must not count on it too much. It was true! Quite as a matter of course, the ticket agent sold us first-class tickets to Hankow. Yes, at 4 p.m. The Green Express, a good train.

We rushed back to our hotel to pack. Only hand luggage could go with us. Quickly we chose what few essentials to take. Fu Hsing-sen arrived, anxious to be of assistance. Into his hands we thrust the rest of our belongings, to be kept for us until they could be forwarded. They are there still! With suitcases we crossed the ferry and hastened to the station, Fu Hsing-sen accompanying us, bearing farewell gifts of fruit and sweets.

The train was in the station. We entered our car. Outside the window kind Fu Hsing-sen waited on the platform, determined to see us off. There was a long interval of hesitation, stretched out to eternity by our impatience and suspense. I looked at my watch. It was already half-past four. I looked out at the scanty trees about the station, at Hong-Kong Island across the water, the too familiar scene. Minutes dragged by. It was nearly five. We had been too optimistic. They would be coming soon to tell us, "Not today. Not tomorrow. A break in the line. Bombing." We would go wearily back to the hotel with our suitcases. It was too soon to hope.... There was a lurch forward! The trees started to slide away past our window. For a moment the round, pleasant face of Fu Hsing-sen kept pace with us, beaming, then glided away rearward. We leaned to wave to him, waving also a glad farewell to the station, the bay, and the island, then sank back in our seats, relaxed to the train's accelerating motion.

We rush toward the hills; the jewel-blue sea is left behind us. The hills part to receive us and close in again to shut away the view of Hong-Kong. We are on our way to Hankow!

The sun dropped lower, threw long yellow shafts of light and level blue shadows. Dusk sifted down like impalpable grey dust. We rushed on in the twilight through the same low hills, through harvested fields, yellow and brown. Beyond Canton the train halted for a long while in the fields. We stepped down to walk by the tracks. It was the loneliest hour of evening – a warm wind blowing; the strident shrilling of cicadas not yet silenced for the night; a hazy half-moon high in the dim grey sky, small as a segment of an orange. We spoke little. Both were remembering the stark ruins of stations and villages we had seen in jagged outline against the pale sky, and the twisted wreckage of Canton railway yards. In the morning our hopeful young enthusiasm would reassert itself, but in the dusk we felt old with the ancient gentle sadness of China and we understood and shared a little the prevalent quiet fatalism of our race.

The engine hooted with a shrill wail into the evening silence. We returned to our car, walking through the train. Ominously, the cars were almost empty. Most of our fellow-travellers had left the train at Canton. Only five were left in the first class, seven in the second. There was no third class; there were no other women. We wondered, with dubious questionings. Why should they run a train with so few passengers? Perhaps they were moving the rolling stock inland. What new threat? Invasion at Canton?

There was no dining-car. The train boy served us supper at our seats. The food was quite good, but dusty. All that night I lay half awake, uneasily conscious of stopping and starting, indefinite pauses, bridges rumbling with a hollow sound under our cautious, slow-turning wheels. All night the warm, dusty wind blew over the plains of Central China.

We arrived the second evening in Yochow, an important railway junction, where the Canton-Hankow line meets the railroad south to Kweilin. From Yochow it is only a few hours' run to Hankow in normal times. It took us four more days.

CHAPTER FOUR

FESTIVITIES IN HANKOW

Yochow station and the surrounding fields and the streets in the grey evening were alive with a grey flood of soldiers. Strolling along the rails, grinning in at the windows of our train, moving about in sluggish currents, sprawled asleep on the platform or on the bare earth of the fields, seated on the ground dozing, their heads bowed upon their knees – soldiers everywhere. Waiting, with vast patience. Many had bandages, once white, now earth-stained, bloodstained, tied around their arms, heads, or legs – the walking wounded. There was no noise, but a slow, heavy murmur of many voices together. These soldiers were Hunanese, with a great strength and poise about them. They watched us blankly as we paced the platform. They had a look of weariness and acquaintance with danger, and under their indifferent stare we felt like children.

Pao joined a group of their officers who stood a little apart, talking together, and asked where they had been. Hankow. The front. They had been there a month in the fighting. Yes, considerable action. The Japanese were nearer Hankow. They had everything – tanks, planes, heavy artillery, superior equipment. But we had stood them off ten months. These men would be back in the lines again after a rest.

A short, thin young captain with the keen glance of a hawk turned the question back. "Where are you from?"

"We have come home from abroad."

"Where are you going?"

"To Hankow, to report for duty."

"You have come *back* to Hankow, when you might have stayed abroad? You are very brave. I am proud to meet you."

If it had been irony we could have endured it. But his sincere admiration made us abashed. We had done nothing as yet.

In Shanghai and Hong-Kong and in distant foreign lands there are still a few young Chinese – students, dilettantes – who are waiting complacently for the war to end without them. Sometimes we are all judged by these few who lag in ignominious safety. This young officer in Yochow, who had fought since the outbreak of the war, known the privilege of hunger, cold, suffering, wounds, in the cause of our country, and thought nothing of it all – I wished that he might stand representative before our foreign critics who do not know the Chinese truly. We could never do enough to prove worthy of the words he had said to us.

The engine was disconnected from our train. We were abandoned on the tracks. We would not be going on to Hankow that night. Bugles in the dark of morning woke us, vying with cockcrow to announce approaching dawn. Not the brisk, imperious notes of reveille, but now one, now another bugle bleating forth a long, faltering tremolo; then simultaneously but *not* in unison, each bugle striving independently for some stable pitch, all combining in a despairing, moaning chorus. The little bugler boys rise up before light to practise; it is their hour. Diligence is their one virtue.

Grey dawn revealed the same patient grey horde, bivouacked in and around the station. Huge tubs of steaming rice and kettles of soup with floating vegetables were brought for them and the soldiers clustered around to scoop up bowlfuls of the hot food and gulp it down with zest. The sun rose. Shops in the street opened up. About ten o'clock there was a raid alarm. Shops hurriedly closed. The soldiers picked up their rifles and packs, fell into ranks and marched away from the town. Our engine came bustling back to conduct us to safety. The train was run out on a siding in the country. The passengers took refuge among trees and thickets. When Pao and I walked alone we were not afraid. But others kept anxiously searching the sky. They hid under sheltering banks and covered themselves with green branches for camouflage. They had been through the bombings of Canton. It all seemed very curious to us, but after we had endured bombings in Kweilin and Chungking, we understood! Hours passed and no planes came. We wandered back to the train. There was no food served; there was no more water to drink. We subsisted on the last of Fu Hsing-sen's *bon voyage* fruit and sweets.

Back to Yochow, the third night out of Kowloon. The same soldiers, returned from their march into the country, still waiting for their train. In the morning the same weary bugles. All that day refugee trains going south pass through Yochow, cattle trucks filled to overflowing with human salvage. Miserable, with drawn faces, in rags, dirty and thin, clutching their pathetic possessions, tied in bundles. Children, old and wizened with fatigue, long past whimpering, rubbing their trachoma-eaten eyes with their dirty hands, with the rags of their garments. Refugees in a continuous stream, packed into cattle cars, standing; standing for days on end, packed so densely it is impossible to move

53

so much as a hand. Faces blank with utter exhaustion, they are like dumbly suffering animals. Speech and gesture have become for them desperately difficult. They are past emotion, centred upon one terrific effort of endurance. We watch them; this is the reality behind the news reports we read in England, in Hong-Kong. We can say nothing. We can only clench our hands and watch the passing of our people, fleeing from their devastated farms and villages, homeless. Pao's lips are set in that grim expression, the tiny wrinkles radiating about his eyes.

Two days and two nights in Yochow were an eternity of delay. But we had the first-class carriage almost to ourselves; we had soft berths, shelter from the drizzle of rain that began on the second afternoon. We were ashamed of our impatience, for we were so infinitely comfortable in contrast to the refugees in their cattle cars, the soldiers in the open. A short time before our train at last made a definite motion to leave Yochow a troop train came for our friends, the Hunanese soldiers. I was glad. If we had gone and they remained, in my memory they would be for ever waiting in the chill grey rain. Now I could rest my concern for them, having seen them on their way southward to deserved furlough.

Twenty hours to cover the short run from Yochow to Hankow. We moved at the pace of a walk; we were shunted on to sidings to give right of way to refugee trains southward and troop trains northward; we stopped for raid alarms. But in the sunny late afternoon, five days almost to the hour since we left Kowloon, we pulled into Wuchang.

Where the Han River meets the Yangtze there are three cities, separated by the rivers – Wuchang, Hankow, and Hanyang, collectively known as Wuhan, the great industrial area of Central China. Wuhan, hotbed of revolutions, where the republic was brought to birth in 1911, now China's war-time capital – not ancient, hauntingly lovely, dignified, like Peking, nor shining as a new-minted coin, showy with new palaces of government, like Nanking, but grim and raucous, toiling in sweat and mud in the broiling summer sun and the chill, penetrating damp of winter. The unbelievably huge Yangtze, Son of the Ocean, a thousand miles from the coast, winds between the Wuhan cities, coppery brown, turbid with the red soil of the west washed down in its wild course through mountainous Szechwan. Here in the level land of Central China it broadens to a boundless plain of water, stretching away southward into the Poyang Lake, and even at Wuhan almost too wide to see across. Wuchang on the south bank was already bombed to ruins. But Hankow, with its foreign concessions, seemed as we approached it by ferry untouched. The tall buildings along the waterfront stood unshattered. The ships moored at the docks were loading and unloading with customary activity. The foreign consulates on the Bund, huge, old-fashioned mansions in their gardens, seemed serenely unaware of war.

In the streets, in the kind autumn sunlight, women and children were buying round white moon-cakes, for this day, October eighth of the Western calendar, was the fifteenth of the eight month by ancient Chinese reckoning, the Moon Festival. In all homes there would be feasting tonight. The rich would spread banquets and invite their friends. The poor who tasted meat only three times a year would eat meat tonight. Incense and candles would be lighted in the family shrines. People would walk in their gardens or in the streets and parks, singing to the softly breathed music of flutes. They would love the white moonlight for its beauty. They would forget for one night to dread the full moon which lights raiding enemy planes on their course.

We wander with the crowds. Here is no feverish gaiety of a doomed city, but a happy content. They say the city has been ordered evacuated, but the Bund – the broad street along the waterfront – is a moving current of people, strolling, watching the lights of steamers on the river and the silver scribble of moonlight on the water. Families, men and women – women with flowers in their hair – walking with their children. Hankow is to us the last stand of the pre-war China we have known, the China of the coast, rich, amiable, placid. They say the enemy is pressing nearer – but every one is so secure, so confident. Nothing will happen. That is, nothing for months. There are so many people in the streets, buying sweets, laughing, enjoying the moon in Chungshan Park, pushing into cinemas and theatres. Nowhere is there a sign of devastation, fear, or disturbance. Nothing can happen here....Hankow at the eleventh hour, so long threatened, given up for lost in 1937's December, yet safe and serene in the moonlight of 1938's October. ...

Next day Pao reported to General Headquarters. He was at once given a commission and appointed to the General Staff. That meant the rear, not the fighting lines. Pao was disappointed. He would have wished to be sent to the front first, on active duty. But with his knowledge of languages and his specific technical training, the superior officers decided he would be of more value at General Headquarters. "A kind of office job!" Pao commented scornfully. Secretly, and half against my will, I was glad he would not be going to the front immediately. We could be together in Hankow. We could be married! While Pao still grumbled at his luck, my mind raced on planning for our wedding.

In those dim, far-off days on the ship, returning to China, if I thought of our wedding I could never make a picture clear in detail or even in outline. It was not difficult to think of myself as Pao's wife, and the two of us together in China, in a new and exciting life. But for the actual ceremony neither of us made any definite plan. I thought of Peking, always of Peking – I could not have imagined as background this seething, war-time city of Hankow. We would return again to the house by the canal in the Forbidden City; we would taste again of the leisurely ample life of the Capital of the North. But Pao was dubious. Peking – occupied territory. . . . "It will be a long time until Peking is retaken," he said. So I answered, "Anywhere – Canton, Hankow – I do not care. It is all China – home!"

I thought of weddings I had watched as a child, remembering the din of fire-crackers; music of cymbals and drums and tootling wind instruments; a great spread of scarlet silk hangings; feasting; men guests and women guests in gowns of heavy brocades and satins – but against this background I could never imagine Pao and myself. Certainly I could not go to him as a traditional Chinese bride, a stranger contracted for by his family, excessively demure in a red veil (red being the colour for joy), carried to his gates in a gaily festooned sedan chair. Even more certainly I could not see myself as a fashionable Shanghai bride in tinselled velvet, with ten yards of tulle veiling carried by a half-dozen little girls in hair bows and short pink dresses.

Perhaps we should be married in a mass wedding, sponsored by the government. We should march in procession to stirring national airs played by a brass band; we should give our responses in unison with thirty or forty other couples; we should sit down with our guests, with all the other couples and their guests, to a well-regulated banquet. No. That might be patriotic and in accord with the doctrines of economy, but it would not be ours – our own!

I wanted something to remember, a significance, an inner beauty. I wanted . . . Pao is not a Christian, but when I told him what I wished, he consented. We would have a Christian wedding at the mission in Hankow. It would be very simple and quiet. There would be only ourselves and two or three friends for witnesses and the minister.

I told Pao of my own new job. While he had been reporting for duty I had gone to volunteer my services at a hospital for the wounded. Bombed out of its building on the outskirts of Hankow, the hospital had moved down-town, where it was housed in a bank building. So many of the staff had gone, evacuating with their families to provinces farther inland or entering Red Cross service, that the hospital was short-handed. With the increased work of soldier wounded and air-raid casualties, volunteers were welcomed. A few foreign doctors remained. The head nurse, Miss James, was British. She had a very commanding presence and stood at least six feet tall. I felt like a small child before her. I made known to her my qualifications and my wish to be of use, and without further formality was accepted and put to work. Stretcher cases were coming in, wounded who had been given emergency treatment in the first-aid stations just behind the lines, then transported to the rear. Although the front was so near, some were days reaching the hospital. Right then, in my first hour on duty in the receiving ward, I learned the smell of gangrene, that sweetish, sickening stench, warning of an infection almost beyond hope. Those cases had to be isolated promptly, lest the contagion sweep like an uncontrollable fire through a ward.

Most of the wounded, as they were carried in, were silent, and uncomplaining. A few moaned; others were restless with delirium. One with a bullet through the lungs and a fever of 105 degrees – a farmer conscript, not young, with hollowed brown cheeks – conscious enough to be aware of the season of the Moon Feast, begged for moon-cakes and wine and pork, all the good things he had been hungry for during lean months of war and the days of bitter fighting at the front. Perhaps for longer. Perhaps never in his life had he had his fill of good things to eat, in the long, hungry years of his youth and maturity, when he tilled the soil. I would have given him anything he wanted – what difference could it make? He was going to die. But the doctors said no. Soft diet for high temperature. . . . And in all likelihood he would have turned in revulsion from the food had it been offered to him, so desperately ill he was.

October tenth – celebrations! This is the chief holiday of New China. On this day, the Double Tenth, in 1911, the republic was founded. Here – here in Wuhan! The monument to the dead of 1911 stands untouched by the bombing, its tall shaft still erect above the ruins of Wuchang. This is the birthplace of China's freedom. Where else should there be such pride in the day?

Evening, with a waning moon sliding through thin, silvery flakes of cloud, orderly in design as the silver scales of a fish. There was excitement in the dusty air, in contrast to the soft happiness, the calm well-being of the Moon Feast. The laughter had an edge of shrillness; it rang out startling and abrupt. There were no plaintive flutes in the twilight, but drums, band music, cheering, marching songs. There were parades with lanterns and torches. Schoolboys of the Youth Corps marched, shouting slogans – "Resist to the last! Keep Wuhan! Keep Wuhan! Down with the invaders!" The crowd took up the cries, repeating in diminishing echo down the side streets. Troops coming back from the lines, relief troops on their way to the front were marching through Kianghan Road, Hankow's chief thoroughfare. No rest or holiday for them! Guns and ammunition trucks were driving through the streets to the accompaniment of cheers. All the trade guilds marched in procession, each division with the implements of its trade – the merchants with the abacus, carpenters with hammer and saw, masons with chisel and trowel. Huge lighted floats went past, with life-size models of aeroplanes and tanks, with symbolic figures of Peace and Victory – one with a towering twelve-foot effigy of the Generalissimo. The people went mad with enthusiasm. They were jubilant, wild with joy, sure of victory.

This is not the China I knew, the country of easy-going, common-sense people, not readily roused to passion, scornful of emotion. These are not the impassive scholars, the practical merchants, submitting indifferently to any government, however ill. These people of Hankow are immensely stirred, fiercely alive, intense. It is the war that has done this to my people. We are united and determined, as never before. Our will to freedom is aroused.

As we stood watching the parades, a motor-car drew up before the Bank of China, opposite, where there were government offices. Out of the car stepped a lean, uniformed figure. He mounted the flight of steps and turned for a moment, looking out over the crowd, unnoticed by them. A severely simple uniform without decorations, a face serene in the moonlight and torchlight, a face to be marked, with its characteristic long, clean-cut jaw, high, unlined forehead, and deep-set eyes. Pao recognized him at once – the Generalissimo!

Chiang Kai-shek stood on the steps. As the crowd became aware of him there was a murmur, then silence, then a roar, spontaneous as the roar of a forest when a wind goes over it – *"Wei Yuan Chang! Wei Yuan Chang! Linghsiu wan sui!"* "Generalissimo! Ten thousand years!" The man they hailed stood at the salute, acknowledging their cheers, a small, grave smile playing about his lips; then bowed and passed from our sight into the building. I turned to Pao; he stood immobile, straight and still, his face tense with feeling and the effort to hide his feeling. And I remembered this was more than China's leader he saluted. It was his teacher, the master to whom he was bound by a relationship sacred from earliest history – Chiang Kai-shek, head of the Central Military Academy. How often Pao had stood at attention in the ranks with his fellow students in Nanking, learning from this man what it meant to be a soldier of China.

We drifted with the exultant crowd, and, tired, we entered a theatre where the play was *Keep Wuhan!* The acting fell short of the art we were accustomed to in Peking. The modern costumes, the abrupt, unrhythmic speech, seemed strange to us and a little uncouth. But the audience applauded each patriotic utterance with such zeal that it was difficult to hear anything. Half way through the play an announcement was made of fresh victory at the front. The crowd went delirious with joy. Hankow will be saved! Wuhan will be held!

Outside again. The moon is enormous and yellow; the pale silvery clouds have dissolved away in the clear, dark curve of the sky. It is wonderful to be alive and here, in free China, to share this passionate contagion. We are at last one with our people, united by one purpose. Pao and I together and our country around us – we with all China welded into one by the tragedy and sacrifice and glory and all the pitiful blood shed in defence of her freedom. Tonight our fear is gone. We have been troubled and unsure at times, shaken with distrust of the future and dread of the unknown awaiting us. But our fear is gone. Within us springs up strength, like the jet of a fountain rushing upward, straight, tall, powerful. This is the moment of revelation, of completion, toward which all our past was building. We have learned faith in our destiny, to enable us to go forward without fear.

Within three days Pao and I were caught up in the current of a new and strenuous routine. All day we were at work. Our evenings we had free to be together. We were no longer strangers in Hankow. If we walked in the street, went to a restaurant or theatre, we were certain to encounter people we knew, friends and connections, gathered into Hankow from all over China.

One evening Pao took me to call upon his uncle, General Tang, that he might see me and approve. He was the patriarch of the family since Pao's father's death.

General Tang, head of an important department in the General Staff and one of the busiest men in China, is a quiet-mannered man of middle age, slight of build, with an immense innate dignity. He was worn down with work, and thin; one could perceive the strain under which he lived. From the private soldier in the ranks to the Generalissimo, the military man in China gets the least pay and does the most work and makes the greatest sacrifices. For young men like Pao, perhaps it is easily borne, but for those past fifty, with large dependent families, with home and fortune lost, it is a heavier thing.

General Tang's welcome to us was typical of him, reserved but sincere. I had faced this interview with trepidation, but his un-affected graciousness put me at ease. He is not a loquacious man; he is never free with confidences, but he can always be relied upon in time of difficulty, as we learned to know. In his official capacity he never takes praise for anything well done, but leaves the empty glory to others, satisfied, himself, to know that the work *is* done. He is truly representative of Pao's family, who have for centuries kept to the tradition of the old Chinese code of honour and up-rightness.

General Tang, with a flicker of his eyelids and a slight smile for our impatience, gave us the news. The last two days' fighting has gone on steadily, doggedly. The result is quite good – quite good. But on the other hand . . . it may not be necessary to hold Wuhan. . . .

We were struck dumb. We did not understand, for we had not even considered the possibility. I, at least, thought in terms of definitely bounded territories which must be held at all cost, whose loss would mean disaster, utter defeat. General Tang continued in his quiet, unaccented voice: "This war is going to be very long. You have not yet understood the strategy we must use. There is plenty of time. We have plenty of space, plenty of man power . . . plenty. . . ." Again the faint smile for our bewilderment; then he turned the subject and accepted our invitation to be the chief witness at our wedding.

There remained the question of a second witness. Pao learned that his friend Ah Huang was in town, and we looked him up. Ah Huang is a Cantonese who was born and educated in Canada. At the outbreak of the war he left a very lucrative position as an engineer in an aircraft factory there, paid his own way back to China and was now setting up repair shops near the aerodromes. We found Ah Huang in bed at his lodgings, half smothered under two thick quilts, although the day was warm, shuddering and shivering with malaria. Between chattering teeth he cheerfully hailed us "Well, who won't turn up next! When did you arrive?" He would have none of our sympathy. "It's just a matter of getting enough quinine into me. I'll be O.K. in a week." We were regretful; a week would be too late. "What day? The fifteenth? Let's see. . . ." He counted on his fingers. "Today I shake, tomorrow I don't, the next day I shake, the next day I don't. Can do!" But wouldn't it be too much for him to rise up from a sick-bed to attend a wedding, not to mention a wedding dinner? "Oh no. I get up and go to the shop every other day, anyway. I'll be there. You can count on me."

Friends had given us an introduction to the Reverend Dr. Kent at the mission. We called to make our request that he should marry us and to arrange the hour. There was little of outward beauty in the mission-house. It was a small red-brick, two-storied building, enclosed with its garden within walls. The style and furniture were typical of so many missionary houses in China – nondescript colours, walls whitewashed or yellow daubed, rugs, sofas, and arm-chairs all well used and a little faded. But there were flowers from the garden – chrysanthemums, white and red roses, and early narcissi; and here and there a Chinese scroll painting or a vase of pure and lovely line.

We found Dr. Kent a tall, thin man, quite young, with a lean, quiet face and grey eyes. When he spoke, his voice was slow and very kind and understanding. We made the appointment for three-thirty the next afternoon.

At the hospital I told Miss James I should be unavoidably absent for a day. Under her scrutiny I know I burned red. Her eyes said, "Is this an excuse? Will you also leave us?" I stammered that I would certainly be on duty next morning. I do not know whether she believed me. For nothing was stable; no one could be depended upon. We were a heterogeneous group under her orders. A few trained nurses, a number of untrained entrusted with far too much responsibility for their slender experience, and the rest volunteers with or without medical background. With this assorted staff Miss James had to run her hospital and see that the patients were cared for.

Rumours were rife. The nurses met in the corridors to whisper among themselves, repeating hearsay and wild reports. In the morning when we came on duty some would be missing. A sudden contagion of panic and they would be gone without notice. Others continued. They went about their work, grim-lipped, scornful of weakness. Then more rumours and in another day or two these were wavering.

In the clear daylight rumours evaporated. Hankow was impregnable. For so long the enemy had hammered away at it and still it stood. There was no reason why it should not stand indefinitely. But in the evening again, when the lights were low so that the patients might sleep (though all night long there were mutterings and heavy sighs of pain and restlessness), fear stalked the wards, and we would remember the horror tales – true ones – told by women and girls who had come through the sack of Nanking; delicately bred and sheltered women who had been subjected to every indignity. The ring of our enemies closing in on three sides seemed to tighten closer, then in the dusk, and we thought of what might happen if – when – Hankow fell, and we had waited too late for escape. . . .

Pao's duties took him everywhere – to the various offices of the General Staff, to Wuchang across the river, to the defence works. He brought back news not yet released to the papers. "The Japanese have landed at Bias Bay. They are marching upon Canton," he told me in a voice without expression. Almost it might have been the statement of some trivial thing, but that the words came slowly and with difficulty. It is so always when we speak of defeat and reverses. We are stoically matter-of-fact – "Shanghai defence is broken; Nanking is lost" – telling the news in as few words as possible, facing the fact, externally impassive. It is when victory is announced that we let free our emotions. We stand up and cheer wildly for the recapture of some unimportant village, some minor strategic point. And we go mad with joy over the major victory of a Taierchwang or Kunlunkwan, the successful defence of Changsha, the recovery of Nanning. We set off fire-crackers and hang out flags. By this sign only may our hearts be read and our true feelings understood, when we state calmly, "Canton will be lost."

Canton, the gateway to Free China! With the railroad out, our last link with the coast gone, what hope left? Dismay gives way to practical considerations. There are still the rich interior provinces. There is the narrow-gauge railway out through Indo-China and the long, rough road through the Gobi to Russia. The Burma Road through the wild mountains of the south-west is being rushed to completion. We are not defeated; we have resources yet.

Pao had further news: "The General Staff plans to leave Hankow."

I was stunned by the word. "Why? By why? Aren't the lines holding? Couldn't we keep Wuhan?"

With the same curt brevity Pao explained. We were not defeated. This was not rout. But the defence of Wuhan was costing too much. We would need to husband our resources, more than ever now. The High Command had determined upon a strategic retreat. Everything was planned. Already new bases had been established. Each government department would be maintained to cover the retreat.

"But nobody knows of this – the people are so absolutely certain the cities will be held. The government cannot abandon everything without warning!"

"They will be told. There have been warnings. Evacuation of civilians was ordered long ago. If they will not believe, if they will not obey, is it the fault of the government? Industries, factories, and their workers have been moved. Every effort will be made to help those who wish to go. But panic now would hamper troop movements and betray our intention to the enemy."

"Pao, when?"

"I do not know. Soon."

But nothing is changed! Posters – "Keep Wuhan!" – flash out assurance from every vacant wall and bill-board. People stroll along the Bund in the pleasant autumn sunshine, watching the ships loading and unloading. The city is busy and gay, full of people. Children, women with flowers in their hair, merchants at the doors of their flourishing shops – they are all here still. And in a little while . . . "Soon," Pao said . . . Weeks? Or days. . . . It is terrible to know a thing not known to others. The burden of this secret knowledge is so great my mind is unable to accept it. Except when I am with Pao, talking of it, it sinks into the fog of a nightmare too fantastic to be real.

The morning of my wedding day. Sunlight golden on the river and the air all dazzling brightness. Exactly the weather for an air raid, but air raids were something I could not believe in just then. I had the morning leisurely and free. I walked on the Bund, taking pleasure in everything: the trees of the parkway; the song of the carriers loading ship – "Hey-ya! Hai-yah!"; the swift procession of cars and rickshaws; all the teeming, customary life of the city. One could never have guessed the threat of enemy lines closing in upon it.

I bought from a flower vendor small white roses and sweet-scented narcissi, and returned to my room at the hotel to fashion a bouquet. My new gown of modest dark blue silk was laid out on my bed. I laid the flowers against its strong, deep colour – ivory, pearl, on the blue, beautiful! I fastened a small cluster of narcissi, formal, delicate, in the knot of my hair, then reduced it to just two blossoms; I had such fear of being garish, for the women of Pao's family were never ostentatious.

Pao had been away all the morning on duty at the General Staff. There was still time on my hands before I should meet him for lunch. I sent the room boy to bring me Pao's boots, for I remembered the sketchy service they received at this hotel. I attacked them with brown polish and zeal, and although they lacked something of the English lustre of Sandhurst days, they showed improvement.

At one Pao returned and we went out for lunch. There was a curious restraint between us; we were almost shy of each other. We assumed an off-hand manner, talking briskly. I asked him about the events of his morning. He admired the flowers in my hair and gave it as his opinion that a few more blossoms would enhance the effect. When our eyes met, we forgot what it was we had been saying and were overcome with sudden silence in the middle of a sentence. . . .

It was almost three o'clock. Time to be starting for the mission-house. I had made myself quite ready to face the critical appraisal of Pao's family, in the person of his uncle. General Tang. Enough but not too much of colour on my cheeks and lips; the gown very conservative; the flowers in my hair augmented, but still a little prim. Ah Huang called for us, and I went down to meet him, clutching my bouquet with both hands. Pao came out of his room, belted and booted and full-uniformed, with all the insignia of his new rank, but bareheaded. The cap he held away from him in repulsion. "This cap – it will not do! Green! It no more matches my khaki than grass and corn!"

In China there is no standard dye for uniforms. We are congenitally averse to regimentation. Therefore the various units of a suit may run the gamut from pale yellow, through orange, khaki, and grass colour, to deep holly green. Pao's cap had never been through the same dye bath as his suit. "Your old one?" I suggested weakly.

"But the regulation style has been changed. Also it is too yellow

64

and does not match my dress uniform. That was why I ordered a new one. The tailor was instructed; he made promises; and this is what he delivers at the last possible moment!"

The matter was of importance. An officer cannot go bare-headed; it is not done. There *must* be a cap, and Pao is not one to compromise with conditions. Nothing less than the exact article would do honour to the occasion. "You go ahead with Ah Huang," he said. "I'll meet you there and buy a cap on the way. There must be shops." And Pao rushed out in search of perfection.

Ah Huang and I called rickshaws and proceeded to the mission. Dr. Kent greeted us, for the moment taking my escort for Pao. Then, with some confusion, he realized it was not the same young man who had accompanied me previously. I came to his rescue with an introduction of Ah Huang and an explanation, "My fiancé has gone to buy a cap."

"Oh yes, of course, naturally," Dr. Kent agreed, as though it were a common occurrence, and invited us upstairs to his study.

We were scarcely inside the house when there was an air-raid alarm. I was not yet accustomed to the sirens, the rush of crowds seeking refuge, shortly followed by complete cessation of traffic and an uncanny stillness, the street lying wide and empty in the sunlight. Dr. Kent and Ah Huang made conversation, uncon-cerned. I stood by the window, watching. My white roses were drooping a little; my hands were too hot. I put the bouquet down upon a chair. The hour set for our wedding came – and went. I do not think I was afraid, either for myself or for Pao (the Han-kow concessions had never been bombed), but I felt rather for-lorn.

An hour went by. I memorized the room – its whitewashed walls, a blue sofa, two arm-chairs, and a desk with roses in a bowl, a clock on the mantelpiece (especially the clock with its hands that never seemed to move!) flanked by vases of white flowers. I watched the shadow of the garden gate and wall lengthen across the deserted pavement. The day's bright quality of joy was dulled to a flat monotony, measured off by the slow tick of a clock and the impatient beat of my own pulses.

At five the all-clear signal was given. Into the oppressive silence the siren shrilled and hooted. Before its long-drawn note had subsided, the street was filled with a jostling crowd. In a moment all was normal, noisy and free.

General Tang arrived with apologies for the unavoidable delay. Still no Pao. It seemed to me that all looked at me a little strangely. Their eyes were embarrassed, almost pitying. It is possible they were thinking Pao would not come; he had changed his mind; he had decided not to marry me. But I was untroubled by any such misgivings. Trust is the basis of everything we mean to each other.

As the clock on the mantelpiece strikes six – only two and a half hours late – a rickshaw rounds the corner on one wheel and comes to a halt at the mission gate. First there is a view of the top of a fine new khaki cap. Then Pao glances up and there is the flash of his smile, when he sees us all leaning from the windows. Dr. Kent hurries downstairs to greet him. Ah Huang is close behind. Boots clatter on the steps, ascending. Only General Tang and I sit sedately, waiting. I could not have walked to meet Pao if I would, my knees were shaking so. Pao enters, quite unabashed. There is a dancing devil of laughter in his eyes as he shares with me in a glance his amusement at the obvious relief of all the rest.

It is growing dark. They light candles. Dr. Kent opens his Bible. . . .

This was our marriage. Candle-light. Dr. Kent speaking the solemn, thought-weighted words of the ceremony, his voice quiet and low with authority. Pao and I standing before him, trying to hold ourselves straight and still, but shaking with excitement and wishing we could cling together (but that would not be dignified), our hearts beating terribly, choking the breath in our throats, so that we could scarcely answer when it was expected of us, "I do." (Pao added a muttered "Of course!" under his breath, with a *hsiung* look.) When he put on my finger a flat, dark gold ring engraved with his name, our hands trembled as they touched.

Dr. Kent presented us with two small Bibles, inscribed with our names and wishes for our happiness. I meant to keep mine for ever as a talisman, but I lost it the following spring in a bombing in Chungking. General Tang spread out upon the desk the two copies of the marriage contract. These were to be signed and stamped in red with our personal seals. It was a detail I had forgotten, but Pao, at the last moment remembering, had spent the two hours of the raid alarm in the shop of a seal carver. He now produced the two little wooden seals, one cut with his name, one with mine. After us, our witnesses also signed and sealed the certificates. When General Tang rolled them up into little scrolls and gave them to us and I held mine in my hands – this legal contract in the essential form which is as old as the civilization of China – I realized that I was now Pao's wife, accepted by his family.

Through streets gay in the dusk with millions of electric globes like glittering beads and the hot red blaze of neon tubes we drove with our guests – General Tang, Dr. Kent, Ah Huang, and two or three friends who had arrived late for the ceremony – to the Kuan Sun Yuan, the famous Cantonese restaurant, for the feast indispensable to every Chinese wedding, whether rich or poor. Pao's uncle, who is a connoisseur of food and wines, had selected the menu. It was a modest repast, as feasts go, but we were at the table an hour or more eating course after course. I was remarkably hungry – no proper Chinese bride of the old style who, as custom prescribed, would have touched no food for three days. We had not risen from the table when Pao was called to the telephone. He returned to us, grave, with knit brows. He was ordered to report to Marshal Pai Chung-hsi at nine in the morning.

"But his headquarters are across the Yangtze and miles beyond!" Ah Huang exclaimed. "You cannot possibly make it by nine in the morning unless you cross the river to Wuchang tonight."

"Tonight!" we echoed blankly. We looked at each other in consternation.

"Tonight by the eight-o'clock ferry," they told us. "There is no boat leaving in the morning that will get you there in time."

"Before daylight, then!" said Pao.

Inquiry revealed that the earliest ferry was at 4.30 a.m. We made our farewells, left the restaurant rather soberly, and drove to the hotel. At the desk we gave instructions to call us at four in the morning.

It is an astonishing apartment, our suite in the hotel. One room is huge, as big as a banquet hall, with three tables, sixteen chairs, a bed large enough for four stout men, lots of settees, windows, and mosquitoes. The other room is room-size, packed with furniture of every description and use. The bathroom plumbing makes noises all night like bombing planes.

Our windows look out on Kianghan Road. We can see the river far off. The night is even noisier, busier, and dustier than the day. The clamour of the city rises up to us – street cries; wireless and phonograph singsong; the clang and clash of rickshaw gongs; shouts, laughter; loud voices; the shuffle of marching

67

troops, sandal-shod, so strangely different from the smart click of leather heels on the pavement. Far away the shrill whistle of a river steamer bound for the ports of the upper Yangtze. . . .

I have folded away my blue silk wedding dress. On the table lie the two small wooden seals, the little watch Pao bought me in Hong-Kong, the narcissi in a saucer with water, the certificates that prove all this is real. "In ten years," says Pao, "when this war will be over, I shall marry you all over again, and we'll continue to do so from time to time as long as we live. It is a charming custom, marriage. We'll have our children attend too, I think." We laugh together; isn't it insane to be so happy?

All night the rumble of traffic, the blended dissonance of voices below our windows . . . I did not know I had slept – the noises went on and on in a heavy dream – until I struggled awake to the sound of knocking and the harsh glare of the electric light. Pao was already up, putting on his clothes. I crawled out of bed, determined to dress and walk with him to the ferry. I was shivering, my teeth chattering uncontrollably, with chill that was more of the spirit than of the body. There was no dawn as yet; the red and yellow lights blazing all night made a lurid haze into the sky, as over a burning city. "Go back to bed, Suyin," Pao ordered sternly. He pressed the quilts warm around me, kissed me, and was gone. I lay, still shivering, while new voices shouted in the street, and the red glow flickered out and the windows outlined squares of the bleak grey morning. Alone. . . .

CHAPTER FIVE

RETREAT FROM WUHAN

There was a chill in the air that day, a raw wind blowing. October's encore of summer was over; the wind had a knife edge of winter. There was something else, something more than the turn in the weather – a new, vague feeling of apprehension abroad. It was not my secret knowledge of the impending fall of Hankow that made me imagine things. The people were beginning to know; a whisper ran among them; many shared my knowledge. The shops were not so busy; some were closed, fronting the street with blank, boarded-up façades. From the hospital windows I watched the beginnings of exodus, people going by, carrying their meagre belongings in bundles and baskets slung to the two ends of a bamboo pole. People going away, patiently moving westward to escape invasion.

Ships bound for the ports of the upper Yangtze – Ichang, Chungking – had long waiting queues of deck passengers. Trains going south had been packed with refugees for weeks. Those who had hesitated were without means of transportation. Everything was sold out for months ahead. They were setting forth on foot upon the long trek westward, loaded with their scanty household goods, leading their children by the hand, carrying the smallest ones. My heart tightened a little as I looked at the familiar scene.

So it was in the north when I was a little child and famine stalked the land. For three years no rain had fallen. All the reserves of grain were gone. The people had eaten everything, even to the bark of trees. Their faithful work animals were killed for food. They had drunk the blood of the last water buffalo. At last when the fearful alternative of cannibalism faced them, those who could still walk rose and set out on foot, staggering under the loads swung from bamboo poles across their lean shoulders, leaving their land to seek work and food in regions not forgotten by the clouds and rain of heaven. Many fell by the way, many died; a few reached the lands of plenty, found food, and were strengthened to return again to their homes when the drought years had passed. I had seen them going away. . . . But this man-made disaster was more terrible because it was not a thing decreed by fate, but caused deliberately. It was an act of war against these helpless people, these small, hurrying children. . . .

I turned back to my work. I was on duty in the women's ward then, but there was no escape from war casualties. Women and children, victims of air raids on the borders of Hankow or brought in from Hanyang and Wuchang across the rivers, filled the beds. There were even two girl soldiers. With cropped heads and their ears standing out on each side so nakedly, they looked like boys. One had a bullet through the arm, the other had a leg torn to shreds by machine-gun fire. I envied them their hardihood. Sometimes in idle imagination I have seen myself striding the long roads with a soldier pack on my back, carrying a rifle, fighting for my country like a man. But I shall never do anything so adventurous. When occasion comes to prove myself in stress of physical hardship and danger I usually begin by being miserably ill! I am impatient with my uselessness!

Pao returned from Wuchang. Of his interview with Pai Chung-hsi his diary tells with a soldierly brevity:

At 8.30 I arrive and am told the Marshal will receive me. I knock at the door and enter. Marshal Pai is seated. He is all, thin, his head clean-shaven. His nose is high-bridged and strong, his chin prominent. His eyes are dartingly quick. They will stare reflectingly past your shoulder, focused on distance, then pounce upon you, sharpened to keen points that bore into you. We have twenty minutes' interview. Marshal Pai, as chief of the Military Training Department, is interested to know what I have gained from my work in England. He asks me questions on the European situation, revealing his own thorough knowledge of the critical balance there. He demands accurate and concise replies, nods in comprehension with narrowed eyes. When I leave he has clearly indicated his saisfaction.

Pai Chung-hsi, the strong man of Kwangsi, was until a few years ago an irreconcilable opponent of Chiang Kai-shek. But with the outbreak of the war he laid aside these personal and political differences and put himself and his forces at the service of the Generalissimo. He has been utterly devoted, upholding the military policies of the leader with self-effacing loyalty. He is a great strategist, an upright man and a born commander. Kwangsi, once a barren, bandit-infested region, under his rule became China's model province. Within a few weeks we were to see and know Kwangsi for ourselves, though at this time we had no thought of going there.

October seventeenth. Midnight. Pao has gone away. He is gone and I let him go alone. . . .

Here on the table are the narcissi, still sweet though a little yellowed. The watch, Pao's gift. And my little wooden seal cut with the name no longer mine – Han Suyin. I am not Han Suyin; I am Tang Fu-jen. Pao and I have been married two days.

At dusk I came off duty and returned to this odd apartment that was home for us. Pao had not yet come in. I started out with the hope of meeting him. It was growing dark. I fought the cold wind that swirled up eddies of street dust against me. Down Kianghan Road the glitter of neon shop signs and lighted windows was broken by sudden gaps of darkness where buildings were left closed and empty. I had not gone far when I had a premonition of something wrong. I hurried back, almost running before the wind, my heart beating fast with some vague dread. The lights were on in our apartment. I flung open the door. Pao was there, bending over his suitcase, packing. He looked up.

"Suyin, sweet, I am going away. The boat leaves at eight."

In a few hours everything had been decided. The General Staff was to leave that night. The ship was waiting at the dock. They would cross the Tungting Lake to Changsha, from there travelling by rail to Hengshan in Hunan and across country to a village called Nanyu.

Pao told me in clipped sentences as I helped him to fold away his things. After the first blow of surprise, it was as though we had known it for a long time. We spoke in few words and unemotionally of commonplace matters. The shirts are not back from the laundry. I will send them to you later. How long will you be on the way? Write back from Changsha of your safe arrival. How many days before I can expect a letter? How shall I address my letters? I shall give up this apartment and move into the nurses' quarters in the hospital. It will be more convenient.

To neither of us did it occur that I might go with him – now, tonight! I had my work. The hospital was crowded and shorthanded. Fighting continued; all night and morning the wounded were being brought in from the front lines. There was still need for me in Hankow. I had returned from England for this purpose, to find a place where I could be of use. I would stay on until

71

the troops were actually being withdrawn, the defence works abandoned. But this seemed so remote, so unlikely an eventuality. We spoke as though it would be weeks – months, even. Pao would come back for me when conditions really became critical. Or, as we both believed still in our hearts, despite all warnings, Wuhan's long resistance must be at last successful, the Japanese driven back. I would wait in Hankow for Pao. The government would return again.

We took rickshaws for the Bund. I went with him for good-bye. Down on the docks, by violet-white arc light or the dim yellow flare of kerosene lamps, there was a chaos of embarkation. Rickshaws arriving on the dead run, motor-cars blasting their way through the press with loudly blaring horns. Officers in uniform and gentlemen in suits of European style or long Chinese gowns, herding their families aboard or looking to the bestowal of their hastily assembled baggage. Ladies, slender and elegant in their silk *shan,* their eyebrows pencilled delicately and their lips painted full and red. Raucous-voiced servant-women. Children, heavy with sleep. Crying babies and their imperturbable wet-nurses, with bovine calm unbuttoning their loose blouses to give suck. Carriers staggering under mountainous loads.

Pao and I picked our way across the deck of an intervening ship to reach the small steamer reserved for the General Staff and their families. Iron rails stacked loosely gave insecure footing, rocking and rolling beneath our tread with infernal clankings. Below, the wide doors of the hold were open; through them filed endless double line of carriers, like a two-way procession of ants, going in loaded, coming out empty-handed, transferring from the dock great stacks of equipment and machinery. Between the two ships, close-moored though they were, a woman with tiny bound feet had stumbled and fallen into the water and was being rescued with great outcry to the entertainment of many watchers. People who did not belong on the ship were determinedly fighting to force their way on board and, meeting equally determined resistance, were being pushed off. Porters were hurling baggage through the air – furniture, chairs and tables even.

We stepped aboard the ship of the General Staff. The decks were choked with dumped baggage and piles of machinery, over which people stumbled in the dim light of kerosene lamps. The electricity would not come on until the engines started up. There was a confusion of shouldering, shoving bodies, of voices raised

72

in altercation and voices calling for someone lost. Washbasins clattered from poorly tied bundles and huge net-covered baskets spilled their contents. Blankets were strewn about to entangle one's feet. In dark passages one almost trod on sick people, lying on quilts. We wormed our way through the crush and emerged on the upper deck, where Pao's uncle, General Tang, had reserved a claim for us, a blanket spread out on the floor.

A great despondency overwhelmed us. We sat silent, our shoulders touching. There was nothing we could say to each other. Below they were still loading ship. It was already nine-thirty and no sign of casting off. The song of the carriers – "Hey-yah! Hai-yah!" – was a rhythmic pulse through the din. When the last of the cargo was stored the ship would move.

"This is no good!" Pao exclaimed. "Waiting here until the last moment. We'll not be gone before midnight, and you have to-morrow's work at the hospital. Good-bye is just good-bye. We may as well say it now as later, and you can go back to the hotel and get some sleep." We made our farewells; we tasted the salt of tears with our kisses. We left the deep shadows of the upper deck, fought our way through the pandemonium, down steep, narrow stairways, through the dense crowd clogging the lower deck, to the gang-plank. Ashore we bought some biscuits and sesame-seed cakes, for we had had no supper. When we had eaten them Pao called a rickshaw for me. "Good night, Suyin." "Good-bye, Pao." That was all. The arc light's glare and the stares of passers-by forbade any further gesture of affection. My rickshaw puller raced off with me. Pao turned and was gone, swallowed up by the crowd.

I entered the lonely room which had so briefly been our home. We had laughed together over its absurdities. Tonight it was merely hideous, with its gaunt furniture, its heavily framed, cheap pictures hung at an acute slant forward, its harsh electric bulb in a shade of ruffled pinkish glass. Dust, inescapable this windy weather, made a film over everything, gritty to the finger-tips on every surface one touched.

I moved as though sleep-walking, still dazed by the swift turn of events. This is a dream, a dream! Pao is not really gone. I shall wake in this enormous bed to find him beside me. I lay in the darkness, sleepless, perhaps an hour, too desolate for tears.

Suddenly, as one wakes to reality out of a slow nightmare, my mood of compulsion, of acquiescence, was dispelled. What am I doing in Hankow, and Pao on his way to Changsha? Is there no work for me in all China except in Hankow? Nothing matters – nothing – but that we should be together. Why had I not gone with him? Why had I let him go without me? I sprang up – it was not quite midnight – dressed, threw a few things into a suitcase, snatched up my handbag and ran down the stairs, my feet scarcely touching the steps. I called a rickshaw – "Quickly! Quickly!" We swung into the Bund, sprinted for the wharf – faster! – the ship was gone! The ship of the General Staff was gone, and Pao with it. Black, empty water only, shot with the moving glitter of reflected lights. . . .

Next morning from the windows of the nurses' quarters on the top floor of the hospital, where I had moved, I watched an air raid. From the relative safety of this tall building in the foreign concession one could see the Japanese planes, like a file of migrating birds, small in the distance, raiding the air-field. Around them the shells of our anti-aircraft batteries burst in balls of white smoke, sudden as popcorn. Black smoke of the demolition bombs fountained from the ground and floated away on the wind; seconds later, windows rattled to vibration in the air and there came the dull, heavy thud of the bombing. Then the sustained, singing thunder of the bombing squadron's engines (once heard never forgotten!) hovered under the sky for long moments after the planes had disappeared, dissolved into the light.

In Shanghai, Canton, Hankow, the Japanese usually avoided bombing the foreign concessions. Barring accident, it was quite safe to watch from windows or roof-tops the adjacent war, sometimes only a few blocks away. It gives one an uncanny feeling to be so close to danger, yet insulated. Foreigners in Shanghai watching with detachment the bombardment and burning of Chapei across the Soochow Creek; foreigners holding roof parties at night for the thrill of seeing the fire sweeping through densely populated streets of the Native City – how is this different from Chinese thronging to the Tu-ti Miao in Peking to witness executions? One does not see the blood; that is all.

When I came off duty in the afternoon there was a lost, empty feeling where there had been expectancy at this hour. I should be hurrying to meet Pao for our evening together. But Pao was gone. I went for a walk, alone, upon the Bund, drawn irresistibly to the place where I had seen him last. Again the dense crowd on the docks, the motor-cars and rickshaws, the carriers with their song, the women clutching babies – all the noise and excite-

74

ment of embarkation. It was yesterday repeated. It seemed impossible that Pao should not be there.

On the dock I found Ah Huang, surrounded by stacked machinery. He was supervising its loading, sixteen carriers to one massive fly-wheel. The huge mass was intricately rigged with poles and ropes to distribute the weight evenly among the carriers. Ah Huang grinned at me. "Moving day," he said. "We're setting up shop again at Ichang and all points west. You know how the Japanese stripped the factories of Shanghai of every scrap of metal. They won't get this!" His ship was sailing that night. He asked after Pao; I told him. He looked at me keenly and said, "Well, I suppose you two know what you are doing. But if I had a wife I'd keep her with me. Hankow is going to be increasingly unhealthy very soon."

Next morning I waked to a strange, ominous, rumbling sound, a subdued roar of unrest. The people knew the worst now. They were in full flight, but there was no disorder, no panic. Their myriad voices and the pad and shuffle of their soft-shod feet made up the noise I heard. I watched them from my window. They would walk hundreds of miles – to Ichang, to Szechwan. They would meet winter. The streets were bright with sunlight. There was wind in the blue sky, wind swooping about the tall buildings with a swift, shrill cry, wind promising winter whipping the garments of these homeless thousands setting forth on an unknown trail.

I went out to buy a newspaper – no more newspapers being sold. The *Ta Kung Pao*, leading daily, had put out its last issue in Hankow, with a message for the soldiers at the front blazoned across its first page and an announcement within that the presses were being moved to Chungking. There were rumours concerning Canton – nothing known certainly but hints of treachery. Perhaps Canton had already fallen.

Hankow looked very bleak and it was suddenly cold in the shadow, too warm in the sun. The streets were unfamiliar with blank, boarded-up shop fronts, where yesterday all had been thriving trade. Some shops were in the act of closing. The proprietor could be seen hastily fitting the long wooden boards into their slot, driving them home with a bang, locking the doors, pocketing the keys, and, fan in hand, walking unconcernedly away.

Every one knows. All are leaving. Yet there is no panic. Everywhere the most perfect order and discipline – the carriers in their customary alignment, the wounded on stretchers being carried in at the head of the street. All is quiet, calm, except for the wind and the shuffling of the many feet.

Fighting was still going on, they said, the rear-guard covering the orderly withdrawal of the main army. Our leaders were determined this time that it should not be as it was when our long resistance at Shanghai broke without warning, and the retreat mired down in the swampy land between Shanghai and Nanking, and men and equipment were needlessly sacrificed in the deep, churned mud of the roads for lack of plan. There must be no repetition of that retreat, nor of the stampede of fear-mad civilians at the Nanking-Pukow ferry, when the weak were trampled or pushed into the river and drowned, and families were wrenched apart in the struggling mass, never to find each other again.

Since there was no need to keep silence longer on the information Pao had given me days before, since every one knew and we talked among ourselves at the hospital with the same strange calm of the refugees in the street, I mentioned casually to Miss James, the head nurse, that Hankow was expected to fall at any minute now. She flushed with the high colour the English show under their fair skin and in a rather dogmatic voice refuted me. "You shouldn't give yourself to such rumour-mongering; why, I don't mind telling you I was at the tea given for Madame Chiang only yesterday, and she promised us that she and the Generalissimo would not be leaving Hankow until the last moment. They are still here, so you can see there cannot possibly be any critical danger!"

No, Miss James, you are entirely wrong. You do not know the Generalissimo and Madame Chiang. Their presence is no guarantee of perfect safety. On the contrary; where conditions are most insecure they are there, organizing, directing, holding everything steady with their coolness and courage. They will stay until the last minute – yes. The Generalissimo, like a good master of the house, will stay until almost every one else has sought safety. He and his wife with him will be here, watching, supervising the removal; then, after a final inspection to see that everything is taken away that can be moved and everything destroyed that should be destroyed, so that nothing of use or value may fall into the enemy's hands – then they will go. They will take their plane and be off, satisfied that the job has been well done.

I did not speak aloud; time and the event alone would convince Miss James. But as my thought revolved about the theme, it suddenly became real to me – *Hankow is falling!* This is the crisis – now! The troops are being withdrawn; the government has already gone. Hankow is being abandoned. Hankow, defended for ten months against the constricting loop of enemy lines, is lost. In a few days Japanese troops will march through these familiar streets. The scenes of horror that occurred at Nanking will be re-enacted. There will be mass executions, perhaps – looting, raping, and murder certainly. The imperial armies in victory seem forced to these excesses by some inner compulsion; this wanton use of power seems necessary to them to convince them again of their strength, of their irresistible might. They have to get themselves drunk on it, as they do on saké.

For the first time I faced without unbelief and without the anaesthetic of an unnatural calm this fact of Hankow's imminent fall. Perhaps the concessions would offer sanctuary as in Shanghai. But even so, safe from physical harm, it would be to wear my heart away, cut off from the clean air of Free China. It would mean separation from Pao, my husband of two days only. It might mean, as to some of my friends in Peking, despair and recourse to drugs. To endure this aimless, dreary life of submission – bowing humbly to the sentinels in the street, afraid to speak freely – one could not be too keenly awake, too much aware. It would be easy to drift into the limbo of an opium dream, dulled and only half alive. . . .

When I remained on duty in Hankow I had not taken into account the swift course of events. Looking back, it seemed almost bravado that I had thought I could stay on until the last moment. That moment had come, far sooner than we had foreseen. I was trapped. There was no possibility of getting tickets for train or boat so late. I could not shoulder my pack and walk a few hundred miles to Changsha or Chungking, as many others were doing; I had not the stamina. There was no one to whom I could turn; Pao's friends were gone.

Dr. Kent's lean face with its kindness and understanding flashed to my mind. I scarcely knew him; I was only one of hundreds he had touched in the routine of his work. But remembering his voice of quiet authority, I felt confident he would help me. I went to him, and he was as kind as I had hoped. He had resources, though it took all that day with an exhausting round of calls and interviews before he was successful. But that night I could sleep in utter relief, in the knowledge that Dr. Kent had secured for me a berth on the ship of the International Red Cross, leaving for Changsha in three days, the twenty-second of October.

Still the wounded came in. Fighting had not ceased. But there were official visitors at the hospital, supervising the evacuation of such cases as could be moved. This retreat was so orderly one could not feel it, but by now it was unmistakable. When I went to Miss James to tell her I had to go, she said nothing. She understood now that there was more going on than she could see. I felt almost a deserter, there was so much to be done. But I knew all this activity would die down to stagnation once the Japanese entered Hankow. Miss James would carry on, I was certain, even if she had to do it alone and single-handed. Though the Japanese came, her duty was with her hospital. They might try to interfere, but I could not imagine the most hardened and high-handed of Japanese officers being rude to her six-feet-odd of imperturbable bulk, or outfacing her steely blue eyes. She would be in command of any situation.

With my plans clear I could throw all my strength into my job, trying to pack a month's work into these last two days. Outside in the streets the shuffling of feet went on without pause. Other traffic sounds were few. Most of the trucks had left. There was occasionally the swift rush of a speeding car on some last urgent errand. All the rickshaws were gone, requisitioned for moving army supplies. Sometimes for minutes at a time I forgot all about the retreat going on, in the absorption of my work. In a world gone insane with slaughter we fought for a single life as a thing precious and irreplaceable. Often we lost. It was an unequal battle we fought, to resore what steel and explosives had wrecked.

At night I dropped into bed, drugged with weariness. The last night. . . . Tomorrow I was going away. This job was over. Long before daylight I was awakened by a tap at my door and the voice of a servant-woman mumbling something indistinctly – "Telegram," I thought she said. The word is *tien-pao*. I stumbled to the door, dizzy with fatigue, with a clutch of terror at my heart. I flashed on my light, pulled at the bolt. In the dim light of the hall the servant-woman was trudging away; she had left no ominous envelope on my door-sill.

"Suyin!"

Pressed against the wall in the half dark of the hall-way stood Pao! His face was turned toward me, very pale, with big, glowing eyes, tight lips. I stared, as though at a ghost. "Oh, Pao, it's you," I said. So stupidly. . . .

78

Then I was in his arms, sobbing, shaking with a joy and relief so intense it was like pain. His arms were like hard bands. The cloth of his uniform smelled of outdoors and of night. Pao thought I was cold, I trembled so uncontrollably. I was cold, though I had not known it. I slipped into bed and pulled him in with me, all dressed as he was, and we clung together.

The first intensity of our excitement spent itself. We talked together in low voices of the four days, long as years. "I came back for you," Pao said. "The river is being closed against the Japanese warships. They say after today no ships can pass. This is the end for Hankow."

"Every one knows the city is falling," I answered. "For days people have been going away."

When Pao returned to the ship after sending me home in the rickshaw that night (that night which seemed months and years, not days, ago!) he made his way back to the upper deck. There was yet no sign of any end to the interminable business of loading. Pao joined his uncle, General Tang, who was in conversation with friends. Pao stood deferentially aside, not entering into their discussion. Some twenty minutes elapsed. The carriers' song had stopped. Suddenly the electricity flashed on; the decks throbbed to the engines' rhythm. General Tang turned genially to Pao. "Are you and your wife settled – as comfortably as possible under the circumstances?"

Pao answered, "I am comfortably fixed, but my wife is not with me. She is staying in Hankow."

General Tang's face grew dark with consternation. "What! You've left her?"

"Yes, she stayed on for work in the hospital."

"You must both be mad!" exclaimed his uncle vehemently. "Don't you know Hankow is going to fall? This is retreat!"

"Why, yes. But –"

"Hankow is going to fall immediately! Within a week the Japanese will be in possession!"

Pao must have turned white. He says it felt like a shot through the heart. He sprang for the companion-way, dived down the narrow stairs into the maelstrom of the crowded lower decks, thrust his way desperately toward the gang-plank. But the engines were turning; the moorings were already cast off. As he set foot on the first rung of the steps to the after-deck the ship with a jerk moved clear. By the time he had reached the rail there was a broadening strip of open water between ship and dock, too wide for a jump. Pao whirled back, made for the engine-room through corridors packed solid with people and baggage. "Turn back!" he pleaded. "Turn back the ship!"

But for one man they could not turn back the whole ship. It was impossible. Pao understood there was nothing further to be done. He walked slowly back to his place on the upper deck. The lights of Hankow spun long, wavering threads of brilliance down into the water. He watched the glittering shore line, until there was left only a dim skyward glow, as of the red and yellow haze over a burning city.

The night and the next day were a terrific ordeal for him, with distance ever widening between us. Among the officers on the General Staff on board the ship he kept hearing the most sinister rumours, some true, some false, and no way to prove which. Canton was lost, they said. Unbelieving until the last, the people of Canton rose up from their dinner and fled empty-handed, leaving the meal still on the table. At Hankow the defence works were already abandoned; the lines were broken. The Japanese had only to walk into Hankow; there was nothing to prevent them, just as there had been no resistance when they took Canton. The entrance to the Poyang Lake was to be blocked. Already a boom was laid; it would be closed immediately to prevent enemy shipping from sailing down to Changsha. Even among the General Staff much was not known certainly, though they were well informed beyond the common knowledge.

About noon next day enemy planes sighted the ship. They circled about it like birds of prey. The massed passengers pressed back under shelter, out of sight. The ship carried no special flag of sign by which it might be identified. There was nothing to be seen from above but a small steamer, ploughing along unprotected. Evidently the Japanese decided it was too insignificant a vessel to be carrying important persons. The planes wheeled and flew away. Later we learned that they machine-gunned and sank a ship with five thousand refugees, mostly women and children. At such appalling cost the General Staff and their families escaped.

As soon as they reached port, Pao asked for three days' leave, inquired where he was to rejoin the General Staff, put his baggage into the hands of his uncle, and boarded a British steamer which was going back to Hankow from Changsha. He and a tactiturn Englishman were the only passengers. The silence and loneliness must have been uncanny after the turmoil of the ship he had left. Pao roamed the ship, seething within. He descended to the engine-room a dozen times a day to urge more speed, in dread that the boom might be already closed. He came upon two deck hands sharing an opium pipe in some secluded corner, and with all the pent energy in him he put the fear of hell into them, picturing the awful fate awaiting drug addicts, so that they swore to reform from that day forth. He paced the deck in a fever of restlessness; he could not sleep. On the fourth night after he had left he returned to Hankow. The grey profile of tall buildings lay stretched along the shore, with lights few and dim. The ship docked; Pao jumped ashore. There was an unwonted silence over the half-deserted city. It was three o'clock in the morning, the twenty-second.

Pao finished his story. "They say nobody can get away after today. The boom will be closed." I told him of my reservation on the Red Cross ship. He made a slight grimace. "Where does that leave me?" But I felt certain with his General Staff connections we could get him a place also. "One man more will not sink the ship. We'll go in the morning and make arrangements. You must go away now and try to get some sleep. I cannot keep you here in the nurses' quarters. It's against regulations!"

"If I can get a room at the hotel!" Pao remarked.

"You can get the whole hotel! Everybody's gone," I said.

At eight I called for him. He had not slept; neither had I in the few hours since we had parted. Sharing his room was a friend he met in the hotel lobby, just arrived from Hong-Kong the evening before. He had come to Hankow expecting to meet important people with whom he had business; he found the city emptied. He was utterly in the dark as to the situation – which indicates the speed and secrecy with which the evacuation was carried out.

The streets were almost empty. No traffic of any kind. The refugees with their packs and bundles were only a thin trickle; the flood had passed. All stores were closed. Wayside vendors with their portable charcoal stoves sold hot noodles, hot boiled eggs, cakes. We picked up the elements of a breakfast as we walked down the street toward the Red Cross office. This was in a building which housed numerous other welfare and patriotic organizations, among them the girls' division of the Three Principles Youth Corps. In a large room where we waited while Pao's application for a ticket was being dealt with, there were about a hundred girls having an early lunch. They had finished only the day before the last of a half-million padded winter garments for the soldiers at the front. Thousands of the bulky grey coats were

81

stacked and tied in bundles, filling all one end of the room.

As Pao and I were waiting, in came a slim, youthful-looking woman, dressed in slacks and a woollen sweater. Her dark, shining hair was caught in a knot at the nape of her neck. Her pale, smooth skin was untouched by make-up. Her black eyes were, I think, the most beautiful I have ever seen, and alight with keen vitality. It was Madame Chiang Kai-shek.

She spoke to the girls in her lovely voice, giving them instructions for packing the piled garments after their lunch. Then, seeing me, she was immediately solicitous – all China is her family! – and asked, "Is everything all right? Have you anyone looking after you? I can arrange for you to go with these girls." I told her I was going away with my husband that afternoon; she seemed relieved. I knew from her manner that the fall of Hankow was very near. I asked when she was leaving.

"When all these are safely on their way," she said, with a gesture toward the roomful of girls. "We need all young people in Free China, to work, to organize, to continue the struggle of resistance. We need all of you!"

I told her we had returned to China for that reason, that we had done what we could in Hankow in the two weeks we had been here.

"Wherever you go with that spirit," she said, "you will find service to do for China." She smiled and her eyes shone with animation. Impulsively I told her how much I admired her. She murmured some Chinese phrase, turning aside the praise.

Many people have written of Chiang Soong Mei-ling; her American education, her work, her wit, her beauty, her poise, her patriotic devotion. Every one has heard of her courage, when she took a plane and flew to the north-west, into the stronghold of revolt where the Generalissimo was held a prisoner in Sian, to live or die with him. She has proved it again a hundred times over, staying at his side through this war, braving air raids and hardship with him. This is what the world sees – a beautiful, spirited woman, a heroine of New China. There is more than this. All the traditions of Chinse womanhood meet in her. Famous and unknown, thousands – millions – of Chinese women, pretty and sparkling, clever and feminine, all velvet and silk without, but with souls like steel blades, souls of an utter constancy, the souls of the mothers and wives of China. Mothers who taught their sons the stern lesson of loyalty, as did the mother of Yueh Fei, engraving the words with a sharp point on his skin that he might never forget – "Faithful to country until death." Wives who have killed themselves to free their soldier husbands from all hampering ties that might restrain them from giving everything for China. Widows vowed to lifelong faithfulness. Chiang Soong Mei-ling is of these. She is not only modern; that is the lesser part. She is Chinese.

On the Yangtze. Late afternoon. Hankow recedes into the past. Yellow haze of the sun softens the proud skyline. Empty of feeling, submissive to the force which carries us further and further from war and cruelty and reality – from all the tragedy of China – we watch the city which is to be given over to death and terror on the morrow. Suddenly the passivity of our mood is dispelled like fog. We are quickened with new resolve. For – tall, dark, stern – the Wuhan monument, erected to those who died in 1911 for freedom from tyranny, stands black against the fold of the sunlight, a challenge. Wuhan is lost. But the stronghold of Free China – that is impregnable, for it exists in the hearts of many million freedom-loving Chinese.

It was four o'clock of the twenty-second of October that we sailed. Pao shared my cabin; someone assigned to the other bunk had graciously withdrawn to yield him place. We had clean beds, white sheets, baths and showers, dinner on plates and with forks. Unbelievable luxury. There was an air of comfort everywhere, though the ship was overcrowded. Many of the girls we had met in the workroom were on board. Our ship passed through the boom just before it was closed.

On the twenty-sixth Hankow was entered by the enemy. The Generalissimo and his wife were in the city until the last. At the final moment, when nothing remained for them to do, when to delay an hour would have meant capture, they took flight, their plane eluding enemy fighting planes that pursued them.

CHAPTER SIX

NANYU – HEART OF CHINA

A ship is a little world, sufficient in itself. It is a planet, moving in space. One is caught up out of time, and there is only the now, the here. The wind blows over the face of Tungting Lake, and the red-brown ripples break in flashes of white, and the water birds fly solitary overhead or in formation like planes. We rest our elbows on the rail of the after-deck and watch the wake, boiling and churning to foam that lies in a widening path all the way back to Wuhan – to lost Wuhan. We do not talk, but our shoulders touch, and Pao's hand covers mine on the rail. We are together and quiet, in this wide plain of water, shoreless, brown, fading to sky colour. Slowly, out of the haze of light, along the horizon there is defined the wavy blue outline of low hills. . . .

We had sailed away on a Saturday. On Monday we took up life again. We landed in Changsha to find the city in turmoil, like an ants' nest which has been kicked open by rude trampling boots. Such a running to and fro with bundles and babies, such a scattering and panic haste and flight. News of the fall of Hankow had struck Changsha like a thunderbolt, and every one was leaving. Buses were crammed to overflowing, loaded down so heavily that they slid backward on hills or broke down helplessly in the middle of the road. On the railway there was no time-table. Trains would hesitate for hours before deciding to move away, crawling like half-dead centipedes swarming with ants. Refugees were packed in the cars, hanging from the windows, standing on one another's feet on the platforms, clinging precariously to the steps and huddled solid on the roofs.

All that day and the next we spent following every clue which might offer a possibility of transportation. The special train which was to take the General Staff to their new headquarters had left three days ago. In returning to Hankow for me, Pao had missed it. But it was imperative that he should be on duty when the Staff resumed work in Nanyu. He was one link of a chain which must be whole in order to function. We used this line of argument unavailingly as we tried to cajole and persuade the harassed railway office to make an exception for us, to give us tickets on the train which was to leave that night.

Midnight. We walked the platform hopelessly, threading our way among small mountains of baggage and tangled heaps of crowding refugees, even more hopeless and weary than we. On the track stand goods trucks, cattle trucks, coal wagons, packed solid with people who have waited all day – waited day after day – and the outline of each car was a row of human heads against the dim night sky. . . . No train left the station that night.

But we were lucky again. We found a friend of Pao's who gave him a card of introduction and the address of a friend of his, who was in charge of the wagon-loading in the military transport department. (This amazing institution of friendship again! If you can only find a friend with the right connections, you will be passed from hand to hand by an endless chain of friends' friends across China!) We went there and roused our friend's friend from sleep. Yes, he said, there would be a wagon-load of equipment leaving in the morning for Hengshan. The road went through Nanyu. If we could manage to squeeze into the scant available space – the wagon would be very full, he warned – we were welcome.

We snatched a few hours of sleep before we heard the horn blaring at the door of our lodging. We hurried out with suitcases. The wagon body was covered with olive-drab canvas on half-hoops. The driver opened the flaps behind and motioned us to enter. Enter! Every cubic inch seemed filled with square wood crates, metal ammunition boxes, canvas sacks, saddles, and other equipment. Then we saw that, high in the curve of the top, there was a kind of interstice; and, climbing up, we peered into this narrow, dark cave – to discover that no less than four passengers were already crouching in this slit of space! Four men, quite large and stout and incompressible. It seemed impossible that we should insert ourselves into the press. But in our necessity we did.

One man amiably disappeared into a crevice between two sacks. Another with his chin between his knees wedged himself into a far corner. A third rolled full length into a ten-inch crack along one side, with his nose against the canvas. Pao and I, as the latest arrivals, were assigned to the tail of the truck, over the rear wheels, barely inside the flaps of the canvas. In the matter of fresh air we were at an advantage, but this was offset by more of our share of bumping and dust. Also, the space at our disposal was adapted neither for sitting nor for lying. We

85

crouched, legs folded, spine bent, chin on chest, both hands gripping the framework of the canvas roof. The car jolted into motion.

Through the flaps of the canvas we gazed out on a world of dust, nothing but dense red dust, with sometimes the flicker of ghost-like trees or the roofs of a village, dim in the cloud. When we slacked speed at all, the dust eddied into our crevice, penetrating everywhere about us. After half an hour hair, eyes, ears, noses, mouths, were full of dust. After an hour it had worked through our clothing; it was ground into our skin. It got into shoes and gritted dry between the toes. Everything we touched was dust. We sat in drifts of it, and I could imagine it piling over us, burying us, burying the truck and everything out of sight in a huge grave mound. After years they would dig us out, as they excavated Pompeii – "Chinese officer and wife, 1938, found between Changsha and Nanyu. . . ."

After an eternity – or, to be exact, at five o'clock in the afternoon – the truck stood throbbing and panting its petrol-scented exhaust into the whirlwind of dust thrown up about us. I was quite beyond sensation. Fighting through the red storm, someone was tugging at the canvas, a shadowy figure, bawling and coughing. Then Pao was shaking me. "The driver – he says this is where we get off. We're there!" He let himself down and I slid like a sack into his arms. We spat. We wavered a few steps uncertainly on feet and legs which we were not sure belonged to us, and spat again, red mud and grit.

Someone stacked our suitcases by the roadside, and I dropped down gracefully, as though I had no bones – then recollected myself, for Pao was voicing our most hearty thanks to every one, our apologies for putting them to trouble, with all the bows and gracious, formal phrases of a day antedating uniforms. I rose to add my word to his, for I was truly grateful – at least, I would be when I had time to realize that the journey was over. But our life gave no leisure for protracted ceremonies. The truck was a diminishing cyclone upon the road to Hengshan, and we two were left, sitting upon our luggage, making an attempt with what was once a handkerchief to clean our faces of a half-inch mask of perspiration-caked dust.

On the map of all China you will not find Nanyu, so small a place it is. But if you study a detailed map of Hunan province you will find it, a dot and a name in two small Chinese characters. When the General Staff first came, the village was as it had been for a thousand years, Nanyu of the holy Hengshan ranges, where pilgrims came to buy incense sticks, yellow or dull pink, to buy bright scarlet candles and paper stamped and cut with the pattern of the old, square-holed coins we used for centuries – all for sacrifice in the temples. For this was one of the five holy mountain shrines of China.

The forests of the mountain-side pressed in upon the village where it lay, clasped in a horseshoe curve of hills, and trees over-spread the one street, and the leaves of the trees moved with a constant rustle in the winds of the ranges. There was also the sound of water in Nanyu, for streams flowed down through the village, clear torrents washing great boulders, blue and pink coloured, and watering green, deep-piled moss and banks of fern. Above the village the rock path led up by many steps unevenly through ravines, over ridges, visiting one by one the many temples of Buddha, where they clung against the cliffs or spread out on mounting terraces up the hillsides.

Nanyu, with its five hundred yards of main street, was a fragile, isolated star-world, ancient, lovely. Our coming destroyed it. Our coming changed its gentle order, wrenched away its centuries-old accustomed way, drowned out with raucous noise the low chant of pilgrims and priests, the soft, hovering tolling of temple bells – and before the month was past brought down upon it fire and bombs to shatter for ever all its immemorial peace and beauty. . . .

We had been put down at the gate of the China Travel Service Hostel, a mile from the village proper. The hostel was a white, low building, wide-eaved, set in a garden of many-scented flowers, with a great twisted wisteria vine climbing over the gate, and hedges of tea bushes bordering the walk. Clad in immaculate white, an hotel boy ran down the path to meet us and take charge of us and our luggage. We were given tea to drink, to clear our throats of the dust. Floating in the clear dark-gold fluid, flowers unfurled, thin and frail, and their fragrance mingled with the aroma of the infused tea leaves. We were given basins of water and hot, steaming towels. There in the hall of the hostel we went about cleaning our eyes and ears and necks, and the boy obligingly brought fresh basins of hot water as often as required.

Emerging from a towel no longer white, I was startled to find myself facing Pao's uncle, General Tang. He seemed to have materialized out of thin air, but there he stood, with his small, reserved, amused smile and his eyes twinkling welcome.

But there was no place for us here. All rooms had been pre-empted immediately when the General Staff arrived. Important heads of departments, great generals of the Military Council, were already ensconced, many of them two to the room. General Tang had secured for himself a small cubicle with one high window. Through the window, the sky was green to blue, with a scrawl of violet mountain silhouette and a branch of acacia across it. We sat in a row along the edge of his narrow cot in the bare little cell, and talked of ways and means. We would have to seek accommodation in the village. General Tang lent us an orderly to help in our search.

Through fallow rice fields, terraced, contoured to the fall of the land, with low, tree-grown dykes between, the road wound toward Nanyu. Red sand, red clay, dried and deeply rutted as it was, it seemed no longer the unending, jolting road of our torment, but a pleasant walk of a mile in the freshness of the evening. Along the edge, a footpath was easy to our feet, packed earth and short, smooth grass. The sun was slowly sinking into a horizon on fire with gold and pink. The air was delicate, icy, sweet to taste, with the chill of high mountains and the warm scent of flowers mingled. Bird song from a hedge – a long, fine-drawn flute note, ending in a trill. Water, swift and crystalline, under the little bridge whose piers were carved with old stone dragons for ever swimming upstream. Beyond the bridge the road led straight between tall acacias to the first houses of the village. Trees, road, and houses, all looked and felt golden, smooth, sweet to the senses.

We entered the village. Its one street was paved with great blocks of hewn stone, blue, pink, or buff coloured, worn smooth and hollowed by the naked feet or the soft straw sandals of generations of pilgrims. On either hand the little wooden houses, all one-storied, stood graciously open to the street, a double row of little box stages, each with its own quaint setting and its play. There was the smell of incense smoke and that other incense, almost as sweet, of cooking fires burning dry leaves and twigs. The smoke drifted in strands, white and blue in the air. The sun's last light struck through tree branches with sword blades of red gold. Shadows were blue and hazy.

Before their houses under the eaves, the people of Nanyu sat on benches, taking their ease in the evening as they and their fathers before them had done for a thousand years. Their faces were darkly tanned; their gowns were a deep, vivid blue; their hands, brown and calloused but finely made, lay folded in their

88

laps. They watched with a certain bewilderment the influx of strangers in uniform, striding about, busy upon concerns of national importance. War until now had been so alien and so distant from this village, holy to the calm Gautama Buddha. More than a year of the conflict which had ravaged so much of our country had scarcely touched the life of Nanyu. The few conscripts taken from among its young men for the army had only left the village a little quieter, a little more gentle. In its shrines the smoke of incense rose unshaken to the gold-faced images, and priests recited scriptures to the beat of little wooden drums, and the common folk sat at their thresholds in the evening, and all was as it had always been.

We walked through the village, making inquiry where lodging might be found, but every house, every room, every bed, every corner, had been taken by the newcomers. There was the sound of hammering and the smell of fresh-sawed boards, where new structures were being hurried to completion. There was no place for us. Yet for some reason we could not feel anxious about where we should sleep that night. We walked on, the full length of the village street, our eyes fixed upon the mountains, where the tall spire of Tou Yun Feng towered red violet in the sunset, circled about with the last clouds of evening, amber-coloured.

At the far end of the street a stream flowed transversely, spanned by three little white marble bridges, and beyond there faced us the red screen wall of a temple. Dark pines and cypresses of the sacred grove massed sombrely in the gathering dusk, but the temple roofs were yellow glazed, glittering with light through the dark foliage.

But now the orderly came running to tell us he had found a room for us at the Grand Nanyu Hotel. We turned away reluctantly from that enchanted scene to follow him to something more prosaic. The hotel, only by a great stretch of courtesy to be called "Grand", was a rickety modern affair of wood and plaster, built around three sides of a courtyard, entered by an imposing gateway, adorned with its name in characters a foot high. There were eighteen rooms in all, upstairs and down. The ground-floor rooms were level with the courtyard or even lower, with floors of beaten earth. All opened inward with windows and doors, directly upon the court. Upstairs was a similar arrangement, with a wooden gallery all round. The courtyard served as a garage. A dozen or more motor-cars and trucks, caked with dust and mud, looking most dejected and weary, were lined up along the sides. No walk led through the court-yard, but even in dry weather one picked one's steps warily through the perpetual mud puddle which occupied its centre. The reason for this morass was obvious. The Grand Nanyu Hotel possessed no plumbing. From the gallery the occupants of the upstairs rooms emptied their water-basins upon the tar-paulins of the cars parked beneath; while downstairs the tenants casually tossed out their dirty water between the wheels.

With all its deficiencies the Grand Nanyu Hotel had no dearth of patronage. It had a roof and walls; it was shelter; it was a place to sleep, and already it was filled to the doors with officers. The room which the orderly had obtained for us was not exactly vacant when we took it over. A bachelor friend of General Tang's was living there, but when he heard of our plight he relinquished it to Pao and myself and moved in with two other bachelors.

It was a small room on the second floor. One climbed by a stairway, so steep and narrow it could better be called a ladder, to the gallery upon which all the upper rooms opened. There was one window, without any glass panes. The thin lath-and-plaster panels of the wall had shrunk away from the timber framework everywhere, leaving wide cracks through which day-light and weather might enter. We were also in communication with the room below through finger-wide cracks in the floor. Our furniture consisted of a plank bed, a single chair, and a table with no two legs the same length. The best feature of the accommodation we had taken proved to be the room boy.

This room boy of ours was a thin, sleepy-looking lad whose only qualification was his skill in tossing the contents of wash-basins farther and with more splash than anyone else, accurately upon the tarpaulins of cars parked on the opposite side of the courtyard. We took the matter of his education in hand. We conveyed to him our disgust for flies, mosquitoes, and fat, greasy meat. After that, he would blow gently above the food he served us, to eliminate invisible insects, and he was careful never to set before us the least trace of fat. I cannot say but that there may have been tit-bits of fat pork in our bowls when they left the kitchen, but if so they never reached our table, but were disposed of *en route* in the most simple and obvious manner.

We taught him that we wanted water, large quantities of warm water for washing and bathing, especially whenever we came in hot and dusty. When this lesson had been sufficiently impressed upon him we could not leave the room for so much as five minutes without his coming beamingly to greet us on our return, bearing a full basin of warm water. We did not need to wash our faces so many times a day, but we went through the motions in order not to discourage his commendable impulse or confuse his ideas. He was most anxious to please. When he discovered that Pao required eggs as an opium smoker requires opium, he scoured the village for them, bringing them to us, ten or a dozen a day, until our room was full of eggs and we gave them away to children.

We taught him elementary sanitation. We taught him how to sweep the floor, which had to be done carefully to avoid showering all our dust and dirt through the cracks upon the heads of the family below. From time to time he dusted, and the more accessible of our festoons of cobwebs disappeared. He also did our washing, with moderate success, although sometimes he mixed the white and coloured clothes, so that Pao's shirts came out streaked and spotted with the blue from my dark cotton homespun gowns.

Daily the aspect of Nanyu was changing. Uniformed labour gangs worked day and night, building roads, stringing telephone and telegraph lines which radiated in all directions like a spiderweb. This had become the nerve centre of China. The Great Ones of the military organization were here: Minister of War Ho Ying-Ching, General Feng Yu-hsiang, General Cheng Cheng, others of high rank, and in supreme command the Generalissimo, together with a horde of lesser people like ourselves – each individual, high or low, an essential unit in a central government which lived and functioned, though the Japanese thought they had destroyed it when they took Nanking, and again when Hankow fell.

The generals of the High Command had their quarters in temples on the hillsides. The rest distributed themselves as best they could, crowding the village, overflowing into the farm country for miles around. At the beginning, when we were few and Nanyu knew nothing yet of rising prices and falling currency, the people doubtfully asked as much as five dollars a month rent for a whole house with courtyard and well. But when every house was filled up and beds were being shared in shifts, and still the outside world poured in, they grew more assured and demanded a dollar, three dollars, ten dollars a day for the most meagre accommodation. New houses were run up; they took two days to be completed and were rented to the last square foot of floor space from the moment the plan was staked out on the ground. People continued to crowd into the already overcrowded village, six and seven to a tiny room that normally would hold two at most. Pao and I felt almost guilty in our comparative luxury.

Even in the outlying country staff officers and heads of departments competed for rooms with bare earthen floors and thatched roofs. Their womenfolk learned the life of the farmyards – the low, mud-walled homes, the ducks and geese waddling about the courtyard, the water buffalo in the stall, the straw stacks and manure pits, the roosters crowing before dawn and the dogs barking at night. Slender, aristocratic ladies and young girls, accustomed to the soft silks and heavy, rich brocades of Nanking – one met them walking the narrow paths along the dykes between rice fields. They were dressed in coarse and common blue home-spun, but still graceful, aristocratic, with their hair combed smooth and shining, and a flower behind the ear, with their lips and cheeks touched with bright colour, with gaiety and valour in their eyes.

The world poured in. The war was brought to Nanyu. Contingents of troops arrived and were quartered around the village in mat sheds, in tents. They dug trenches and installed anti-aircraft guns. They marched, singing:—

> "Great Wall of China, not crumbling stone;
> Great Wall of China – living flesh, staunch hearts!
> Defend our fields of grain, now battle-fields,
> Land we have tilled for generations.
> Sons, be worthy of your fathers!
> Stand firm against the invader,
> Great Wall of China!"

There is a harshness in the soldiers' songs, a savagery, but sung in unison by five hundred untrained voices, shouted to the rhythm of a long stride, the myriad tread muffled by straw sandals, there is an arresting, heart-stopping beauty and excitement to them.

More and more people came – merchants, cooks, artisans, craftsmen, refugee workmen with their families, pedlars with their packs. They came in rickshaws, in carts, by car, on foot. They set up booths and stalls and little shops, bearing boastful signs with the names of famous Shanghai and Hankow firms. Most numerous and popular were the restaurants and tailors' shops. War or no war, men must eat and women must dress.

The whir of the Singer sewing machine went on into the

night, by the light of little vegetable oil lamps. Above the trestle tables, where skilled apprentices worked over buttons of hand-made cording, bamboo rods suspended lengthwise were hung with swaths of many-coloured materials, some in the flower hues we love so well, but more of sombre blue, fitted to our new circumstances.

All kinds of food shops flourished. There was the humble noodle pedlar, clinking a spoon and bowl to advertise his wares, his whole establishment of portable stove and cupboard, slung at the two ends of a shoulder-pole. There was the famous restaurateur from Nanking, who had escaped from that city with no other equipment than the marvellous recipes he carried in his head, now setting up shop in a mat shed and instantly besieged with customers. From morning until near midnight they were busy. They were at their best in the evenings, when crowds off duty thronged Nanyu's one street and all the little new alleys leading off into suburbs of sudden growth. There was always a crush of people around the food shops, some to talk and laugh and eat, others attracted by the noises and good odours to stand watching, fascinated. Fires crackled and blazed red in the clay cooking stoves under wide iron pans. The delicate savour of rice exhaled from the big covered wooden steamers. There was a hiss and sputter of frying, the smell of oil and peppers and spices. In almost any market town in China it is like this in the evening, a mingling of people in the street, with good fellowship and heartiness of enjoyment. Men who had spent years abroad and knew the celebrated restaurants of Europe participated in Nanyu's village night life with gusto.

When at last the cooking fires were out and the shop fronts boarded up, still with a ceaseless drive the work went on. Trucks and cars rolled incessantly along the roads, their headlights piercing the velvet night with shafts of golden light. A subdued shuffling, the clink of metal and rub of leather – troops night-marching, company after company, swung through the street. Road construction went on twenty-four hours a day. Sometimes the blasting would startle us from sleep with an earth-shaking boom, terrifyingly reminiscent to most of us of air raids.

New roads in all directions, a network of communication wires, newspapers, non-existent until we came – from day to day these increased. To the General Staff in Nanyu came reports from the whole country, news of fighting on all fronts, telegrams announcing victories and defeats, intelligence from abroad by wireless. The General Staff worked on, in its offices established in what had been the Middle School, receiving and co-ordinating all that came in, reporting regularly to the Generalissimo in his temple on the hill. Their uniformed dispatch carriers could be seen going up and down the steep pilgrim paths that led to his quarters. Many times a day our eyes unconsciously turned toward that half-hidden temple, serene roofs with slow curves in a close, dark grove. He is there, Chiang Kai-shek, directing the war with steady, unshaken resolve never to yield, in weakness and cowardice, to armed force. We are strengthened, reassured.

For here in Nanyu beats the heart of China. Here is the determination that has stirred the whole country, willed China to rise from her torpor, given her consciousness of her past glory and future dignity and greatness. One man, yet not one man alone. A spiritual force, a symbol, an integration of us all.

We have lost proud and stately cities. The earth drinks the blood of our dead. The smoke of our burning homes is black and tawny against the sky. But history is not determined by captured cities, burning towns, farm lands laid waste. China is not lost when territory is lost. Where there is an indomitable heart, there is China, unconquerable. This truth is her invisible strength, a thing more concrete than the steel of guns and the stone of fortifications. It exists, this secret power, unlinked to any specific city, harbour, mountain, or river. So long as there remains one Chinese alive to say, like Chiang Kai-shek, "We will not yield to armed force because we refuse to recognize the power of such force. However great the suffering and sacrifice imposed, there is nothing that can conquer the soul!" – so long will China remain essentially free.

Nanyu, sleepy village at the foot of Tou Yun Feng, the Summit of Many Prayers, hazy with smoke of incense, visited by pilgrims for a thousand years, for three brief weeks in the autumn of 1938 rang to the songs of marching men, resounded to the hammering and blasting of construction, and was more significant than Shanghai, Nanking, or Hankow. It held the living heart of war-time China.

CHAPTER SEVEN

MOUNTAINS, TEMPLES, BOMBERS OF HENGSHAN

It is the beginning of November, but journeying southward we have returned to days of soft golden sun again, though the nights are chill. Mornings we are up at first light. In the mysterious whiteness of thick fog we step into the street which lies asleep with all the little shop fronts boarded up. Past the temple with its red screen-wall, out of the village and up the hillside we climb, along a steep, rough path that leads to the torrent where we bathe. Here, high in the hills, the stream cuts its way among huge rocks tumbled from the cliffs above, granite boulders of rose or green or flecked colours, wet and bright. The water pours over rolling pebbles in a strong, rough, white current, or drops from level to level in the white arc of a waterfall.

But all is shrouded in mist. Mist clings like a garment to the mountain flank. Along the course of the torrent on either side marching pines are shadow-grey, dim in the white of the fog. A waterfall leaps out of the void to shatter upon the rocks before us in foaming, milky jade-green. We track upstream, wading the icy current. Our bare feet are sentient as hands, curving to the round of water-worn boulders, feeling the grain and the slipperiness of moss on the rock. Gravel creeping beneath the soles, the smooth, firm clasp of sand under the arches, the swirl of swift water at the ankles – these are all part of our pleasure. We plunge into the pools and come up gasping with shock, laughing to each other. We thrust our way against the rush of the stream to the base of a rock where the current foams, half air, half water, with millions of bubbles alive and tingling to the skin.

The sun rises. Along the ravine trailing shreds of the mist thin and disperse into the morning light. We look down upon the roofs of Nanyu among its tall trees and the soldier camps around it. Nanyu still sleeps, except where wayward smoke of the first cooking fires drifts level among the trees; but from new-made drill grounds rise to us the sharp command, the shouted response of hundreds of voices, where troops are drilling. The plain beyond is coloured like an opal – green, blue, dull gold in a smoke-white haze – with ranges of low hills curving inward on the east and west, pale in gradations of fading blue.

Sometimes in the evenings we romp like children in excess of high spirits, racing each other round and round the village in the dark, ending in the crowded main street, helpless with laughter. People must think us a little crazy and very indecorous. Beyond the blended clamour of voices and the calls of vendors there is the sound of the stream rushing under its bridges. There is the soft distant sound of temple bells and drums celebrating the rites of the moon. There is the weary dissonance of evening bugles.

The bare little room at the Grand Nanyu Hotel was our first home, for the two days together in our Hankow apartment were of the nature of a troubled dream. We settled down to being married. We felt established and secure for a little while, not knowing how short the time would be – three weeks – until we should be again uprooted. Pao's duties with the General Staff were urgent and arduous, but we had all the early mornings together and the evenings and all the lengthening nights. Our home offered little scope for housekeeping and there was no hospital to demand my services, so I spent the daytime of Pao's absence roaming the pathways on the lower slopes of the mountain, climbing among tall pines and firs and flowering gardenia bushes. For hours in the long afternoons I lay in the sunlight, stretched out on a patch of short, sweet-smelling bracken or on some great smooth boulder. Relaxed in such utter well-being it was impossible to think of war. I brought home armfuls of wild flowers of varieties unknown to me, to make gay our crudely ugly little room. From flower vendors in the street we bought chrysanthemums, purple and pale gold, plants in bloom to put in boxes of earth on the gallery before our door. Against the rickety wood rail their flowers stood up gay and tall and valiant. "It looks better so," said Pao admiringly.

The moon of the Ninth Month (November) increased each night until it swung like a great round paper lantern over the hills at twilight. We remembered the Eighth Moon Feast, so long ago in Hankow. Thirty days. . . . Where were they scattered now, the men and women with their laughing children who kept the festival in Hankow a month ago? The moon lit up the hills. We followed a path far from the commotion and crowds of the street. We came to a favourite retreat of ours, a grove of cypress planted in a circle as in old family burial grounds, though here there was no grave in the centre, but only an open, level space. We lay in the ferns, watching the moon clear the tree-tops and float higher and higher, serene and white.

A distant song impinged upon our meditations, a strange, wild chant of many voices in broken rhythm. It drew nearer. We looked down upon the road that ran below our grove and saw a burial procession – monks with shaven heads and gowned in yellow silk, with linen cloaks of rust-red over one shoulder, striking their small silver bells in time with the chant, torch-bearers and lantern-bearers, mourners in white turbans carrying lighted incense, bearers with the huge timber coffin, covered with a red satin pall – all chanting in this strange, swift, irregular rhythm, breaking into long, minor wailing at intervals. Incense smoke blended with the smell of crushed fern. Dim yellow rays slanted between the close-set tree trunks, and shadows moved fanwise with the moving lights. The procession passed like an apparition, winding with the path beyond a spur of the mountain, and the wailing faded into the moonlight and stillness. . . .

Another night while the moon was still huge and brilliant we could not endure to waste the night in sleep, pent within walls. We made our way up the stream, jumping from rock to rock across dark chasms between. We spread blankets on a great level stone, around whose base the torrent swirled, roaring. The constant, unvarying thunder of water seemed to close us in together in a centre of silence. We sat shoulder to shoulder, watching the moonlight and shadow, grey and silver, the soft colourless loveliness of trees and hills in a silver haze. The very mountains were less tall; they crouched like sleeping beasts, their craggy profile smoothed to gently moulded contours. For hours we watched the climbing moon, the imperceptible shifting of shadows; then fell asleep at last to the wild sound of water. In the morning our faces were wet with dew.

At the season of the full moon the temple bells were to be heard at midnight and before dawn – slow, slow, then in quickening rhythm joined with the rapid thud of drums and a strange wailing chant of many voices. The priests performed the ancient ceremonies still, unperturbed. Pilgrims, both men and women, still went from shrine to shrine in fulfilment of their vows, leaving two or three sticks of incense to smoulder before each image. The temple gates stood open to all who would enter. Pao and I spent long hours wandering through the many courtyards.

Pilgrims and guests thronged the temple by day. Temples in

China are for gaiety as well as for worship. In the High Hall, dim with scented smoke, priests struck the bronze bells and read the omens for the pilgrims who knelt before the Buddhas on cushions of stitched coir – brown fibre of the Chinese palm tree – lighting their incense and candles, telling their beads. Out of doors in the sunlight casual guests wandered along the marble terraces, admiring the carved balustrades. Each pillar was capped with a frost-white lotus and the panels between were carved in infinite variety with clouds, fantastic rocks and trees, leaping leopards, delicate, startled deer, riderless horses proudly stamping, mythical fire-breathing *chi-lin*, all kinds of birds and beasts as on the pages of a painted book.

We became devotees of the temple's beauty and peace. Before sunrise we would come, to sit cross-legged in the attitude of meditation upon the marble terrace before the High Hall, watching the incense smoke from the great bronze burner rise in the still air. It was the hour for morning worship. The priests in their wide grey robes would pass in solemn file along the colonnaded porches and through the open doors of the pavilion. Small gold flames of candles burned in a row at the shrine, where the Buddhas sat on their lotus thrones, with hands and feet and faces gilded, their eyes downcast, their lips benignly smiling in the gloom, their hands making mystic gestures of benediction. Before them the priests, ranged in rows, chanted the sutras to the click of small hand drums, in a rhythm as steady and pauseless as the pulse beat. The cool courtyards lay in shadow, pillared by the straight shafts of tree trunks, silver pine and cypress. The highest branches of the trees, the yellow roofs of the pavilions, were gilded with sunrise. Along the roof ridges went coiling, sinuous dragons of yellow glaze and processions of small beasts following each other toward the corners of the roofs and from the eaves hung bells, silent in that still morning air. Incense smoke rose in a slim, unwavering column from the huge burner on the terrace, up through the cypress boughs into the white sky, to ravel and fray into nothingness. So with our thoughts, as we sat in meditation; the world receded; self was lost in a tranquil oneness with the all-pervasive peace.

One night when the evening chant was finished we tarried late when all others had gone, walking the marble paths patterned with moonlight. At the doors of the High Wall we paused and peered within, where a single red lamp burned before the shrine, a heart of faint radiance in the cavernous darkness of the immense hall. A black-robed priest sat cross-legged on his cushion, fingering his yellow-tasselled prayer beads, murmuring in monotone. Drawn by some indefinable impulse, we advanced together to the altar and stood gazing up into the symmetrical, dimly golden face of the tall central Buddha. We are not Buddhists, Pao and I. But moved by the thought of centuries of prayers poured forth in longing and faith to this image of all good, of spiritual peace, Pao spoke: "If you represent that principle of righteousness which alone we recognize supreme and regnant in this world, then protect us, for we have pure intentions." And we bowed in respect, as we would bow to a prince.

In the insecurity of our existence we enjoyed this lovely interlude of Nanyu, knowing it for what it was, a temporary armistice with fate. But in this breathing space we gained strength against future need. We hoarded these days – smooth and sun-coloured as amber beads strung together on a cord – to be remembered when we should be separated. But it was inevitable, even in this brief interval when we were sufficient each to the other and needed no one else for our happiness, that we should in casual contact meet old friends and make agreeable new acquaintances. We avoided, so far as possible, invitations to dull feasts and stupid, prolonged mah-jongg parties. But with two or three friends we planned an ascent of Tou Yun Feng while the weather still held fair.

Pao had obtained two days' leave. We would take the whole day for the long climb up the pilgrim road to the temple at the summit, spend the night there and return tomorrow. Early in the morning Pao went out to buy oranges and returned to peel them for me, as I lay still drowsily abed. Clear, cool sunlight streamed level in a broad ray through the open door. The chrysanthemums made a tracery of shadows on the floor. Pao sat on the edge of my bed, scorning the chill of the air, stripped to the waist. The sunlight slanted upon the golden, smooth skin of his shoulders and the play of the long delicate muscles of his arms; on his hair, blue-black, springing crisp from the forehead with a little peak at the front – the same as mine. I could see the gilding of light on the small wrinkles at the corners of his eyes as he laughed. . . . Today, after four years of war, the lines are deeper; they are there without laughter, engraved by thought and experience.

Our friends, Wu Kwei-fan and Wang Yu-lin, called for us. Let me tell about Wu Kwei-fan, for he went with us through a trying ordeal later, a bulwark of dependable strength, his laughter never failing. He was about forty-five, tall, well-built if a little stout, with a big round face and round horn-rimmed spectacles. The most generous of men, he was always ready to lavish his last dollar on a dinner for his friends. He had married late; his beautiful wife and three-year-old son were in Shanghai in the relative safety of the International Settlement, while he followed the peregrinations of the General Staff. He carried their photographs always in his pockets, and within fifteen minutes after your introduction to him he would have them out for your admiration. Except for the horn-rimmed glasses, the face of his small son was the same guileless round, beaming countenance as his own. Wu Kwei-fan was an unquenchable talker, the wit of the General Staff; later we were to discover that he talked even in his sleep. A lovable man, a thoroughly good man, typically Chinese in his huge zest for life and his invincible cheerfulness. He would never be a success in a worldly sense. He was too good-natured to push his way ahead with the necessary ruthlessness; he was too wise and philosophic for the discontent that spurs ambition.

Wang Yu-lin also was to be with us on another and a graver journey. She was a small, slender girl, whose elaborately curled locks, patterned after the coiffure of the latest American movie star, contrasted oddly with her straight, plain *shan* of peasant blue cloth. Her fiancé, Pu Kuang-ti, worked in the same office as Pao. He was to have joined our mountain-climbing party, but withdrew at the last moment, pronouncing such excessive exercise bad for the reasoning faculties. He was a bit of a dandy, willowy of figure, and wore his hair long, swept back from his brow with a suspiciously perfect wave in it.

We left the Grand Nanyu Hotel about seven. We crossed the central marble bridge at the head of the street. Sentries with rifles and bayonets stood on guard at the bridges and at the gates of the temple. Since the evening before, the temple had been closed to visitors and pilgrims, for a contingent of troops was being temporarily quartered there. It is a common practice, for temples are considered public domain and since the early years of the war lords have been summarily taken over for billets whenever necessity arises. It seems a pity and quite inconsistent with the pacifist teachings of Buddhism. Usually only the galleries of the outer courtyards are occupied, and the resident monks are left to their devotions in the High Hall. Whatever their inner feelings, the monks seem to ignore the intrusion, going about their ceremonies and meditations indifferent to the hubbub in the outer courts.

100

Sometimes as we climbed the sun was hot on our backs; sometimes we plunged into shadow, dense and cool as water. We crossed and recrossed the stream and its tributaries, following the pilgrim road with its irregular steps and hollowed flagstones. Small covered bridges offered benches where we could rest and look out through the dark cleft of the ravine to the distant, glimmering, sunlit plain. Stepping-stones were our path across the smaller streams. Reaching the vantage point of a shoulder of the mountain, we paused to look back over the widening view and ahead to the cliffs that grew steeper as we neared them. We stopped for our noon rice at a wayside hut roofed with bark shakes and open to the road. A *hua-kan,* which is a crude species of sedan chair, toiled up the steps toward us. The occupant lay back at ease, head lower than his legs, which were draped about the poles of the *hua-kan,* so that all we saw of him, past the shoulders of the front bearer, was a pair of plus-fours and dangling, rubber-soled shoes. The conveyance came to a halt beside us; the languid passenger reared himself up from his semi-reclining posture and hailed us.

"It was such a beautiful day, and I missed you all so much, and the office was dull, so I took a holiday and a *hua-kan* and decided to join you after all." It was Pu Kuang-ti. He was dressed in a Norfolk jacket, pith topi, sun glasses, and the aforementioned plus-fours. He was provided also with an extra pair of boots, hot-water bottles, thermos bottles, a heavy cane, and a rope — ready for big things in the way of mountaineering. He surveyed with some scorn our inadequate equipment. There was not a stick or a staff or a hat among us. Pao carried the only haversack. He was in shorts and a sleeveless shirt, with a sweater tied round his neck. Yu-lin and I wore our everyday costume, long blue gowns slit to the thigh at the sides, practical and easy. Wu Kwei-fan had made no concession to sport and was perspiring freely in his woollen uniform.

The chair-bearers put down the *hua-kan* and settled to rest and smoke and eat. Pu Kuang-ti declined our offer of lunch; he had come liberally supplied with provisions and had already dined on a balanced ration suitable for heavy muscular activity. He flourished his cane and marched ahead, challenging us to overtake him. Wu Kwei-fan watched him out of sight round a bend. "I wonder which of those cliffs he plans to scale," he murmured reflectively. "If he keeps to the road, the rope, at least, would seem superfluous."

We paid for our meal and resumed our walk. Round the

second bend of the road we came upon Pu Kuang-ti, collapsed gracefully against a bank of fern. "Where is my *hua-kan*?" he inquired plaintively. "Couldn't you have hurried the bearers with their meal?" Then, recovering his urbanity, he resolved to sacrifice himself and offered a lift to his fiancée. But Yu-lin was having too much fun with us in Wu Kwei-fan's merry company to accept, so we left Pu Kuang-ti behind to continue his mountaineering in a manner not injurious to the reasoning faculties.

There were no more steps; there were no more dark cliffs bending over us. This was the summit. The road ended here at the threshold of the last temple. We sank down upon the door-step. Pao produced tangerines from his pack, and we peeled the fruit and ate it, tasting its acid freshness, sweet to our dry throats. The sun dropped swiftly to a cloudless horizon; the light was rose and copper red on our faces. Suddenly wind swooped about the peak, striking cold to the bone. We shivered and stood up, and turned to the dark, gaping doors of the temple.

We walked through the many halls, shadowy and mysterious with dusk, past the menacing gods of the gate, enormous armed giants riding upon elephants and tigers and brandishing weapons, past the sprawling obese figure of the laughing Buddha, past Kuanyin of the hundred hands, Kuanyin the All-Merciful. Fluttering like bats out of the dimness, the monks in their voluminous grey robes gathered about us, welcoming Pilgrims knelt at the shrines. The bells and the immense ox-hide drums sounded softly; the wind rushed through the cavernous halls, stirring the red banners hanging from the rafters, blowing about the flames of the candles. All this was so familiar, so remote from alarms of war. Yet even here the monks, as they conducted us to the guest hall, asked news of the fighting and exclaimed in dismay at the report of Wuhan's fall, though they must have heard it many times in the past ten days from pilgrims and travellers.

Monasteries in China are the best of hostels, open to every one, from the humblest old woman on a pilgrimage to the most exalted general. And of the latter they have harboured many. In Szechwan, in a monastery near Kuan-hsien, later, I saw Sun Chuen-fang, a war lord of the north, once a trusted high officer in the national army. When Japan invaded the north he "slept on his sword" – let pass the opportunity when he might have stemmed the advance, and with his armies made a craven retreat. He had to resign his commission and was living in exile, a guest of the monks of this distant province. He was old and broken; he walked painfully with the aid of a cane. Though he had four bodyguards always with him, so that it might be seen he was a person of importance, no one heeded him, no one saluted him. He was forgotten because he had failed his trust. He died some months later. His meditations must have been bitter with remorse.

We sat on stiff, high carved chairs in the immense *keh-tang*, the guest hall, and a small boy-priest brought tea-cups to us. Into each cup he dropped tea leaves, then poured over them boiling water from a huge kettle, the water arching from its spout. Wind tore the steam from our cups as we sipped the scalding tea. Through the round moon-doorway opening upon the courtyard we watched the twilight deepen like multiple veils of shadow. Shuffling footsteps of the monks in their felt shoes, the muffled note of a distant drum, and the long sigh of the wind were not sound but rather accents to the silence.

The abbot of the monastery appeared in the moon-doorway. He was a small, gnome-like creature with the bright, curious, darting eyes of a sparrow. His tiny thin hands with their long nails emerge from many layers of sleeves like the claws of a little bird. He was quite lost in his ample robes and his wind bonnet that buttoned under the chin with red lappets and spread in a wide cape behind the shoulders. He sidled towards us engagingly, with bows and greetings which we returned in kind. He hopped into a tall chair and perched there, his feet in preposterously large felt boots swinging clear of the floor.

Conversation opened with the customary polite interchanges, but once past the preliminaries, our host launched into a narrative so continuous and fluent that even Wu Kwei-fan was unable to put in a word. He told us the whole history of his temple. It had been built hundreds of years ago, and he spared us no detail of its chronicle. He told us of his illustrious predecessors, his taloned forefinger pointing to one and another of the dusty scrolls that hung on the walls of the chamber, legacy of their sacred wisdom. Coming at last to his own times, he told us of famous men who had visited the mountain and tarried here for a day or a year or longer. They came with that mixture of scepticism and credulity which is the typical Chinese approach to any spiritual manifestation. According to the abbot, they departed edified and impressed. War lords had come, striding into the temple halls, booted and sabred and shouting orders. Met with generosity and mildness, served with courtesy which is extended to high or low alike, they had been humbled and abashed and had gone away chastened, to amend their ways. They had offered gifts to appease the gods. One and another had renounced the world, to live out their lives in meditation.

The abbot talked on and on. Blue shadows of the wind whipped through the open doors. Politeness forbade us to cut short the discourse, though we were famished and chilled and it was already dark. He continued with the roster of renowned visitors, naming the great names over. In praise of one he waxed eloquent –Wu Pei-fu. What an abbot *he* would have made. A scholar, a very great and learned man. He had left a scroll of his own magnificent calligraphy in acknowledgement of the temple's hospitality. But though the abbot pointed it out to us, a dim whiteness on the wall, we could not read it, for the light was gone. His high, thin voice declaimed it for us. His small withered face framed in the cowl of the wind bonnet was only a patch of paler shadow in the darkness.

To our vast relief, for we were starving, monks at last appeared with lighted pewter lamps, bringing in our supper. No meat, of course, was permitted, since true Buddhists hold all life holy. But with bean curd – *tou-fu* – and mushrooms and savoury sauces and vegetable oils the many dishes customarily served at feasts were simulated, and the vegetarian banquets of this monastery were famous. The monks spread the table, heaped the fragrant rice in bowls, and murmured, "The meal is opened," which is the signal to fall to. But the abbot, although he made vague gestures of invitation, had not ended his story. Etiquette demanded that we feign indifference to the food, which was giving off maddeningly appetizing odours, and hear him through. For another quarter of an hour he held us with his bird-like gaze and flood of words. "And even tonight," he said in climax, his voice low and impressive, "in the upper guest-house we shelter greatness. You have seen his bodyguards about the courtyards. It is General Feng Yu-hsiang, second in command of the armies of China!" He delivered this with an air of triumph, as though all that went before were but an introduction.

Wu Kwei-fan leaped into the dramatic pause. "But we must not detain you! You do us too much honour. Pardon us that we have taken up so much of your invaluable time, and do not let us keep you longer from your more important obligations." All the time he was gently urging the abbot toward the door, as one would herd a refractory goat through a gateway. As for us, the canons of decorum could restrain us no longer. We snatched up bowls and chopsticks and were eating ravenously. The abbot faded into the darkness.

During the night the wind died down to a still, penetrating cold. We slept restlessly among quilts of infinite age and heaviness, stiff as wood. Wu Kwei-fan thundered at our door before light. "All out for sunrise!" It was four-thirty. In some far hall of the temple the priests' chanting was low and monotonous as the lap of calm water along a shore. Shivering, manacled with sleep and the ache of over-taxed muscles, I stumbled to the window. Stars were steely cold in a clear, dark sky paling to the colourless lustre of pearl at the horizon. Pao wrapped the least rigid of the ancient quilts about my shoulders and we went out with our friends to the brow of the mountain. As we walked over the short grass, each blade crisp and silvered with dew, the light was already whitening, and one blazing planet alone remained of the stars, and we saw each other's faces clear-cut and fresh in the first daylight.

Tou Yun Feng stood isolated in a world submerged, its peak a rugged island, solid and alone, looming above cloud. Cloud flowed about its cliffs, level as the sea. The smooth whiteness stretched away to phantom-grey mountains, less substantial than the cloud itself. Overhead the sky arched flawless, blue burning to cold, pale fire at the eastern rim. The sun rose with serene and lordly leisure, coming up through the cloud. The sun entered upon the still expectancy of morning like a prince taking possession. At once the white level of cloud broke into long ripples of light, and drifts of cumulus mounded upward into the brightness. It was difficult to believe that all the mornings we had groped in wet mist on the mountain-side there existed this calm and shining splendour above us.

When we had breakfasted and given our contribution to the temple (it is their rule to accept what is offered and never ask for more) we made our farewell to the monks. The abbot was concerned elsewhere – fortunately, for we wished to reach home by afternoon. We left a message of gratitude for his kindness and began our descent. The steep downward path called other muscles into play; it was less arduous than the climb, yet Wang Yu-lin and I trailed along slowly, a little weary with yesterday's exertions. Pu Kuang-ti was with us today, feeling virile and hardy and urging one or the other of us to accept a ride in his *hua-kan,* for it was a pity to encourage idleness of the chair-bearers.

Boot heels and spurs rang on the stone steps. Attended by eight bodyguards, General Feng Yu-Hsiang came down the mountain. Older, but the same stalwart figure and broad, honest face I remembered. We stood and bowed; the General acknowledged our salutation with a nod and a wide smile. He was bronzed, unshaven, his small keen eyes alert. He strode by, not half as well dressed as his guard, wearing the creased and faded grey cotton uniform of a common soldier and black cloth shoes, his shoulders squared, his nostrils flaring, sniffing the air, peasant fashion.

I thought of that evening in Sinyang when General Feng, a secondary war lord then, had taken supper in our home. He was now high in the military Council, second in command to the Generalissimo himself, yet he remained the same plain, straightforward soldier, despising pomp and display. He kept no private motor-car. He had come to Nanyu on an army truck and set up his headquarters in a mud-walled farm-house. In his tastes he was still a northerner; he could not satisfy his great appetite with rice as the Chinese of the south and central provinces do, but had to have cakes of wheat flour sent in each day from the newly opened Peking restaurant in Nanyu. Feng Yu-hsiang, once a war lord in his own right, was one of the central government of China now, pushing with all the immense vitality of his huge body and the strength of his adoring army against a common enemy.

We rounded a spur of the mountain. Nanyu came into sight below us, grey roofs and gold roofs and dark trees, radiating red and yellow roads, and the plain beyond the embracing ranges and the river coursing among foothills, bright as a satin ribbon. Somewhere to the southward lay Hengshan, indistinguishable in the haze, where the railroad passed on its way from Changsha to Kweilin.

"Listen!" Yu-lin held up a hand for silence. We stood still. Only the faint rustle of leaves in the wind; only the sound of the stream in the ravine.... No! A drone; a distant, singing thunder; a sputter as of fire-crackers, but very faint and far; then dull detonations and a shiver in the air. Out of the haze where Hengshan should be sprang up dim black smoke. Air raid!

The planes were coming toward us – the droning of their engines increased to a roar and seemed to come from every

106

quarter of the compass at once. We strained our gaze to find them; our eyes must have passed over them in the bright void of the sky. . . . "There!" We dived into the tall grass by the road. The terrible music beat in waves about us. . . . Distinct and nearby, our anti-aircraft guns barked. Then something slid down the air with a shrill sibilance and crashed. . . . We felt the ground tremble. The roar of the planes increased until it was more than sound – a vibration against the skin that the deaf would perceive. Pao and I, lying together in the long grass, turned our faces upward to stare in a fascination stronger than fear. The Japanese bombers flew directly overhead, ten planes in formation, three, four, and three. They moved steadily, swiftly, with effortless power, with a proud, indifferent assurance, glittering like white fire in the sun, unimaginably beautiful. We watched them as they rose above the mountains and were gone.

We stood up, a little pale, and brushed grass seed from our clothing. "Now they have learned the Generalissimo is here," said Pao thoughtfully. We looked about for our companions. Wang Yu-lin crept from under a rock, somewhat dishevelled; there were twigs and lichen in her hair. Wu Kwei-fan pushed his way out of a thorn thicket where he had taken refuge, turning and twisting about to detach the hooked barbs that still detained him. Pu Kuang-ti was not to be found; Yu-lin had seen him last scurrying down the path like a startled hare. We went in that direction, calling his name. At the turn of the road stood a small edifice of mud and thatch, erected by some public-spirited citizen for the convenience of passers-by; before we came to the corner the wind brought unmistakable evidence of its purpose. From its doorway now issued Pu Kuang-ti, green as a grasshopper, holding to his nose a white silk handkerchief. He groped to meet us. We shouted with laughter. He emerged from the handkerchief to glare at us reproachfully.

"I see nothing amusing. When it is a question of saving one's life, fastidiousness is out of place. If we *had* been bombed, your tall grass wouldn't have stopped shrapnel, while the thick walls of that privy. . . . And you needn't have bawled after me so rudely. I heard you the first time, but since I could not be certain the raid was over I was unable to answer you; the air in there was rather . . . dense. . . ."

We laughed until we were weak. Not very subtle humour, no. But when you have just seen death pass overhead on blazingly silver wings your emotional equilibrium is apt to be unstable, to be thrown off balance by the lightest touch. Suddenly we were sober again.

From this high distance it was impossible to determine how seriously the raid had harmed Nanyu. Smoke and dust spread in the air above its roofs – it was not ten minutes since the explosion – concealing what devastation it might have suffered. We hurried on downwards, not pausing for rest, and one hour later came out on the hillside directly above Nanyu. The deep, confused murmur of a crowd, like the hum of a swarm of angry bees disturbed, rose to our ears, and thin cries shrill above the communal voice of excitement. We looked down into the village. "No!" I cried out in protest. "No! No!"

It is our temple that has been bombed! Our temple, that was the shrine of eternal calm. The golden roofs of the High Hall gaped open to the sky and the marble terrace before it was shattered, with a huge crater in the centre where the incense burner had stood. Through a breach in the red walls we press in among the agitated crowds. The slender cypresses of the courtyard are slashed and splintered. The skyward-curving eaves with their bells and processions of friendly little beasts lie in dust. The marble balustrades are demolished, with all their graceful carvings of startled and leaping deer, of birds in harmonious flight and leopards springing among clouds. Rescue squads are delving in the disorder of broken beams and rubble, while onlookers watch in hypnotized horror.

For the moment this is as much as my stunned mind can accept. But there is more. Pao stoops to pick up a long, jagged fragment of metal. There is a stain of dull red left on his fingers; he drops it with a shudder. On the white marble there are other stains, torn bits of clothing scattered, bomb shards and . . . an arm torn off at the shoulder. I shut my eyes, sick with horror, and turn to go quickly away from this place. But as we go down the marble steps to the lower courtyard, men wearing the insignia of the Red Cross pass us hurriedly, carrying between them a human body, ripped and disembowelled. They place it on the ground at the foot of the wide flight of stairs, in a row with other motionless heaps, and hastily draw over it a piece of faded red cloth from one of the long banners of the High Hall. An officer's boot protrudes. From the next covered form beside it project the sandalled feet of a common soldier, and from the next beyond the thick-soled cloth shoes of a priest.

The monks run to and fro, their wide garments flying in the winds of their agitation, their prayers and laments a keening wail, shrill above the low moanings of the wounded. They bring lighted incense and burning candles to thrust upright in the earth at the feet of each of the dead. An officer in command of rescue work shouts to them to bring out straw and mats and quilts for the injured. They hasten, distracted as dusk-loving birds rudely awakened to harsh sunlight.

War's intrusion has brought havoc to our temple's ancient guarded security of peace. In the wreckage of the High Hall the severed head of the great Buddha lies among scattered ashes of incense, smiling still its golden, contemplative smile. One huge hand, flung twenty yards away in a garden of crushed flowers, points upwards in solemn admonition. . . .

CHAPTER EIGHT

SOUTHBOUND FOR KWANGSI

Change came quickly for us after this. Work was interrupted by raid warnings daily and twice a day. It came to be so customary and expected a routine that the people of Nanyu, who had learned what bombing was like, would not wait for the siren's alarm, but each morning closed their shops, locked their doors, and fled into the folds of the hills until night, when they returned fearfully to their homes to sleep. The tradesmen and hangers-on who had followed the government offices to Nanyu in the way of business left their sheds and booths empty and decamped with their stock in trade for safer regions. The tailor ran away with two dresses of mine and never returned. In three days Pao and I were left almost in sole possession of the Grand Nanyu Hotel. Everybody had gone out of the village to live in isolated farm-houses high up in the hills.

There was a daily tide as definite as the tides of the sea. At first daylight there were stirrings and shouts and footsteps in the street. Men, women, and children streamed out of the village, carrying whatever they valued most tied up in bundles, for no one knew whether they would return to find their homes still standing. Along with them went the pedlars of oranges and cakes and the little portable restaurants. By eight o'clock the street lay empty between blank boarded shop fronts, and a vast silence overhung the village. One could walk from end to end and meet no one but a sentry or two on patrol. Where the country people had come each morning to hold market, with their clean-scrubbed vegetables laid out in flat baskets – smooth purple egg-plant, carrots red as coral, the pale green of leeks; where there had been the din of bargaining and the call of vendors, all was deserted and still, except for a stray cur nosing in the refuse of the ditches. Nanyu was like a fairground when the fair is over, with empty, unswept booths, abandoned.

At sunset the tide turned. The people of Nanyu came home, opened their shops, and lighted their lamps. Down from the hill farmsteads came all the officers and clerks from General Headquarters, hungry for noise and companionship and good food. The restaurants that remained kindled up the fires and were riotously busy, crowding the day's business into three or four hours. Day and night were reversed; there would be loud laughter and singing and traffic in the street until late. Then, of a sudden, the din would be silenced, for we had martial law and curfew was at eleven.

Pao's work, of course, continued, though interrupted constantly. We stayed on in our room at the hotel, clinging to its relative comfort and privacy, preferring this to the meagre accommodation we might or might not have been able to find elsewhere. As long as the hotel maintained a roof over us, it was luxury indeed as compared to lodging in the country, where we could not hope for a room to ourselves.

Our sleepy-eyed room boy stayed on with us. I do not know what motives of loyalty constrained him; certainly our tips were too insignificant to command such devotion. He rose to the emergency with unsuspected fires of energy. He waited upon us morning and night with basins of hot water. He swept the floor unprompted. There was no longer need to worry about the dirt going down through the cracks. When the alarm sounded, although he was terribly afraid, he would never leave before we did. It was his responsibility to lock the doors behind us. He disapproved strongly of our habit of sitting under a tree during the alarm, just outside the village. But even so he would not desert us, compromising on a dry ditch in our vicinity for his shelter. He invariably went to sleep, but after the all-clear signal we would shake him awake and he would stir himself with remarkable success to find food for us. There was almost a touch of magic in the well-seasoned hot meals he conjured up for us when there was not so much as an egg or a bowl of dry rice to be bought in the village until evening. We grew exceedingly fond of him and parted from him sorrowfully when we left Nanyu. Pao gave him his tennis-racket as a token of our esteem; it needed re-stringing, but the boy had always admired it enormously as an emblem of gentility and he was most pleased with the present.

We left Nanyu on the 16th November. On the 12th Changsha had been burned.... It is difficult to write of that needless tragedy. Those who should have kept sane, holding the balance steady as the Generalissimo did at Hankow, failed in the crisis. The enemy were in Yochow! They were pushing down into Hunan; their ships were on the Poyang Lake; nothing could hold them back from Changsha! A contagion of wild terror swept the city. Scorched earth! Let nothing be left to fall into

111

the hands of the Japanese! No chance was given for orderly evacuation. Men ran from street to street with torches; whoever would hinder them was shot down. The frantic people were cut off from escape; thousands died in the fire. Those who reached open country fled destitute, empty-handed, all they possessed lost in the blaze. The roads were black with refugees fleeing from the fire. Japanese planes swooped low to machine-gun the desperate, struggling crowds. . . .

Changsha did not fall then. The Generalissimo sped to the scene and rallied the defence. The attack was halted. Next year when the Japanese again attempted the assault they were flung back in a decisive defeat. To this day Changsha has been successfully defended. That reckless sacrifice was utterly unnecessary. The guilty leaders who had made no effort to hold the city were brought to account for their mad act of panic. Their sentence was severe – death. They had deserved it. Through their hasty and cowardly action Changsha was destroyed. As a strategic point it was still of military importance, but the city with its temples and schools, its fine shops, its old courtyards and gardens and homes, was reduced to ruins. No city in Free China, unless it is Chungking, has suffered more terribly from the war.

Almost overnight Nanyu was abandoned. It was not taken by the Japanese, then or later. But the panic in Changsha, the fall of Yochow, had rendered it too vulnerable. A council was held and it was decided to move the General Staff to Chungking where the civil government had already gone. But the direct route to Chungking was a hazardous road skirting the edge of battle and in danger of being cut at any time. Therefore it was planned to move south to Kweilin, which was to be temporary headquarters until arrangements could be made for highway transport to Chungking.

When I write of this southward journey I would not give a wrong impression of its hardships. Actually it was nothing. If I seem to make much of its distresses, that is my own lack of fortitude. More, a thousand times more, has been endured uncomplainingly by my people, driven before the winds of war. At one time and another there have been fifty million refugees on the roads of China. . . . This journey that I tell of was a minor incident in the saga of migration.

One thing remains vivid to me in retrospect: despite the nightmare of those ten days on the way – the wretchedness, the sleeplessness, the filth, the crowding – no one lost temper, no one complained. Myself excepted (for I was acutely miserable most of the time and none too successful in concealing my feelings), these hundreds of travellers met all the discomforts of the move to Kweilin, not with stoic resignation, but with cheerfulness and good humour.

That is perhaps our outstanding and most excellent Chinese trait, our sense of humour. Chinese laughter, sometimes mellow, sometimes acrid, lightens the most tense situation with appreciation of the ludicrous. It saves us from the solemn absurdities of the Japanese. It gives us a sense of proportion. It is the secret of our resiliency. We endure; we come through. After catastrophe we rise up and build again out of the fragments, as I have seen people in Chungking putting up shelters of broken brick and splintered wood salvaged from their bomb-wrecked homes. Our sense of humour makes us accept things as they are; our cheerfulness makes us laugh at inconveniences; our good temper helps us to put up with discomforts. We are not as progressive and efficient as we might be if we took all seriously, but we are happier.

We can adapt to circumstances. Today we may be guests in a Nanking flower garden. Tomorrow we may be refugees, crowded a dozen in one squalid, earth-floored room. But we laugh. It is free, spontaneous laughter. If we win this war – and we shall! – it will be through our sense of humour.

It was a raw, rainy day when we waited with hundreds of others to leave Nanyu. The golden weather had broken at last in a sullen drizzle and searching gusts of wind. The pavement was damp and slimy; wet dripped from the overshadowing eaves. Dusk fell in mid-afternoon, but no lamps were lighted in the houses. The aspect of Nanyu was changed, like the face of a woman grown old and slatternly. We remembered that first evening – the smell of incense and flowers, the red sunlight through the tree branches, the gardenias in bloom on the hillside, the ancient, unshaken peace of this quiet village dreaming at the foot of holy Tou Yun Feng. We remembered, also, when every day was like market day and every night like the fifteenth of the New Year, with lamps and candles alight all the length of the street, the red glow of cooking fires, the friendly, jostling crowds, the noise of festivity in the air. All was changed. Neither the ineffable peace of Nanyu as we had seen it first nor the bustle and gaiety of succeeding days had anything to do with this drab huddle of roofs, grey under a grey rain.

We had been given orders to be ready at noon to leave Nanyu. Hundreds of officers and their families, with the equipment and archives of various government offices, were to be moved for hundreds of miles over a single-track railroad already choked with troop trains and refugees. But first we must reach the railway. There were almost no private cars. The army trucks were busy moving the camps. Ten buses had been assigned to transfer the General Staff with their families and baggage to Hengyang or some other station, where they would entrain for Kweilin – ten ancient and infirm buses, shuttling between Nanyu and the railroad, going endlessly to and fro.

We were tired and dispirited. Since two in the afternoon we had waited, standing in the rain with our luggage beside us, hoping for a seat in a bus. By eleven o'clock that night the crowd and their mountainous piles of baggage were not perceptibly diminished. There were too many people, too much dunnage – leather boxes, enormous netted baskets, rolled quilts tied up in yellow oiled sheeting. There was even furniture. People who had rescued chairs and tables in their flight from home and brought them all the way from Nanking or Shanghai did not see fit to part with them at this point. They clung to these bulky and non-essential impediments at great inconvenience to themselves and hindrance to all others.

There was no order of precedence. As people arrived they dumped down their luggage by the side of the road and sat upon it. There was no station, no shelter. We waited on the bare hillside above the village, under umbrellas or exposed to the steady rain. The crowd waited in apathy and silence for the most part, at intervals waking to excited anticipation at the sound of a motor horn, the flare of headlights whipping down the road, or the rattle of an approaching car. Each bus as it came in was taken by assault. Men leaped upon it before it had come to a halt, fought at the doors, struggled through the windows. Those who gained a foothold hauled their families and possession in after them, pushing and dragging, shouting, becoming entangled with each other's baggage and clogging the way with their own, all with a great waste of effort. Pao and I let bus after bus go by, making no attempt to join the *mêlée*, unwilling to push and shove for place. I take no credit for patience or politeness. A kind of physical inertia possessed me. No advantage, no destination, seemed worth such frenzied struggle.

Near midnight. . . . Rain fell ever more heavily; brown water ran in the ruts of the road. Lanterns made circles of wan radiance, slanted across with rain, in the vast, hollow dark. Faces were pale and still with weariness in the dim light. We were caught in a slowly eddying backwater of time. Minutes, hours, passed; but the night and rain were timeless, unending, and the long wait brought us no nearer hope. But finally some semblance of order had been evolved among us. Someone in authority had at last convinced the waiting crowd that loading and dispatching would be expedited if we formed a queue and took our turn. It was no longer a question of rightful precedence. It would be idle to argue that point; we had all waited half the day and half the night. . . .

Less and less frequently now the buses came in. They returned to us, bodies plastered with red mud where they had gone hub-deep in the thick mire of the new-made, unsurfaced roads. They were spattered to the wind-shields. They came in coughing and rattling, growing visibly older and more decrepit with each round trip. Or they failed to return at all. Somewhere along the road they lay down in discouragement. They developed internal disorders. They blundered into ditches. We were scarcely more uncomfortable under our umbrellas than those who had fought for a seat, only to spend the night wedged in with their baggage in a stalled bus by the roadside in the rain. If we had known it, we were as well off as those others who had reached the railway.

For an hour or two we had moved gradually toward the head of the line. The end of our wait was in sight – the next bus would be ours. We would quietly enter and take our seats and tremble and move off down the road and we would be on our way to Kweilin!

No bus came. . . . At eleven o'clock, with the rain drumming on our umbrellas and the road racing with muddy rivers, an official announcement was made. No more buses. Bad weather. Traffic suspended until tomorrow. No more buses tonight. . . . Almost with relief we abandoned the long wait to go in search of a place to sleep. It was hardly a disappointment, expectation had already flickered so dim with the hours.

We took shelter in the schoolhouse which had served as the offices of the General Staff. Here history had been determined. Reports from all over China and from the outside world had been received here, and from this room had gone out orders that controlled the movements of hundreds of thousands of troops. It was a large, shabby, whitewashed room, bare except for a few desks and tables. Scattered lights – candles stuck upright in cracks – relieved a little the darkness. Wind pouring through empty window-frames, where the glass had been shattered by concussion in the bombing, blew the flames to streaming pennants but could not extinguish them.

We unrolled our bedding and lay down. At intervals in the hours between midnight and morning we lost consciousness, yet we were somehow aware of the interminable passage of time, the grunts and snores and mutterings of many people stretched in uneasy rest, the ache of our cramped muscles, the unyielding hardness of the plank floor, the sound of the rain and the wind. . . .

Morning. Cold grey daylight filtered through fog at the window. The air was still and cold; the rain had ceased. Children awoke, crying; the smallest were comforted with the breast. We sat up and looked about us with distaste. It is a fortunate thing we do our sleeping, as a rule, in privacy. This mass sleeping and waking, this enforced intimacy of an improvised dormitory, is too disillusioning. There is no dignity in the slack, defenceless, stupid faces of strangers asleep, nor any charm in the first bewildered, groping moments of their rousing.

I waked unrested and feverish. I did not share Pao's healthy morning hunger but I went with him into the street to look for something to eat. We walked the length of the village in the fog. We passed mat sheds where once thriving restaurants had fed hundreds every day. The clay stoves were broken; the great iron cooking-pans had been carried away. We passed tea-shops, boarded up. We came to the Grand Nanyu Hotel. Already it looked strange and alien. The courtyard was empty. The doors swung open on the galleries. In front of the room which had been ours the beheaded stems of chrysanthemums stood up gaunt and forlorn where someone had picked off all the flowers. We prowled about the place. There was no one to hinder us but a solitary servant, the gatekeeper, and he gave us no more than an indifferent glance that scarcely took notice of our existence. There was no fire in the kitchen, no food in the larder; the cooks were gone. Our room boy, who surely would have found food for us, was gone. We felt like ghosts revisiting a place after many years. We felt invisible. Nanyu had forgotten us.

We returned to the schoolhouse. Still no bus. The fog thinned and the sun, already high in the east, shone small and round like the moon, wanly white through the drifting vapour. The usual morning air-raid alarm then sounded. People scattered to the country. Pao and I went farther up the hill and lay in the damp

116

grass under the trees and drank from the torrent to quench our thirst. The sun grew warm toward noon. We slept a little. It is all confused in my mind with disquieting dreams, for by this time I was quite ill and slightly light-headed. The all-clear siren must have sounded about noon. We returned to our post by the roadside. At three in the afternoon a bus came in and we were assigned places.

The bus was a home-made wooden body mounted on a very weary and much-abused chassis, with an engine suffering from cardiac decomposition, hiccoughs, and the heaves. At twenty miles an hour it creaked and groaned and strained in every joint as though it would wrench itself to pieces. On that rough road it behaved like an unseaworthy sailing ship in a typhoon. We were flung from side to side and bounced out of our seats to bump our heads on the ceiling.

The seat in front of us was occupied by a petty officer with his family – his wife and two small children. The husband was doing his best to protect the woman against the violent motion of the car. She herself clutched with both hands at the window-frame, which was without glass. I saw at a glance that she was well advanced in pregnancy. Suddenly her face went grey, distorted with a spasm of pain. She gasped, "It won't be long now if it goes on like that!"

It went on like that for another half-hour. Then with a lurch the bus came to a standstill. In the abrupt silence we could hear the far-off drone of aeroplanes. "Get out and run!" the driver shouted to us, as he leaped for the nearest thicket. "Bombers!" We swarmed out by every exit. The woman ran – or, rather, hobbled awkwardly, doubled over and whining a little with pain. Her husband could not give her much help, burdened as he was with the two children. I might have offered aid, but the ground tilted and rocked this way and that under my feet and the landscape was blurred with flashes of light. I could not tell whether the roaring in my ears was the sound of the planes or the thunder of my own heart and blood. We made for a farmhouse some distance from the road, well sheltered among bamboos. There was a mad barking of dogs. The ragged people of the farm gathered about us in the courtyard; I heard their voices as a formless gabble. The sky swung around; there was the roaring of a great black whirlpool swirling about me, dragging me down into the black oblivion. When I came to I was lying on straw under the eaves and Pao was sponging my face with his handkerchief wet with cold tea. Near by, the woman crouched on the

117

kerbing of the courtyard, preoccupied with her own suffering.

The bombers passed high overhead, so high that they were indistinguishable in the blue haze of the sky. Hengyang had been bombed, we learned later, but we were too far away to hear the explosions. When the last reverberation of their engines had died in silence, a blast of the motor horn called us back to the bus. If we did not come the bus would go without us. The jolting journey was resumed and in another half-hour we came to Santang on the railroad.

Santang was a name, little more. Here the highway met the railroad and there was a station building. Straggling along both sides of the road for a few rods were shabby little shops of thatch and matting, where food of the simplest description was to be had. We had eaten nothing since yesterday. They brought us bowls of rice and bland white *tou-fu* and red pepper. Trucks rushed by in the road, swirling up dust, for it had rained less here. The dust settled on our food as we ate, but we were past caring. We plied our chopsticks busily, pushing in great mouthfuls of the coarse rice and *tou-fu*, hot with the sharp bite of red pepper. At least a part of my indisposition must have been sheer hunger, for after I had eaten I felt a little better.

We walked to the station past mat sheds where wounded soldiers lay in rows, waiting for a train to take them to hospitals at the rear. They lay on a thin layer of straw spread on the bare earth, some few with quilts, but most of them uncovered. They watched us with dull, patient eyes, or they slept with heavy breathing. Some lay so still, so rigidly unmoving, they might have been already dead. Seeing these wounded, the reports and rumours of a battle around Yochow became real to us.

In the waiting-room of the station officers were busy checking over the files and documents of the General Staff by the simple expedient of weighing them by the basketful as they arrived. They had been hastily packed in bamboo basket-loads and brought from Nanyu by carrier. By this most ancient transport system – coolie carriers with their shoulder-poles, taking a hundred pounds twenty-five miles a day – all kinds of freight and express have been brought through war zones, safe to their destination. When modern mechanized transport breaks down and roads are cut and bridges bombed, the dependable old carrier system takes over the task. Mail, machinery, salt, iron, petrol for aeroplanes, munitions, supplies of every kind, swing along narrow paths between fields and over mountains, twenty-five miles a day, and nothing can stop them.

A loud, cheerful voice hailed us – Wu Kwei-fan, who had arrived earlier. "No use to ask about trains – everything goes north, rushing troops to the front. They say our train is on a siding somewhere, waiting for a clear track. It will not go to-night. Perhaps tomorrow. Or the day after that. It depends on the battle around Yochow. No chance until that crisis eases. Meanwhile, where are you lodging?"

We looked about helplessly. Where? Every inch in Sangtang where a person might stretch out to sleep was already pre-empted. Wu Kwei-fan had rescued and assembled a small group and he now introduced us all round. "Here is Wang Yu-lin also. She does not know where Pu Kuang-ti is, and there is no one to take care of her. Colonel and Madame Huang" – a middle-aged couple, he very tall and thin, she a short, round, prim little woman. "Miss Han and her fiancé, Captain Lo." These two I knew slightly. Captain Lo was a friend of Pao's. The girl was a frail and tragic figure, fatally ill with tuberculosis. They sat or reclined on some quilts against the wall. She lay in his arms, both of them oblivious of anyone else, set apart in a circle of doom. She coughed rackingly, stifling the spasm with her hand-kerchief, and lay spent, eyes closed. They understood the danger of contagion but would not be separated. It was a love match between them. In the Chinese conception of betrothal there is a finality as binding as marriage. The engaged refer to each other in formal speech as "not-yet-wedded wife" and "not-yet-wedded husband." It was doubtless madness for Miss Han to undertake the arduous journey from Nanking to Hankow, from Hankow to Nanyu, from Nanyu to Kweilin, from Kweilin to Chung-king, refusing to leave her lover, only to die at the last in Chung-king. Reason condemns it, yet there was something touching and lovely in their unquestioning mutual devotion. Now, as Wu Kwei-fan urged us all to set out in search of lodgings, Captain Lo shook his head slightly and motioned us to go without them. Miss Han lay unheeding, too weak to move.

We left Santang with its overcrowded sheds and struck out into the country to find shelter in some farm-house. Dusk and a fine grey misty rain – "feather rain" we call it in Chinese – dimmed the scene. The mountains on the horizon were gone, dissolved into the dull sky, and fields lay level in the thickening gloom, interspersed with huddled burial mounds and mud-walled farmsteads. We walked single-file among the narrow paths, the men loaded with suitcases and bedding rolls. We were silent with fatigue and with the pervasive mood of dejection

– all but Wu Kwei-fan, who was still in the best of spirits, He strode along singing snatches from Chinese theatrical arias, odd falsetto music with a wild minor strain. When we were turned away from house after house already filled with transients to the last available corner, he refused to be discouraged but cheered us on, guaranteeing to find us lodgings and offering to carry any or all of us who were too spent to continue.

We walked on, deeper into the fields. It was now dark. I carried nothing; it was all I could do to plod empty-handed, seeing nothing now but the faint trace of the path. Beyond my utter exhaustion I became aware of vague pains that gripped me with a sudden cold fear. At first indefinite, they grew more intense, agonizing and rhythmic. I clenched my teeth to check the sob of terror that rose to my throat. For the past two weeks I had cherished a small secret hope and wonder. I had not dared to tell Pao until I knew with more certainty. Now, from my training in England, I realized what was happening. The touch of fever, the prolonged jolting of the bus journey, the raid alarm, and my fainting in the farm courtyard. . . . I knew that unless I could have absolute rest I would lose my hope of a child now. And I could not have rest. . . .

I was shaking with most bitter disappointment and with suffering. In the darkness I let the tears come, mingling with the dampness of rain on my face, and did not wipe them away. I stumbled along, holding my place in the line. We walked seven li, which is more than two miles, and came at last to a farmhouse where barking dogs rushed upon us and recoiled at Colonel Huang's flash-light. The house was dark; the doors were bolted, the inhabitants asleep. Wu Kwei-fan shouted at the door and pounded with his fists. The dogs circled us warily, growling and barking with redoubled frenzy. After long minutes the door creaked cautiously and opened enough for a head to be thrust out. The beam of the flash-light showed us an old, old peasant woman with red-rimmed eyes peering suspiciously, with pendulous lower lip, two or three yellow fangs of teeth, and the wrinkled skin running in two great folds from the outstretched jaw to the haggard throat. Before we could speak she made gestures of refusal, but Wu Kwei-fan would not take no for an answer. There *was* room, he insisted. We must have shelter. With a flourish he produced his visiting card inscribed with all his degrees and offices and waved it under the old woman's nose. He was a personage of importance (here Wu Kwei-fan drew himself up grandly tall and made his voice deep and impressive), and if we were not received, he would return tomorrow with soldiers and there would be consequences!

The woman's head popped in again, there was a parley, then she came out with a lamp. "Follow me," she said sullenly, and led us to the rear of the house to a storage room half filled with sacks of rice, beans, and seeds. At the left of the entrance was a cesspit. In the right wall a small door opened into the room where the old woman and her family of six had their sleeping quarters. Beyond was a lean-to for rakes, ploughs, and other farm implements. "There," said the old woman. "That's space if you want it. Ten dollars."

"It will do very well," said Wu Kwei-fan, rubbing his hands. "Now we will just pile these sacks at one side against the inner wall; then we'll put down straw – a lot of it – on the ground, and we'll put our bedding on that. But we shall pay only five dollars." The men were already putting the plan into execution, tearing straw from the dry underside of the stacks behind the house. The old woman screamed and protested. The money was too little. We were ruining the straw stacks. We must go; the room was not to let. But we had already occupied the premises; we were not to be turned out. We went on with our preparations for the night, deaf to her wrath, even when a man, two boys, another woman, and two small children came out to add their voice to her objections. I do not know whether it was all for effect, to force a better bargain on the rental, or whether it was actually in fear we might have designs on their reserves of grain.

At this point a diversion occurred. There were a renewed uproar of the dogs and voices shouting from the road – other benighted travellers who had followed the same path (no coincidence, for it was the clearest path out of Santang), who had been turned away from door after door, to come at last to this same cold welcome. They would have to go on farther. Here there was no room but the one we had taken. When the six of us had laid down our quilts side by side there was not space to set one's foot.

The old woman went to the front of the house in reply to the hail. We heard a man's voice pleading with peculiar urgency and her shrill refusals – then, in a momentary pause of the barking, we heard a cry, not quite human, a rising crescendo of agony breaking in a shriek. I knew that cry. It was the voice of a woman in labour. It is a sound unlike any other. "Quick!" I said to Pao and Wu Kwei-fan. "It must be the woman who came on the bus with us. Make them take her in here!" For we could

121

hear the old woman vehemently objecting: "Go away! There is no room. We do not want your pollution here. No, not for any money. Go away quickly!"

It may seem utmost callousness. It is not quite that. For superstition has created an aura of mystery and terror about the act of childbirth. Despite the Chinese desire for children and joy in them, the birth itself is accounted vile and degrading. Afterward ceremonies of cleansing must be performed, burning of cedar twigs, lighting of incense and fire-crackers. For thirty days there are taboos to be observed. Until the cycle of the moon is complete, the woman who has borne a child may not cross the threshold of door or gate, lest ill luck come upon all who are in the household. With such dread dangers involved, it is not strange if people like these peasants refuse to take the risk for a passing stranger.

But I could not acquiesce in their superstition. I could not let them drive the poor woman away, to give birth to her child in the wet fields. All my professional instincts were aroused; I was a midwife. "The tool shed!" I cried. "It will be shelter. And she need cross no threshold." Wu Kwei-fan went to bring her. We heard his strong, cheerful voice overriding all protest. I took a candle and went to the lean-to. Pao and Colonel Huang moved the farm implements and spread down straw. Wu Kwei-fan returned, guiding the new arrivals. It was, as I had guessed, the family who had been our fellow travellers on the bus. The husband was half carrying the woman. The children stumbled after, blind for want of sleep.

The baby was born about a quarter of an hour later. In all my time of training in England I could never have imagined this, my first delivery in China. Stuck into a crack, the tallow candle guttered in the wind, making a fitful, smoky light, hollowing a cave of faint visibility in the night's great darkness. The woman lay on the quilt on the ground; I knelt in the straw before her. The two children were curled together like puppies, instantly asleep. The man crouched by his wife, gripping her hands, as she put forth her strength to bring the child to birth. I had nothing to work with, not even a fire for warmth or hot water to wash with. I could do nothing but receive the child as it was born and tie the cord with a bit of string dipped in iodine. The mother's gasping cries ceased with the sudden relief, and there was a thin, weak wail of the newborn. It lay in my two palms, a boy child, a tiny, premature infant, unready yet for life. The little, aged face puckered as with pain; the small chest strained for air; the spidery limbs clutched in terror of falling. I wrapped it quickly in some old clothing the father took out from a bundle and laid it by the mother.

I stood up and the dim, shadowy room spun around me. The strong, clean smell of iodine mingled with the stench from the cesspit at the door, the warm, steamy reek of fresh blood, the sharp sweetness of eau-de-Cologne I had used to disinfect my hands in lieu of alcohol. I was suddenly shaken with nausea. I groped my way across the door-yard to our shelter and sank down on the quilts beside Pao. I cried myself to sleep, relaxed to suffering. But I muffled the sobs and held myself from trembling, that Pao might not know.

I slept late into the morning, numbed in a kind of stupor. When I awoke, Wang Yu-lin was sitting beside me. The others were gone. They had walked to Santang to find out about the train. Yu-lin went to bring me something to eat. I sat on the floor, staring up at the thatch above me, listless. The racking pains had ebbed, leaving me weak and aching, and I knew the worst was over, but the child I had hoped for would not be. How I should have welcomed it, no matter if I had to give birth in a hovel, like the woman I had tended the night before!

Wang Yu-lin brought me rice gruel and when I had swallowed it I got up from my bed. We might resume our journey at any time; I dared not be ill. I combed my hair and washed. I smoothed my bed. I would go presently and call upon my patient in the lean-to opposite. When my knees ceased trembling I would go.... I glanced across the door-yard. The man came out of the lean-to. He was carrying a small bundle about fifteen inches long, wrapped in old blue cloth and tied with wisps of straw, and over his shoulder he had a hoe. Behind him followed the two children. They went beyond a clump of bamboos at the edge of a grave plot. The man laid the small, stiff bundle on the ground and began to dig a hole. The children watched, with blank, uncomprehending curiosity. The father put the baby's body into the hole and made a little mound of earth over it, then trudged back to the shed.... When, later, I went across to see how the mother fared, neither she nor I made mention of the child. She accepted the birth and death impassively. I never knew whether she grieved. Probably she thought it best that the baby had died.

Wang Yu-lin had made a fire of sticks and charcoal outside our door and we prepared a meal. We borrowed a rickety table and an assortment of benches and stools. Pao and Wu Kwei-fan came back, with Madame Huang. They reported no train would be leaving today. The line was congested with troop trains still. In the station at Santang a skeleton staff was carrying on office work of a kind, on improvised desks of piled packing cases. Colonel Huang had stayed to work on some papers.

We settled to an interim existence. The men took hoes and worked on the farm with the peasants. We lived on red-pepper, *tou-fu*, and turnips dug from the fields. I could eat nothing that first day but a little brown sugar and ginseng in rice water. I was still weak and wretched, but I could not give in to illness. I moved about slowly, careful not to wake the latent pain that waited its occasion. Wang Yu-lin and Madame Huang attended to our primitive housekeeping. At night we lit a little earthenware lamp of vegetable oil, shaped like a small teapot with a spout for the wick. We shared one basin, washing our faces in turn, then crept between our quilts. We lay in a row across the small room, except for Wu Kwei-fan, who placed himself athwart the doorway for guard. Bandits could have trodden on him without rousing him! He slept soundly and never woke himself up even though he indulged in long, unintelligible, one-sided conversations in his dreams. When the light was out, noises began – rustling in the thatch; small scratching, gnawing sounds; a chattering and squeaking. Rats. They nibbled at the leather of our suitcases; they ran across us as we lay on the ground. I was in deadly fear that they would bite me as I slept.

The next day, still, there was no train, nor the next. We fought flies in the daytime (the cesspit bred them) and rats at night. The men hoed weeds in the fields for exercise. The people of the farm warmed to us after a time, all but the old woman, who viewed us still with suspicion and dislike. To our requests for hot water, for fuel, for a rag with which to clean our table, she turned a deaf ear. But Wu Kwei-fan made it his special task to woo the old termagant from her cold hostility, and he succeeded to a certain extent. "Come now, old mother," he would plead, "there is the mark of luck in your face, the sign of a merciful heart. Be kind to us poor travellers, and your grandsons and great-grandsons will multiply and grow rich, and you will be the most honoured ancestor in the province." Then she would smile a crooked, wide-mouthed smile, revealing uneven yellow teeth, the arch of the palate, and a pink, surprisingly clean tongue.

On the fourth morning we were told the train would leave at four that afternoon. The release was welcome as a wind to a sailing ship becalmed and tangled in the weed of the Sargasso Sea. It dispelled the lost and aimless mood of these long days of delay. We rolled up our bedding, collected our baggage, and bade farewell to rats, red pepper, and cesspits.

We set out, walking single-file between the stubble fields. From a long way off we saw the crowds swarming the village, like clustered dark insects, like ants or bees. Not only our companions of the General Staff, but refugees from Changsha and the invaded regions to the northward. They had walked, following the railway tracks, thronging aboard trains at every opportunity, no matter what destination, refusing to be dislodged. We thrust our way through the milling crowd. They were everywhere, refugees in grey or dull blue, faded and dirty colours of poverty, a flood of humanity seeping into every crevice and space, pressing for place on outgoing trains.

We made our way to the train reserved for us. Ours was a second-class carriage, with two rows of narrow wooden seats, facing each other in pairs. Some first-class carriages had been provided, but these were first in demand, and sixteen and twenty people were jammed into small, airless compartments meant for eight. We chose second-class by preference. Wu Kwei-fan, Wang Yu-lin, Pao, and I made up one foursome.

When the car was filled to the last seat and children crammed in where there were no seats, the baggage was carried in and stowed underfoot and overhead, where huge bundles toppled perilously in the racks above us. A man with six children walked up and down the congested aisle, depositing a child here and a child there, upon the hospitable laps of strangers. After the inside of the car was thus packed solid with people and their personal property, the refugees rushed upon the train and climbed on top, jammed the vestibules and clung to the steps, in a densely amalgamated mass, too close-packed for movement. There was no system of organization. In fact, the officer who had been put in charge of transportation arrangements was to be seen at the last moment, running to and fro looking for a place for himself, and there was no place, so he travelled all the way to Kweilin in the engine cab.

We waited from four until midnight. The sun had blazed all day on the roof of the car, and within it was like an oven. When darkness came a hanging kerosene lamp was lighted. Children fretted with weariness and hunger, or sprawled asleep on the stacked bundles. The family who had lived in the tool shed at the farm were with us in the same car. The mother opened her dress and gave her breast to one child, then to the other, and they were soothed and fell asleep in her arms. No one dared to leave the train in search of food or water, for it was due to start at any moment. At midnight it did start. Immediately it became cool, then very cold. Windows were slammed down. The air, breathed over and over, became suffocatingly dense. For a time we kept our window open, but people with children in the seat behind us objected so much we had to close it.

We were five days on the train. It was a little lifetime, set off by itself from time before and after. There were eighty-seven people in our car, not including the adherent refugees. Each had space enough to sit, no more, and in that space we lived five days. When the train stopped at a station we sometimes had a chance to get out, to buy water, wash our faces, eat a meal. But the steps and vestibule were jammed with crates, bundles, and refugees, so that it was always a struggle to drive one's way through, getting off or on the train. Also, we never knew how long the train would stop. Once a whole crowd of passengers were left behind. The train went off without warning and they pursued it along the track, shouting and waving. Because they were so many, the train waited for them a mile down the way. Often we were stalled for hours at a time, half a day, in the open country, where no food or water was to be had. We subsisted on dry, unleavened cakes, sprinkled with sesame seed. It was very hot in the daytime, but cold at night, so that we piled on clothing as it grew dark. There was no space to spread out quilts. There was not even room to wrap ourselves in quilts, for the seats were not wide enough both for us and such padding.

People slept upright in their seats, or leaned forward on folded arms to rest their heads on the small tables between each pair of seats. Pao and I took turns sleeping in two-hour shifts. One would lie sidewise, head in the other's lap. Since Wang Yu-lin and Wu Kwei-fan could not thus reciprocate, he gallantly relinquished his place to her and folded himself up with bent knees upon his large leather suitcase in the aisle. This arrangement had its disadvantages. There was constant traffic to and fro between the rows of seats and Wu Kwei-fan was walked on in his sleep many times a night. It troubled him less than it would most people. He slept, as he did everything else, with a wholehearted concentration that ignored small inconveniences.

Bu the end of the second day of our loitering journey the floor of the car was ankle-deep in litter – orange peel, paper, pea-nut shells, chewed refuse of sugar cane. It was never swept. Gradually, too, the atmosphere grew fetid with a stench that was more than the odour of close-crowded, unwashed bodies and re-breathed air. There was but one privy for the use of eighty-seven people. Dysentery was prevalent (due, no doubt, to red pepper, flies, and erratic diet) and day and night there was a waiting line. Presently the privy clogged and overflowed. The door jammed and could never be completely closed. There was no water for flushing or cleaning up. The smell became over-powering, yet the to-and-fro procession, of necessity, continued.

For the refugees clinging to the roof of the car the problem was even more acute. One evening, during a long run between stops, a man on top who could not get down relieved himself. The urine trickled down to the sill of our open window and spattered upon some seed-cakes I had in my lap. It was the last straw. I lost control of my nerves. I became hysterical, sobbing and shuddering with disgust. Pao went clean mad. Gripping his cane, his face *hsiung*, he climbed to the roof of the moving train and laid about him, furious, lashing the crouched shoulders of the refugees and calling them animals and savages. Afterward we were both ashamed. I was at fault. I should have kept mastery of my feelings. Pao cannot endure to see me cry.

Except for this breach in self-discipline, we lived together for five days, eighty-seven people, enduring thirst, stench, crowding, lack of sleep, yet preserving courtesy toward each other, exchanging jokes, and in general behaving as though we were on a pleasure excursion. Courtesy is, I think, one of the highest virtues in time of stress, the pattern of decorum that is so emphasized in Chinese tradition. The surface gloss of good manners smooths away friction. We smile and bow and murmur the prescribed polite phrases, and miraculously the thousand annoyances of our environment melt away.

We had no books or magazines to read. We amused ourselves and each other with stories, verses, and conversations with different people up and down the car. Of course we talked about the war, yet never once did I hear the Japanese reviled and blamed for our present discomfort. Almost to the last one, these people had lost home and fortune in the invasion. Most had been living in Nanking. But they scorned to make much of their material losses. One thing alone provoked their deep, slow-burning anger – the wholesale violation of Chinese women. That is the one thing that will not be forgiven. Yet even here there was no threat of revenge or vowing of everlasting hatred – only a conviction, a sure belief, that these atrocities stem from something in Japanese character and outlook, a fundamental immorality, and because of this decadence of character the Japanese are doomed. They cannot win this war. They cannot endure. They lack the stability that inheres in Chinese traditions of family and home. The Japanese have no virtue (this was the conclusion of our fellow-passengers); they have no morality. Therefore they and their nation are doomed. It may take a hundred years; it may take longer, but no one of us can doubt the outcome. Japan must fall.

Our train crawled on through the plains of Hunan, with its double-deck load – General Staff below, refugees above. These refugees, unlike those we had seen at Yochow, were not stamped with hopeless misery. They were ragged but not too ragged, and only moderately hungry, not starving. But their number! Their number was the appalling thing. There were so many of them; they overran everything; they were everywhere. At first I could see nothing else. Then, progressively, I ceased to be aware of them. Not that they were not there – they still clustered on the roof of our train, clung to the steps, filled the vestibules, thronged the station platforms. But they had become a part of our environment, a thing of everyday life, lived with, along with thirst, smells, heat, bombings, crying babies – they were no longer a thing to attract attention.

On the third morning we were stopped for repairs at a small village. Our progress had grown more erratic and intermittent. There was dissension between the engineer and fireman, which at times amounted to complete non-co-operation. When it came to the point of blows between them, the gentle officer in charge of transportation was compelled to mediate in order to prevent a wreck. The situation becoming known to the whole train, we discussed whether it might not make for better speed if we took up a collection and invited the engineer and crew to a fine dinner to be given when and if we reached our destination.

On this morning, since some essential part of the engine was under repair, we knew we had an hour or more of delay. At once everybody, refugees and General Staff, scattered into the village and surrounding fields. The landscape was full of people busy with intimate personal affairs – washing, scratching, disrobing for a flea hunt, searching the seams of their shirts for lice or, unmindful of unlookers, engaged in other functions usually performed less publicly. After some experience in communal living, I have observed that men are far more apt to degenerate in manners and lose their civilized sense of modesty than are women.

Pao and I seized our wash-basins and hurried into the village in search of hot water. Hundreds of our fellow travellers had the same thought. At the first tea-shop we found the kettles already emptied and ten or a dozen people standing around the great shallow cooking-pan, waiting for the water to heat. At the next place it was the same. People clamoured at every restaurant and tea-shop, wherever there was a stove. They invaded private kitchens, waving towels and basins and dollar bills, calling for hot water. We followed the current. Pushing into a courtyard, we met people coming out carrying full basins, but when we reached the stove the last of the hot water had just been scooped from the cooking-pan and the woman of the house was pouring in a bucket of cold water. Pao firmly took the bucket from her and thrust me toward a door. "In you go, Suyin." He bolted the door and stood guard. I found myself in a small, dark bedroom. I poured the water into my basin. I took off all my clothes and bathed. The sting of cold, clean water was startling but delightful. I scrubbed until my skin glowed warm. When I had done and dressed again, Pao took his turn. The people whose bedroom it was vociferously objected. I stood them off while Pao washed, but when we left they were still grumbling, though less bitterly once they had satisfied themselves we had stolen nothing.

Unexpectedly the whistle shrilled for all to return. We went through the car window to our places, Pao lifting me up, then swinging himself over the sill. This had become our customary mode of entry and exit, for it was all but impossible to force one's way through the compact mass of refugees at the doors. We were shining with cleanliness and conscious virtue. The air about me was sweet with eau-de-Cologne, for I had emptied the last of my bottle into my wash-basin. We smugly announced that we had bathed. While others thought only of breakfast, *we* had taken baths! There was odd silence around us. Envy or amazement – I do not know.

A bath does not last long. There were two days more of this travelling slum. We were hot, sweaty, and itchy. Our clothing clung to us, clammy and exuding an acid odour. Our hair was matted with sweat, dust, and soot. Our throats felt constricted with thirst, our eyes smarted with wind and cinders. Yet it was really nothing.

Whenever, now, we meet friends we know in Peking, their tales of hardships on the way outmatch anything we have experienced. A friend of mine with four small children went from Hankow to Ichang, two days and two nights, on a river steamer so jammed with refugees there was only standing room. Crushed against the rail, they stood on their feet two days and two nights and not even the children made complaint. Another girl, who was at the university with me, slipped out of Peking one night and walked to Free China, six hundred miles, through devastated cities, through the Japanese lines, through guerilla territory. No, what we endured was nothing.

It is the fifth day. The softly undulating horizon of Hunan, the wide rivers and rich fields, give place to a terrain as strange and wild as legend could devise. First hinted at with isolated rocks jutting up through the flat green fields, a change comes over the placid landscape. A plain as level as the sea is broken by sudden, improbable hills, thrusting up through the crust of the earth in sharp cliffs and pinnacles. The sea was here once, washing between these islands of stone; it has left long reaches of shingle, pebbles rolled and rounded by water. The hills press closer about us – queer, unbelievable shapes, stark under the hot light of afternoon. They seem alive – fantastic monsters that rush toward us and past us with a snarl and roar. It is only the clangour of iron wheels on iron rails flung back at us from the impending cliffs, but in this violent and unnatural scene it seems to emanate from some sinister life in the very rock. The near-by hills leap at us, roaring. In the middle distance they pace the train, prowling beasts stalking us. On the horizon they stand silent, menacing.

Sunset fills the sky with a glare of magenta-red light. The cliffs close in, more and more savage, tall and threatening, the colour of blood and flame. It is almost impossible to breathe, they press in upon us so frighteningly. The train rushes on in the waning daylight, through purple-dark shadows, the whistle shrilling in a long, despairing wail between wild hills crested still with red-violet light. The colour in the sky dulls to ash. Without warning the train stops dead, with a jerk that throws us out of our seats. We are at Kweilin.

CHAPTER NINE

THROUGH KWEILIN

In the dusk of our arrival at Kweilin we descended from the train in the manner which had become natural to us, Pao leaping out of the window to the platform and I handing down our luggage to him. When I followed the last of the suitcases, sliding into his arms, we were at once beset by porters, mostly women with raucous voices, but among them a few timid men. The women were astonishing, almost as tall as the men, and their equal for strength – heavy-set, deep-bosomed, muscular, barefoot, free-striding. They have never followed the custom of footbinding. They carry loads, till the fields, contribute their share of labour to public works – repairing roads, breaking stone for the railway. They wear short coats and trousers, the usual peasant dress, with a distinctive apron of blue cloth fastened at the neck with thin silver chains. A tall, gaunt amazon of forty took charge of our things, wresting them forcibly from the men carriers and scornfully saying, "We'll do this work; you go away and fight!"

It becomes monotonous to state that we arrived in a certain place and looked for lodgings and there was no room. But in a life where all landmarks are lost it means much to have a room and a home, no matter how impermanent.

Kweilin was already full of refugees; for months people had been flocking here from war-threatened and invaded areas. We went first to the Laughing Multitude Hotel, a very good government-run hostelry not far from the station. Of course such splendid accommodation was not for us. All the rooms were occupied or reserved by high government officials, foreign newspaper correspondents, and similar favoured persons. But three hundred people from our train swarmed into the place and made ready to sleep on the floor of the dining-hall that night, if no better arrangement could be made. Pao was one of the few who found any other place. While he and Wu Kwei-fan were out looking for lodgings, Yu-lin and I and all the baggage belonging to our party obstructed a passage-way in the Laughing Multitude Hotel, until we prevailed upon the hotel boys to give us a room, if only for a few hours. It was incredible luxury to be in a room with a door that we could shut and be alone! The

131

apartment was already bespoken for some important personage; we could not stay the night. But we made the most of our brief tenure. We called for hot water and more hot water. We bathed. We washed our hair. We changed all our clothes for clean things from our suitcases and consigned the evil-smelling, grimy garments of our journey to the hotel laundry to be called for later.

When we were evicted we went down to the common room, where bedding was being unrolled upon the floor, making a huge patchwork of quilts, edge to edge. Wu Kwei-fan came back, unsuccessful. It was late and dark. The inns were full. Near midnight Pao returned. "I've found something," he said a little grimly. "It's long enough to lie down in and wide enough for the two of us. There were three men considering it, but they couldn't all get into the room at once. Besides, they had families."

A small dark door with a sign, "East Gate Hotel," a narrow slit of a courtyard. We were admitted by a sleepy *cha-fang*, the inn servant, who showed us the place. People lived here crowded six and eight to a room, like pigs or sheep in adjoining pens. Darkness and whispering were their only chance of privacy. Yet it was shelter; it was a place to live. It was our home for about twenty days.

The pen we occupied was their very smallest, exactly seven feet square. The bed, six by five, filled it so completely we could never both get up at the same time. "It *is* small," I agreed, "but then, it will be all the easier to keep clean." Each morning at daybreak the *cha-fang* woke up singing, "The Republic of China, having arrived at this dangerous pass" – the first line of a popular war-time song. Then he would break off and begin again. He would repeat the phrase in various keys, experimenting freely with the pitch, but he never got on any further with the song for he knew no more of the words. When he had sung some fifty times about the dangerous pass of our country, he would wait upon the guests with hot water, tea, and a broom. The broom was for our own use; the *cha-fang* never swept the rooms. At ten he would bang on our doors, shouting, "The meal is opened." Pao always left early for the office, but I shared the hotel fare. The lodgers ate together at red-varnished tables, breakfast at ten, the afternoon meal at five. The food was plentiful and good – rice, soup, and two dishes of vegetables seasoned with meat. Prices were reasonable – only a dollar a day for room and board. We were fortunate.

When we went to call on Wu Kwei-fan some days later, we found him lodging with a weaver outside the city. The weaver had two rooms. Wu Kwei-fan had the shed outside, a room to himself. This would have been entirely satisfactory had it not been that a flimsy partition of matting was all that separated it from the pig-pen. Through wide cracks between the mats we stared at the pig, a large, sullen beast who stared back at us with inimical eyes. Wu Kwei-fan said, "When the wind blows from east to west, there is the peaceful, distant murmur of the city. There is the scent of wild flowers and sweet grass. But when it blows from west to east, there is nothing but pig. . . ."

Our first days in Kweilin were quietly uneventful. Pao reported for work in offices established in the beautifully proportioned, pillared halls of an old temple. For a long time there had been no grey-gowned priests there, no idols worshipped with incense and ceremonial chant.

The offices of the General Staff were close by the west gate of the city. It was rumoured that there were great stores of munitions hidden somewhere in this vicinity. Our lodging was within a stone's throw of the east gate. From there the road led across a pontoon bridge to the hills and spacious caves which were better shelter than any man-made dug-out.

The caves of Kweilin are a natural wonder, famous, visited by man travellers. In those first days before the war caught up with us again we made the tour of the caverns of the Seven Star Cliffs, a labyrinth of intercommunicating passages extensive as an underground world. The guides carried torches of twisted rattan. The light was almost lost in the vaulted immensity of the huge, hollow chambers. It flashed back from the scintillant crystal of fluted columns and stalactites. It flickered over fantastic sculpture, built up by the slow drop of lime-laden water through hundreds and hundreds of years – the Prayer Monk, the Frog, the Four Elephants, the Philosopher; our guides named them over for us. They warned us to walk carefully, skirting the brink of an enormous pit going straight down into unfathomable darkness. They leaned to wave their torches dramatically, revealing the edges of the abyss and beyond only black emptiness. These caves were Kweilin's refuge from air raids, large enough to contain the whole population of the city.

There had been no raids before our coming. But the spy service of the Japanese keeps them informed of our movements. They became aware of the presence of important military chiefs in

Kweilin and the second week in December the bombing came.

The day of the first air raid Pao and I were shopping where the two main streets of the city crossed. There was little to buy in Kweilin, the province is so poor. We ransacked the book-shops, spending more money than we could afford on reading. Pao's choice runs to political themes. I prefer novels, but there was almost none, the people of this province were so serious-minded. The best I could find was *The Three Kingdoms*, a famous classic written at least a thousand years ago. I needed, also, a new winter gown, thanks to the absconding tailor at Nanyu. We stopped at a silk shop at the exact geographical centre of the city. The siren sounded.

When that ominous scream swelled above all other sounds, the clerk who was serving us turned white, stood paralysed with terror for a moment, then began hastily folding the silk in packets to carry away from the city. At once there was the clatter of boards slammed into their grooves, closing up shops. Pao and I walked toward our lodging, leisurely, unafraid. We had been through many raid alarms, but only the one raid, and even now that seemed a fact of history, remote, unreal, rather than an event of actual experience.

At our inn the *cha-fang* met us, wearing an odd black-var-nished helmet that proclaimed him a member of the volunteer fire brigade. He would remain on duty, he said. He counselled us to leave our things in his charge, taking with us only our most treasured possessions. Out in the street again we were swept in an irresistible current toward the city gate.

We were a few rods beyond the gate when the second alarm sounded. The planes were near! They were coming to Kweilin; we were to be bombed! It was then terror, panic as I never saw it again until Chungking. As we had been physically swept along in the current of flight, so now we were caught in the tide of mass terror. Had I been alone with Pao, we should have been calm. But panic is contagious. The fear of all around us fright-ened us also. Our hearts beat faster. Instead of being passively borne along, we pressed forward, pushing with all the rest toward the Seven Star Cliffs that fronted us, dark, across the river valley.

We came to the pontoon bridge that swung in an arc from shore to shore, bending with the tug of the stream. Again the road narrowed, for the bridge was only eight or ten feet wide. At either side the supporting sampans thrust prow and stern beyond the planking, but it was not possible to step from boat to boat since they were too widely spaced. Entering upon the bridge we were in the middle of the column, Pao in front breaking the way and I following, holding fast to his belt. But as we advanced toward the curve of the bridge we were forced nearer the perilous edge. Every one shouting, every one pressing, we moved slowly forward, step by step, desperate with the fear that we might be trapped here for the approaching planes to mow down with machine-guns. People were pushed off the causeway into the projecting boats and were fighting to get a foothold again upon the planking. Now a man with an enormous bundle on his back swayed against me, throwing me off my balance. On my other side a woman dropped something and stooped to retrieve it. I lost my grip on Pao's belt, stumbling over the woman, and went down. In such a mob one might be trampled to death in a few moments. I felt my strength going from me in utter horror. I might have fainted but that someone trod on my hand with a hard leather heel and the pain roused me to struggle. I fought blindly to escape – and rolled over the edge of the planking, falling between two boats on the down-stream side. I came up gasping; my hands clutched the side of a boat. "Pao! Pao!" I screamed. Pao heard me, I do not know how. He whirled about, his fists crashed right and left, clearing a momentary space, forcing his way against the onward pressure of the crowd the few steps back to me. He was over me. He sprang down into the boat, bent, and grasped my wrists – and I had never seen his face so white and *hsiung* – dragged me out, caught me up in his arms, and carried me the remaining length of the bridge.

There was discernible a deep vibration of sound, distant but powerful, and even those who had never heard it before recognized its threat. Pao seized my hand and we ran toward the open fields. The path we followed did not lead to the cliffs and sheltering caves, but we ran on, seeking only to escape the pressure and panic of the mob. Although the drone of engines was now very clear we were less afraid. We were free and in command of our own thoughts again, not caught helplessly in that wave of mass terror.

Over the black hills beyond the city we saw the planes coming, thirty-six bombers in a flying wedge. They circled in reconnaissance. The anti-aircraft guns went into action, with their low, thumping report. We saw bombs falling, black, shiny, and small. We could follow their slantwise flight downward to the crackling line of explosions, black smoke, fire at the centre, that sprang up from the ground. The planes continued on toward us, tense wings coasting the air so smoothly there was no effect of speed.

They moved with a proud unconcern, as beyond good and evil, swerving in a curve over the hills and disappearing to eastward.

Smoke surged up in unfolding, uncurling volumes where incendiary bombs had been dropped. From the west came more loud detonations – our ammunition dumps were blowing up. The city was burning. From where we stood in the fields across the river it seemed one seething cauldron of flame within its ancient walls. We watched the fire in a kind of hypnotic excitement, unable to comprehend it in terms of death and loss except as it touched us personally. Probably our inn was burned down and all our scant possessions gone. We should have to go out and look for a room again – I remember that was my chief anxiety at the moment.

We have grown accustomed to it since, yet there is always strangeness in returning to a familiar place changed suddenly beyond recognition. The row of shops, well-known as a string of beads fingered over constantly, breaks off in a space of scattered wreckage. The pavement gapes in a crater and houses on each side lean aslant, skeleton framework without tiles or plaster panelling. The sun shines in, unnaturally bright, where we had known the shadowing eaves of close-built houses. We saw this for the first time, returning to our lodging in the early afternoon. Broken tiles crunched under our heels. The street led into blaze and smoke. Our inn was safe but the row of shops opposite was on fire. We stepped over charred beams and rafters fallen into the street. Our *cha-fang,* mad with excitement, sweating and streaked with soot and looking very much like a devil, wielded a hose impartially upon the smouldering ruins and the hurrying passers-by. Its intermittent spurt of water was fed from a large tub on wheels, containing a pump worked by two assistants. Once behind the doors of our courtyard we could hardly believe anything had happened, for all was exactly as we had left it. Only the tang of smoke in the air, the high-pitched voices of an agitated multitude outside, gave hint of the disaster.

The first raid destroyed accurately the business centre of Kweilin. Next morning when we walked about the streets we came upon the foundations of the shop where we had been buying silk twenty-four hours earlier. As we stood there, like an echo of yesterday, on the hour exactly, came the siren's warning.

There was no repetition of the first day's panic. Already for hours people had been streaming out of the city with their rolled quilts over their shoulders and their hands full of bundles. We walked without haste back to our inn, picked up our small package of valuables, gave the key of our room to the *cha-fang*, and went out of the city and across the pontoon bridge in company with a good number of unhurried, calmly fleeing folk who conversed together with amiable unconcern as they went on their way. Though we had plenty of time to reach the caves, Pao and I turned aside into the fields again. We had no fear because we did not know enough to be intelligently afraid. It is one thing to watch a bombing from a safe distance and quite another to dive for shelter from a bomb plummeting down through the air upon you. After that has happened once your faith in the benevolent law of averages is shaken for ever and you take no more chances. But at this time we were inexperienced and our dislike of crowds was greater than our apprehension of danger. We wandered among the orchards and cassia groves, picking wild flowers. We had brought books with us. Waiting for the planes, which did not come, we lay under the trees until the all-clear siren, reading *The Three Kingdoms* and the speeches of Pai Chung-hsi.

After this we had a raid alarm every day the sun shone.

On one of the rare mornings when we had no visitation of bombers because the sky was low-hung with an even grey cloud ceiling we left Kweilin. The hills around the horizon were like fantastic stage scenery. They stood up in a grey haze, two-dimensional, as though cut from cardboard. On such a day, without the sun's genial warmth, one realized it was winter. We stood shivering in the bus yard. The crowd was smaller than we had been accustomed to, for the General Staff was being sent off in sections over a period of ten days or so. A sufficient number of lorries and buses had been arranged for, to transport us to Chungking in relays. The first two days of the journey we had good drivers and good cars; Kwangsi efficiency prevailed. But after that all the buses were in marked disrepair, with shattered headlights, bashed and rusty hoods, leaking radiators. Their inner works were in as bad condition. They coughed and sputtered on a mixture of alcohol and synthetic petrol extracted from *chin-yu,* vegetable oil. Some were charcoal burners, carrying a large upright cylinder about four feet tall beside the driver's seat, supposed to generate gas from the fumes of smouldering charcoal. These were noticeably short of breath; they gasped and choked and gave up the effort when faced with a moderate up-grade. The men who undertook to pilot these rolling junk heaps had only a smattering knowledge of motor engineering. After we crossed the Kwangsi border into Kweichow, we entrusted our lives to some very erratic drivers.

Yet, compared with the journey to Kweilin, this was a pleasure jaunt. We stopped for hot meals. We stopped every night for rest, though sometimes at very odd places. There was a great deal of scenery along the way which we enjoyed, except when the road went through that scenery in loops and zigzags and flying leaps over cliffs and chasms, and we were at the mercy of a madman who drove without any recognition of the use of brakes. Christmas Eve we slept on the floor of the great hall of the hotel at Yishan, occupying a dais at one end meant for theatricals. The next day we crossed the border into Kweichow, a wild, mountainous province, until recent years cut off from the world, almost inaccessible. In the ravines and remote mountain valleys of Kweichow live many tribes of aborigines, tall, ruddy men wearing short, wide gowns of red, yellow, or violet, fur-lined, and women with heavy bracelets, ear-rings, and chains of silver studded with turquoise and coral. We saw them in the market towns where they had come to barter baskets and coarse pottery and the skins of wild animals. They walked among the Chinese with a freer stride, their slanting eyes having the alert wary gleam of the eyes of leopards.

There are few large towns in Kweichow. But everywhere we heard familiar accents – "That's Hopei! That's Nanking, Ningpo, Hankow." Here in Free China have gathered millions who would not endure the captivity of body and spirit under Japanese domination.

As the road wound northward and ascended to high mountain passes by tortuous loops and turns, we climbed into winter. Hoar-frost silvered the blades of young wheat in the small fields of upland valleys. Snow and sleet blew on the wind. Climbing the dizzy turns of the road higher and higher, the car rocked and spun, until it seemed the mountains were revolving around us while we swayed and trembled at the vortex.

We had a variety of drivers, desperate men who seemingly cared nothing for their lives or ours. One drove with a rash impetuosity appropriate only to level paved highways. He swung us abruptly around sharp turns above cliffs, or escaped collision with cars approaching from the opposite direction only by a sudden twist of the wheel which sent us charging up steep banks. Another was half blind with trachoma. He carried two so-called mechanics in the seat with him, who understood as little about the car as himself. Whenever the engine stalled, which it did quite frequently, the three held solemn consultations under the hood, but could never get it started again without the help of Pao and other passengers familiar with motor vehicles. The car was a perambulating wreck minus horn and headlights; the radiator leaked with a steady dribble. At every stream or puddle the mechanics alighted to scoop up water to replenish it. But their chief function was to compensate for the missing horn. Leaning one from each side at the front of the bus, they whooped and shouted at any stray fowl, hound, or peasant in the road. The high point, the supreme opportunity, came when we passed through villages thronged for market day. Then the two mechanics screamed themselves hoarse, proclaiming the illegitimate pedigree of every person in the scattering crowd. Still another driver was a gambler. He had stayed up half the night before, playing mah-jongg, with the result that we failed to make our stage and had to spend the night in an opium den.

There are still opium dens in some parts of Kweichow, Yunnan and Szechwan, illegal but quite open, like the speak-easies of the prohibition era in the United States. It must be remembered that not many years ago the war lords of this region derived most of their revenues from opium. In March and April the hills were like a huge embroidered robe flung in folds – rose, white, and purple, fields of poppies in bloom; and opium-smoking, though diminished, is not ended.

We had been travelling long after dark without headlights. A thin, cold rain began to sift down. The road, which had been visible as a faint pale streak, became indistinguishable in the blurred darkness. It was evident that we could not reach the town planned for that day's destination, so about nine o'clock we stopped at the first cluster of houses we came to, a queer, crumbling village of a dozen or twenty mud-walled hovels crouched in the darkness on the bare hillside.

We crowded into the only inn the village afforded, asking lodging for the night. A warm, sweetish odour, pungent as the smell of burning orange peel, hung heavy on the air, an odour unforgettable, once known. I was unfamiliar with it as yet, only when I glanced about the room did I guess it for what it was – opium fumes. Mat-spread couches were ranged along the walls, and on them were set low-burning lamps of an odd, squat design, and men were lying on the couches, not asleep, not awake, absorbed as with some secret rite. Hands moving above the small flames cast multiple shadows. Faces leaning toward the lamps were like yellowed ivory – like carved ivory skulls, the skin

139

stretched taut upon the bone. Their lips were dry and pale; their eyes seemed clouded with a yellowish film. They did not stir or crane their necks at our intrusion. They were incurious, still with a deadly apathy. The inn-keeper's wife went from one to another, passing minute cups of the raw opium. She looked a slut, with her unkempt hair and a sly leer on her round, waxen, yellow face. The smokers would take up the black, thick, syrupy opium with a slender implement like a small knitting needle, turn and turn it bubbling over the lamp flame, watching always with that hooded, intent gaze, shape the pellet of gum upon a little tablet of polished stone, then set it into the small aperture of the pewter pipe bowl and sink back to draw in the vapours, heating it again over the flame. Though there were no more than a dozen men in the room they seemed many more in number, with their shadows many times repeated, thrown upward gigantic upon the walls and ceiling.

All the other passengers from our bus went up the narrow stairs to the loft above, but Pao and I took possession of the inn-keeper's ante-room, where we put together two square tables for a bed and spread our quilts. A lamp of *chin-yu* was set upon a stool, making a softly golden centre of radiance with its unshaded flame. The reek of opium was as strong here as in the outer room. It went to our heads a little, thronging the shadows about us with wings of scarlet and darkness. We made our brief preparations for retiring. I wiped my face with a moist cloth, took off my coat, and lay down. Pao sat on the edge of the table, ruddy and golden in his dark red pull-over. The small glimmer of the *chin-yu* lamp made vivid contrast of his black hair, his eyes deep and luminous and dark in the gold-toned warm ivory of his face, and his lips curving and red. He bent above me and I reached up my hands to him. . . .

The door creaked on its wooden hinges and a woman's laugh, raucous and shrill, broke upon the moment of tenderness. Pao leaped down, flung open the door. The inn-keeper's wife, unabashed, stepped over the threshold. She leered at us in the lamplight and said something quite obscene, and stood laughing, expecting us to laugh with her. I did not catch the import of her remark, but Pao without a word caught her by the shoulder, pushed her out, shut the door, and set a chair against it. Savagely he turned, his face burning darkly red. He blew out the lamp, abruptly jumped into bed, and turned his back on me in an agony of humiliation and anger.

In the morning the car would not start. We waited about for

an hour or two while the driver worked on it. After much haggling over the price of breakfast, we were served rice and a little salt pickle and red pepper, with a thin, tasteless soup. Men drifted in for their morning opium – gaunt, haggard creatures, clad in rags against the winter chill, their heads bound with dirty white turbans. Some of our fellow travellers began to exhort and instruct them on the evils of opium. They stared with opaque black eyes, and out of their silence emanated an indefinable threat. We felt we were no longer among normal human beings. It was not that we feared anything they might do to us, for they were harmless, wasted wrecks of human-kind. It was rather an instinctive shudder in the presence of a thing sinister and mysterious. The opium smokers dropped down on the mats and the slatternly woman of the inn lighted the lamps and brought them tiny cups of the drug. They were isolated beyond our touch, deaf to anything we might say. In my mind ran a date of history – 1839, the First Opium War, when Great Britain forced upon China a treaty permitting the introduction of opium from India. . . .

As we approached the Szechwan border, toward the end of our journey, we came into green, fertile country, planted and tilled and thickly populated. Crossing some high range of mountains, we could look down on lesser hills and wide valleys where the black-green of cypresses, the widespreading dark foliage of banyans, and the paler green of bamboos like fern fronds clustered about walled farmsteads. The slopes were terraced and planted to winter crops, bright emerald wheat and blue-green bean fields, and even the dikes and banks between the fields were cultivated. Curving to the slant of valleys, fallow rice fields filled with still water reflected the sky, like bits of broken mirror-glass. We were coming to the rich inland empire of Szechwan.

Our transportation for that day was an old bus with a body made of camphor-wood and kerosene tins. Its self-starter system produced only vague internal rumblings but no explosions in the engine or rotation of the wheels. It required the combined efforts of fifteen or twenty coolies pushing for a few rods along the road before the engine caught the idea and commenced to function. Once started, it ran fairly well, but this initial diffidence held us up at every stop. We had just got going after a half-hour's delay when we sighted a man walking along the highway carrying a basket containing a magnificent live pheasant. The yard-long tail feathers of the bird trailed in the dust behind. Our driver slowed down as we drew near and yelled at the man, "Sell me your pheasant!"

"Five dollars," the man answered over his shoulder.

The engine gave an ominous hiccough; the driver shifted to low gear in time to save it and shouted again, "Too much. I'll give two dollars."

"No sale." The man plodded on.

The car shuddered all over and gave two jerks. We all besought the driver to put on speed before it stopped. He gave no heed. "Two-fifty!"

"Two dollars and seventy-five!"

We groaned as the engine choked finally and then settled in its tracks. The driver, unperturbed, jumped down from his seat and walked over to have a look at the bird which had taken his fancy. After ten minutes of lively bargaining he returned grinning and triumphant, carrying the pheasant by the wings. He seemed so pleased with his purchase we could only laugh. It took a quarter of an hour to start the bus again. The men all had to get out and push. There were several false starts, then unexpectedly the engine responded and we were off, with the men chasing after and scrambling aboard as the car moved.

That night our driver drank wine until a late hour with friends he met at the inn where we stopped. In the morning he had to be roused and hurried for an early start, since this was the last day and Chungking was a long stage distant. Still somewhat fuddled in his mind, he drove out of town, and it was not until we were several miles on our way that he recalled the pheasant. He had hobbled the fowl and placed it for safe keeping in his private wash-basin. Since he had been hustled awake and rushed to the bus, his wits still hazy, he had neglected his morning ablutions, and both basin and bird had been left behind. He swore and would have gone back for them, but in the face of our combined strenuous objections did not dare.

In the haze of a dull winter afternoon already darkening toward dusk we came to the Yangtze, the same proud Son of the Ocean we had last seen at Hankow. Here at Chungking, fifteen hundred miles from the coast, it is still a king of rivers, a massive flood of swift, turbid water red, moving with visible urgency and power. Along the south bank are ranges of tall hills dark with pines. A reef of bare rock runs parellel with the shore; the current mounts against the rock in a white wave. We stood on the foreshore, looking across the mile-wide expanse of dangerous water to the rock which is Chungking.

Grey in the evening mists, Chungking is like the pointed prow of a ship, thrusting downstream between the Kialing and Yangtze Rivers. Tall buildings rise, tier on tier, above the cliffs. Smoke hovers over the city, dimming all detail, but the outline is etched with delicate precision, grey upon grey sky. Seen thus across the water it seems insubstantial, floating in haze, a mirage. Distance lends the illusion of silence. It is impossible to conceive of the din of packed multitudes rising in clamour above its faint grey towers. It is a shadow city, empty of all life. It is a city of our own imagination, silent above the grey waste of water and mist.

CHAPTER TEN

BIG FAMILY IN SZECHWAN

From our sampan we stared up at the cliffs of Chungking, bulking solid against the dull sky. The scene seemed to open and shut like a fan as the river carried us swiftly past. Treacherous undercurrents in the brown water boiled to the surface and swirled in huge circles, and our rowers doubled the stroke, standing to their oars facing forward, stamping on the deck planks and shouting, "*Hai – Hai!*" Gaining a favourable cross-current, we drifted diagonally. The rowers rested; the steersman flung his weight against the stern sweep, turning our blunt bow toward shore. In the abrupt silence after the struggle with the river we heard the sound of the city across the narrowing water. A great roaring voice, continuous, unvarying, emanated from that human hive, thousands on thousands of voices blended into an enormous murmur. We were close enough to see the ant-like activity at the Lung Men Ma-to, the Dragon Gate Anchorage, and on the steps above. Beyond the narrow sand beach which is submerged in high water the cliffs form a palisade. Here, propped up with poles against the rock, clinging like the nests of cliff swallows, were the tenements of the poor. Dark, narrow, stairlike alleys ascended through clefts in the rock, through this accretion of hovels, and lateral passages ran along the ledges, connecting the houses. In some places these perpendicular slums are gone now, tinder to terrific fires sweeping against the cliffs in a roaring updraught, but more have survived the bombings. Now, after three years, the same dark and ancient houses hem in the flight of steps to the Dragon Gate, though these steps lead up to a bomb-wrecked, fire-swept wilderness above.

Our boatmen shipped oars and nosed the sampan in among the river craft that clustered two and three deep along the landing. They worked in slowly, using long bamboo poles like lances, shod with an iron point at one end, a hook at the other. All the boats were scarred and torn by the prod and grapple of these poles, yet no one ever cursed about it, for it was give and take, the rule of the river. A plank was run ashore. We were immediately overrun by piratical turbaned coolies, clamouring to take our baggage, excitable men with shoulder-poles, shouting in

Szechwanese, a crackling speech with none of the soft modulations of the Peking tongue.

Down on the river front the only transport was upon the shoulders of coolies. We went by *hua-kan* for the seven hundred and eighty steps up the cliff. Once, only! Since then I climb the steps afoot! We were carried up through a cleft in the precipice between close-crowding hovels. Semi-liquid black filth drained along open ditches on either side of the road. Huge dumps spread down the cliff; dogs and beggar children dug in the refuse. People turned to stare at us and mutter in their Szechwan accent, "Outsiders. Down-river people." They looked hostile in the dusk. I have realized since that it was merely their dull curiosity and our own sense of strangeness.

A few minutes later our carriers set us down at the foot of a broad paved street lined with shops brightly lighted and displaying a wealth of fine things to buy. Everywhere was the dazzling illumination of electric lights. Our eyes, so long used to the feeble glow of *chin-yu* lamps, blinked at the splendour. Well dressed people thronged the pavements. Newsboys shouted their papers. There were buses – neat, well-kept buses shining with new paint – and handsome private rickshaws with polished fenders dashing past, gongs clanging. At last a big city! We could buy things in the shops. We could go to the theatre and the cinema. For me there was an added thrill – I had come home. In this city, this province I had never seen, I was not a stranger. I had returned to my own people, my father's family.

I had thought to write in this book only of Pao and myself, caught in the turmoil of war-time China. It would be the story of two young Chinese typical of many millions, our life and experiences differing in detail but in broad outline the story of our people. But I find that I cannot make this a faithful reflection of China unless I tell of the Big Family which is the unit of Chinese life. A botanist describing a plant is not content to speak only of a leaf or a petal. He will minutely study the seed, root, stem, foliage, and flower, considering the plant as an entity. So with this story. If I am to tell of China truly, fairly, not in some fragmentary, distorted manner, I must write of my family and its way of living – of thinking, of eating, of enjoyment, of meeting disaster – for it is this which makes up the pattern of existence in my country. I had been too long adrift, thinking myself unique and self-sufficient. I needed to come to Szechwan in order to learn that I *am* myself only because I am a part of the

Big Family. "But of course you would write beautifully with the brush pen," they tell me, unastonished at my accomplishment. "Your First Uncle was a scholar of the second degree and your direct Grandfather was a famous calligrapher." Bowing before the portrait of my grandmother, I discover that I have the modelling of my brows from her, and I see my own smile on the lips of a small cousin. So I am not proud and detached any more, knowing my life incomplete apart from the root and stem which produced it.

The very nomenclature of relationship reflects the Chinese sense of family solidarity. The children of brothers, cousins in actuality, are considered brothers and sisters. From the first-born on, they are numbered in sequence as sons and daughters of the family, irrespective of their individual paternity. Thus my two sisters, the daughters of my own father, are Fifth Sister and Eighth Sister respectively. Elder Sister is the daughter of First Uncle. I am Third Sister. My father had five brothers; all married and produced offspring. Of my generation there are fourteen sons and sixteen daughters living and almost as many dead (also included in the count unless they died in early infancy), so that designation by numerals is practically the only way to avoid getting mixed up.

Similarly with our ancestry, we include not only the direct line. My direct grandfather, who was eldest in his generation, deceased now many years, is called First Grandfather. His brothers we do not call grand-uncles, but Second Grandfather and Third Grandfather in the order of their age. Of that generation Third Grandfather and Fifth Grandfather only survive. Since Third Grandfather married three times, his direct offspring are many; they are all called my aunts and uncles. They are referred to as the generation above mine, although several are of my own age or younger.

In addition to the numerical system, our given names also indicate relationship. All the children of one generation are given names with one of the two characters in common. In my father's generation the character is Ta – "great". In mine it is Kuang, meaning "shining". Shining Wisdom, Shining Pearl, Shining Coral, for the girls. One may carry various names in the course of a lifetime – a baby name, a school name, an official name – but within the family this name with one syllable shared in common with all the brothers and sisters is kept throughout. This character distinctive of a single generation is predetermined far ahead, chosen with regard to abstruse philosophical and religious

146

implications. In our family the characters for descendants of the next twelve generations have already been fixed upon and written down in the family book.

All these members of the Big Family are tied together by the one surname, passed down in the male line. Girls marry into their husband's family, yet remain daughters of their own family. But relationship by marriage is tenuous beyond that first link. My children will be the cousins of my brothers' children. Since cousins bear a different surname there is no bar to intermarriage. Among the children of my aunts this in-breeding has been practised quite frequently. With us the sense of kinship depends more upon the name than upon consanguinity. All of the same surname are regarded as relatives and marriage between such families is frowned upon, even though no blood relation can be traced. Surnames in China are much fewer than in other countries. We have a phrase, "the hundred names," which means inclusively the people. Actually there are two or three hundred names, but at least half the inhabitants of China must be called Wang, Chen, Liu, Li, Chang, Yang, or Wu, the commonest occurring surnames. They are the Smiths and Joneses of China, but infinitely more numerous in proportion.

Although I knew all these facts concerning the Big Family before I came to Szechwan, I had no true comprehension of their meaning for me. Except for Third Uncle, who had come to Peking seven years before to settle up my father's affairs, I knew none of my relatives. The Big Family in Szechwan was an abstraction to me. I confess that, as Pao and I took rickshaws for my uncle's house, my only thought was, "I *hope* Third Uncle is in Chungking; I am so tired of looking for lodgings!"

Third Uncle is manager of a bank with branches in Chungking and Chengtu. He had houses in both cities, though the family lived in Chengtu. We had written to him from Kweilin that we were on our way to Chungking and he had telegraphed a cordial invitation. But of course it was impossible to say what hour or day we should arrive. He might be gone, leaving the house in charge of servants. The gates would be closed, since it was evening, and we would have to seek an inn. . . .

Our rickshaw pullers tugged up a rise, bent double, their heads almost touching their knees. The shafts cocked up at such an angle, the seats canted back so steeply, that we were constrained to sit far forward, necks stiffly out-thrust, to keep the centre of gravity from shifting too far backward and causing an upset. With a shout, "*Shao lai!*" (Come a little less!) – for warning to traffic behind them – our men flung down the shafts before a huge, black-shining gate, pitching us out at my uncle's address. The gate was not closed – Third Uncle was here!

We gave the gateman our names. He conducted us through three courtyards to the *keh-tang*, announcing in a loud voice, "Third Little Mistress has come home, and Third Little Mistress's husband." My uncle came out to meet us, beaming with joy and hospitality, both hands extended in greeting. I introduced Pao, who made a correct and soldierly bow. My uncle bowed in return, but I caught an appraising gleam in his eye as he took my husband's measure. Evidently Pao scored high in his estimation, for he told me privately later that I had good eyesight, which meant that I had chosen well. "All alone and without advice or experience," said Third Uncle, "you might have done far worse!" He deplored, nevertheless, that Pao was not a business man. He hoped Pao would give up soldiering after a few years and turn to finance, since a military career does not bring in sufficient income. I suppressed my inward amusement. Pao does not understand the first thing about money! I am the one responsible for all the saving and disbursing in our family. But I could not tell Third Uncle this, for he is a business man to the core and admires all the practical virtues.

My uncle had aged very little in the seven years since I had seen him last. He is of middle height, wiry, with keen black eyes and a loud, cheerful voice, his whole person alive with energy and common sense. Though he prefers deep-cushioned foreign furniture to the stiff ceremonial chairs bequeathed by my great-grandfather, he will have nothing to do with Western styles in clothing, claiming, with truth, that the Chinese gown is warmer in winter and cooler in summer and all the year round more loosely comfortable. He discards nothing, accepts nothing, at the dictate of fashion, but makes his own decisions. His touch-stone is comfort and good sense. He avoids ostentation. Although he wore a robe of satin lined with squirrel fur and undergarments of fine Kiating silk, revealed at the side slits of his outermost gown, this last was of plain blue cotton cloth.

Third Uncle bows us into the *keh-tang* and calls for tea...
But this is not real! It is a dream and a memory out of a past that is gone, with all its graces and amenities. The clean-swept courtyards, the spacious *keh-tang* with its softly shaded lights, its deep-piled rugs, its chairs and sofas spread with tiger skin

and golden monkey furs, the gleam of lacquer and gilding, the tall blue vase with its great branches of *la-mei*, translucent gold flowers with the scent of spring – all this luxury and comfort are of another world. With the dust of our abominable journey still upon us we lean back in huge, soft arm-chairs and sip tea from cups of thin porcelain that come from Kiukiang. No ships sail up and down the Yangtze now to bring to Chungking rich merchandise from Shanghai and foreign countries and the ports of the lower Yangtse. Kiukiang fell a year ago. The artist who painted with delicately pointed brush the slender ladies and swaying willow-trees on this teacup is dead. Or he is wandering a refugee, starving, with no way to use the skill of his hands. This rose-and-blue rug was woven in Tientsin in the north. These carved lantern shades are from Peking. Here on the silk panels are drawn the gardens of the Summer Palace, the canals and bridges. And Peking is of another life. . . .

My uncle calls, "Lao Li, Lao Tseng, Hong Sao, come all of you! Come and welcome Third Little Mistress and her husband!" The servants kneel to us and kowtow to the floor in respect. They bring large brass basins of steaming water, and perfumed towels and Ivory soap which is almost worth its weight in silver, for it comes from America. They hasten to prepare the evening meal and to heat great cauldrons of hot water for baths. Second Brother, who is the son of First Uncle but lives and works with Third Uncle here in Chungking, comes home from the bank, and we are introduced: "Third Daughter and Third Daughter's husband."

Second Brother bows. "Third Sister and Third Sister's husband, you are most welcome."

All the conversation is of our journeys. Third Uncle shakes his head and makes little clucking sounds of distress and sympathy. Even as we describe the trains and the buses, the execrable food, the filth and the crowding, the fleas, heat, thirst, bombs, and babies, we seem to be repeating a tale at second hand. Everything has become very amusing in retrospect and quite unreal. If we are sitting here in this pleasant *keh-tang* with servants hastening to attend to our every need, if all this luxury of space and cleanliness and privacy is ours, then it is not possible that we – the same two persons – hoed turnips for supper at Santang and lodged in an opium den in Kweichow.

It was New Year's Eve. That night we slept in a room freshly painted jade green, in a huge carved bed, all black and gold, curtained with pink silk. There were white silk sheets and satin quilts of pale green, lavender, ivory, embroidered extravagantly with dragons, chrysanthemums, plum blossoms, and goldfish, warm and incredibly light, for they were stuffed not with cotton but with silk batting. Velvet curtains were drawn across the windows against the winter cold and a fire of glowing charcoal burned in a polished brass basin upon a carved stand. A little maidservant was within call for anything we might want. We were warm and tingling with well-being after bathing in many bucketfuls of hot water in deep Soochow bath-tubs. These are enormous bowls or crocks, three or four feet in diameter, lined with green glaze, originally intended for fish-bowls. Third Uncle kept two in the courtyard for goldfish and two more in the bathroom for baths. They are so deep one sits cross-legged on the bottom and steeps in hot water to the neck. It was the first full and sufficient bath Pao and I had had since we left Hankow. Everything was so wonderful! We stretched out in bed, where hot-water bottles had prepared a warm place for us. We sighed from the depths of our being with vast content and slept without interruption straight through to New Year's afternoon.

When we woke and remembered what day it was we kissed and wished each other a happy New Year, our first together. We felt so rested and clean, so happy to be where war had not yet come to disrupt everything, the day with its implication of a new chapter beginning seemed a good omen. The maidservant brought us tea. She also brought narcissus and *la-mei* for our room, with Third Uncle's New Year greeting. We should have been up early to pay our respects in acknowledgement of his hospitality, but when we made our late appearance he was very understanding and waved aside our apologies. The next three days we rested and amused ourselves. There was holiday in observance of the Western New Year, which is sponsored by the government to supplant the old Chinese New Year. But the people are reluctant to abandon a feast of such ancient significance. The new calendar will do for business purposes, but the First Month of the Moon Calendar is still the true turn of the year and the season of greatest festivity.

We strolled about the streets of Chungking, admiring the handsome shops. We went to cinemas; we went to the theatre; we went to the Kuan Sun Yuan to eat delicious Cantonese breakfasts, pastries stuffed with an infinite variety of savoury mixtures, sweet, salt, or sour, served with scented green tea. This was the same restaurant where we had had our wedding dinner, now moved from Hankow to Chungking. Its signboard was like the face of an old friend. We listened to shrill and scratched records played on old-fashioned phonographs with horns. We listened to the wireless, grand opera from Berlin, monotonous and noisy swing music from San Francisco, the latest popular Chinese songs from Shangahi. Never have the more obvious gifts of civilization appealed more to us. I went into the same orgy of cheap pleasures after the bombing of Chungking that spring. I think it is the instinctive reaction of overstrained nerves to crave such amusement, healthful and diverting.

Pao reported his arrival in Chungking, but was not immediately assigned to duty. It was some days later that the momentous letter came. The envelope was large and impressive, with official seals in red. Within was one thin sheet of paper with two or three lines of writing and another great square seal. Pao read it at a glance and passed it to me with hands that trembled. The letter was an appointment for an interview with the Generalissimo.

This interview is an honour granted to each graduate cadet of the Central Military Academy. Chiang Kai-shek is their teacher; they are his students, his sons, and this is a lifelong relationship, a bond between them. With fast-beating hearts we prepared for Pao's meeting with China's leader. I cleaned and pressed Pao's uniform, polished the leather of belt and boots to a mirror gleam. I persuaded him to have a fresh hair-cut, though both of us refused to consider a clean head-shave.

This custom of shaving the head, practised among officers of the highest rank as well as among common soldiers, has its humorous side. Originally it served a very practical hygienic purpose. Soldiers on active service kept their heads clean-shaven to eliminate lice. With the typical simplicity of the race, many of the highest-ranking officers in China who have seen many campaigns also adopt this measure. Pai Chung-hsi, Li Tsung-jen, the Generalissimo himself, are no exception.

This has given rise to the curious legend that, in order to create a favourable impression upon the Generalissimo, the first requisite is to have a cranium as smooth and hairless as an egg. It is also desirable, so the theory runs, to be well bronzed, as though one had just come from the battlefield. On our ship returning from Europe there were three unremarkable young officers coming back from Germany. They took especial pains to sun themselves well *en route*, and their first act upon arrival at

Hong-Kong was to visit a barber for that invaluable total hair-cut. When we encountered them that evening in the hotel lobby we gazed in frank wonder at their polished, pale, perspiring scalps, scintillating in the glare of the electric lights. We were unable to contain ourselves, but burst out laughing. This was remembered against us when, after many months, we met the gentlemen again in Chungking. . . .

Of course the whole idea is groundless. The Generalissimo is not so superficial in his judgments as to be influenced by such trivial things. Pao has kept his thick, wavy hair and bothered little about tanning, and it has made no difference in his chances of promotion.

While I cleaned and polished to furbish up Pao's appearance, his own preparations for the interview were chiefly in the nature of meditation. He endeavoured in those two days to fix his mind upon the principles inculcated during his years at the Central Military Academy, which have been his guiding rule ever since. *Tso-jen* – to be men – in such dignity and integrity as Chiang Kai-shek himself exemplifies. It was with calm and confidence of spirit he left to meet the Generalissimo. He returned two hours later. He was pale with emotion, his lips compressed, his eyes blazing with excitement. In a voice not quite steady he told me the Generalissimo had temporarily attached him to his private staff as a student officer, after which he would be sent to the north-west, to the front.

"Oh, Suyin," said Pao, "he has become older! He has deep lines about his mouth, but his eyes are the same." Pao made me see the plain, bare room, the huge desk piled with papers, and seated at the desk the man who bears the burden of China's destiny. One man alone. The ultimate responsibility is his. In the crowded ante-room high officers in uniform and a host of lesser persons waited to see him. To each he gave a few minutes, coming to the point without waste of time or indirection. And each one, leaving the inner office, carried with him the memory of deep-set brown eyes, challenging, inspiring with a burning faith and conviction in the justice of the cause. If Pao had already given his fealty to this leader, he returned from head-quarters that day with an intensified hero-worship, a devotion he had not felt for any man since the death of his father.

Third Uncle was going to Chengtu by plane for the Chinese New Year celebrations and I must go with him to meet all the Big Family. It was especially imperative that I should visit my grandmother's grave to burn incense and mourn her, since I had been absent in England at the time of her death. Chinese New Year came late that year, for there had been thirteen months in the previous year. To make up the discrepancy between the Moon Year and the Sun Year an occasional thirteenth month is inserted. There would be festivities and ceremonies for a full fifteen days, beginning with the nineteenth of February. I was a little reluctant to go at this time, for Pao was to leave for the north-west before the New Year season was ended, therefore he could not accompany us to Chengtu. I should have been even more jealous of these last few days we might have had together if I had known how long we were to be apart from each other. Or if I had guessed how nearly final was this parting. . . .

The Chungking airfield is on a strip of level sand, an island near the north shore, which varies in size with the height of the water, but keeps always the shape of a clam shell. Second Brother and Pao and a number of friends came with us to see us off. We sat in a sampan, Pao and I close together on a cross thwart of the boat, for the few minutes' crossing, and we had nothing to say to each other. There was a dense winter fog on the river and over the city. We were alone in a circle of fog. The water had a flat glimmer of light over its muddy colour. The boatman poling at the other end of the sampan was like a ghost, dimly grey. Voices were startlingly near, but the shore, the island, and the other boats with people in them were all invisible.

It was seven o'clock when we came to the airfield. It was eleven when we took off. They waited for the fog to clear. Then they discovered some fault in the plane which needed repair and they worked on that for two or three hours more. We strolled about the island disconsolately. I had sand in my shoes. Everything there was to say had been said. At last the plane was ready to go; the passengers were climbing in. Third Uncle beckoned to me and I said, "Good-bye, Pao," and went up the steps. Pao was still standing where I left him; through the window I smiled at him but his face was very drawn. The plane began to move; I pressed my cheek against the window-pane and waved as we rolled off down the runway. Pao had already turned his back, though he stood in the same spot, unmoving.

We slanted up into the air. Chungking lay below us, shaped like a dog's head, the two rivers meeting at the muzzle. The clear blue-green Kialing poured into the turbid Yangtze. There was a definite line of demarcation where their waters mingled.

We flew to Chengtu in a clear space between two even layers of grey cloud. We could see neither the sun nor the earth. The air was bumpy. Strangely enough, although I am a poor sailor, it did not affect me. Across the aisle sat a woman with a very tiny baby, not a month old. Suddenly, as the plane gave a lurch, she turned to me, her face convulsed with distress, and almost threw the baby into my arms and immediately was sick into the receptacle provided for the purpose. The remainder of the trip she was preoccupied with her nausea and I held the baby. It slept all the way. I enjoyed very much the soft, limp weight in my arms. I made up a fantasy that the plane was wrecked and most of the passengers killed and nobody ever claimed the baby, so I kept it. . . .

Chengtu is one hour's flight from Chungking. We slid down through the grey clouds and flew low over the fields until we sighted the radio towers and the numberless grey roofs of Chengtu, then sloped down to a landing on the north airfield. I returned the borrowed baby to its mother, who was now miraculously restored by contact with the stable earth. The company bus rushed us into the city, depositing us at their office on the main street. We took rickshaws for home – the home I had never seen, the house of the Big Family.

The rickshaws swung into a quiet side-street and drew up at a great roofed gateway. The gates were wide open in ceremonial welcome and servants were lined up at either side, for they were expecting us. They rushed upon us to take our baggage, crying "*Lao-yeh,* you come home! Third Little Mistress, you have come home!" Their glad shouts of greeting echoed under the gate and filled the narrow street with a noise of rejoicing.

We stepped over the high threshold and passed through the outer courtyards, where *mei-hua* trees were in bloom, their dark, angular stems studded with pink flowers like small double roses. In the upper courtyard were assembled Third Uncle's family and about a score of other relatives, ranged upon the terrace before the ancestral hall in formal rows, as though expecting to have a group picture taken. Third Aunt stepped forward to greet us. Third Uncle bowed to her and she to him, both very dignified. Then she turned to me, her round face, smooth and white and merry, all smiles. "Third Daughter, welcome! You have come a long way. We are very happy to have you come to us." I loved her at once. She is a plump and tiny person, much smaller than I am. Her hair is very black, shining as polished lacquer, wound in a smooth coil at the back. Her hands are like a child's,

154

white and small. Her bound feet are neatly shod in tiny pointed shoes.

She took me by the hand and named in turn each of the visiting relatives, the sons and daughters. We exchanged many bows. Since I was the stranger and younger than many of those who had come to meet me, it was I who should have called upon them first to offer my respects. But when Third Uncle wired that I was coming to Chengtu with him, Third Aunt sent messengers hot-foot to all the households of our kin to tell them. I think I was a kind of legend to them, with my foreign education and my romantic marriage.

Their welcome was so gracious that I felt myself received as a daughter of the family. But this acceptance was incomplete until I had been formally presented to the ancestors. I retired to wash and change my travelling dress for a *shan* of heavy dark silk, appropriate to the occasion. Then my aunt and uncle, one on each side of me, conducted me to the ancestral hall.

Placed at the upper end of the innermost court, the room of ceremony, the High Hall, is in the position of honour. It is always a lofty room, going up to the ridge of the roof, for it would be unbefitting to have people walking to and fro above the family altar. Even in poor homes of one room and a loft, the loft does not extend over the Sacred Cupboard, where candles and incense are burned to the spirits. In the house of the Big Family this room is the ancestral hall, where portraits and tablets of the dead are kept and all the descendants do reverence to them. It is the tradition for the whole family of five generations to live under one roof. But our Big Family had grown so numerous that this was impossible. It should have been First Uncle who remained with his household in the courts of his ancestors, but Grandmother, who outlived Grandfather and decided such things, preferred Third Aunt above her other daughters-in-law and elected to keep her as mistress of the home. It was thus Third Uncle came to have the house with the ancestral hall. The other sons moved to new homes, all but my father remaining in Chengtu.

We enter the High Hall. It opens upon the courtyard by screen doors of lattice which fold back, leaving all one side open. It is windowless. The walls are panelled in dark wood. Light streams in from the court, direct, dramatic, in a broad flood, upon the portraits of the ancestors on the wall opposite and the shelves of spirit tablets inscribed with the names of all the dead. My father's tablet is among them. On a great slab of redwood, facing the doors, are the words, "Loyalty and filial piety continue in the family" – written with free, splendid strokes in my grandfather's famous calligraphy and carved in the wood for a legacy. Before this stands the altar, a long, narrow table of dark wood covered with a stone slab. Under it is the Tablet of Earth, with a brass incense burner before it. Above it hangs a lamp of scented oil, kept burning all night, suspended by a chain from the character "Heaven", painted in gold upon the highest roof beam. On the altar are set candlesticks, censers, vases of white *mei-hua* and bowls of narcissus, and a bronze tongueless bell which gives forth a soft note when lightly struck. Here, too, on special feast days are laid out the cups and plates for wine, fruit, and grain offered in sacrifice. The stone floor is clean-swept and cushions of brown coir are placed before the altar for kneeling.

Third Aunt indicates where I should kneel; then, pointing to a scroll painting dim and brown with antiquity, hung in the place of honour immediately above the central incense burner, she says, "This is your great-great-grandfather." He is a very stately old gentleman in robes of plum purple, green, and gold, wearing a mandarin hat with a coral button and satin boots with thick white soles, seated upon a high carved chair, his feet wide apart and his hands upon his knees. Beside him is his wife, with a head-dress of pearl tassels and filigree silver enamelled with an iridescent blue kingfisher feather. She wears a voluminous robe of red traced over with embroidery of gold. All the colours are dulled, the faces are featureless brown ovals, but the gilding of pure metallic gold shines out richly in the old portraits. I bow my head low. Third Aunt then calls in a clear voice, as though speaking to someone very old and revered and a little deaf, "Great-Great-Grandfather, this is Third Grand-daughter of the fifth generation."

In turn I am presented to each generation of my progenitors. They are all here, gentlemen and ladies portrayed in classic paintings or simple drawings or – the more recent – in photographs, enlarged and tinted. They are here in the tablets of black stone engraved with their names. First Grandmother, who died less than a year ago, gazes unsmiling from her portrait. Despite the hollowed temples, the deep-sunken, lidded eyes and withered lips, there is a vitality about her, and a hint of humour and great beauty. It is in mourning for her that the flowers upon the altar and everywhere in the house are white. In the outermost court-yard the pink *mei-hua* trees spread a canopy of luxuriant, sweet-perfumed blossom. Here live the upper servants and the tailor and the concubine of the deceased stepson of a remote cousin. They are permitted to enjoy the bright-coloured flowers; we may not, for red is the colour of joy. No one in the household wears red, and even rouge and lipstick are banned. Paintings, gay hangings, beautiful ornaments, are put away, and in the High Hall and the *keh-tang* the walls are hung with scrolls of white, pale blue, and light yellow, the colours of mourning, inscribed with verses celebrating the virtues of First Grandmother, testimonials sent for her funeral. In her own room the immense carved bed is kept made-up, the embroidered quilts and the linen mosquito-net changed with the season, her water pipe freshly filled and set upon a table convenient to hand. At each meal her place is laid for her at the position of honour, facing the door. Her rice bowl is filled and Third Aunt adds to it the best morsels selected from the dishes of meat and vegetables and politely urges, "Grandmother, please to eat."

All these observances come under the head of mourning, but everything is quite cheerful and matter-of-fact. For twenty-eight months ceremonies of remembrance are performed, in diminishing scale. It is a time of transition, when the dead are thought of as tarrying for a time, pleased with the filial attentions of their children. So slowly do their souls withdraw from their accustomed home, so gently are they loosed into the spirit world.

I was accepted by the Big Family, absorbed into its life. Sometimes I felt as a rather individualistic raindrop might, merging with the sea, losing the laws that held it self-contained, spherical, and submitting to the mass laws of wave and tide. I woke in the morning to the mellow sound of the bell in the ancestral hall, where Fifth Brother, the eldest son of the household, made his obeisances for all of us to heaven, to earth, and to the ancestors. Through my windows I could see the courtyard, with the branches of trees putting forth the first small leaves of spring. Fifth Brother came out to the terrace before the ancestral hall, sticks of incense in his hands, and bowed three times in the direction of the gates. The day was begun.

I lay idly listening to the sounds of the household, the rhythmic swish of brooms sweeping the terraces and courtyard, the gentle thumping of feather dusters run over the window lattices and carving, the creak of the well pulley, the bump of water buckets and the rush of poured water, the voices of the servants. Presently a maid brought hot water in a big enamelled basin, then returned with a brazier of glowing charcoal. I rose and dressed. My aunt's hairdresser then entered, a thin, small, severe-looking widow, an artist to her finger-tips. First carefully applying with a white goose feather a kind of brilliantine made from the extract of pomelo seeds, she combed and smoothed my hair to an ultimate gloss; then, instead of the usual low-placed coil worn by the married woman, she evolved for me a coiffure of six tiny rose-shaped knots, each perfect and intricate, in a half-crown at the back of my head. This done, I spent ten minutes putting on cold cream, rubbing it off, putting on vanishing cream, smoothing it in, brushing powder lightly on my skin, touching brows and eyelids with fragrant oil – a ritual strange to me after these months when the minimum decency of cleanliness was often impossible of achievement.

Third Aunt then entered, smiling, perfumed, powdered, her hair exquisitely precise and gleaming. We saluted each other, then went in to breakfast. All the brothers and sisters sat about a large round table of polished bare wood, Third Uncle and Aunt in the places of secondary honour, and Grandmother's bowl and chopsticks and empty seat in the place of primary honour. The big wooden rice steamer, close-covered to retain the heat, stood on a side table, and a maid scooped up bowlfuls of the freshly fragrant rice. It was a simple meal, *tou-fu* and pickled turnips for seasoning, but for me there was a special bowl of pigeon-egg soup, supposed to be strengthening. Third Uncle rallied me on my slenderness, beaming with fond approval on my aunt and urging me to emulate her plumpness.

All about the house there was a bustle of preparation. Everything must be fresh and immaculate, swept and polished and orderly, that we might befittingly meet the New Year. The plan of the house is the unvarying design of Chinese architecture, a series of courts, each surrounded by rooms all opening upon galleries and narrow terraces roofed by the wide eaves. Only in the side courts is there latitude for improvisation. The smaller courts are paved, with trees growing in circular plots surrounded by a kerb, and flower pots ranged along the edges. The larger courts are gardens, with walks bordered with iris or wild orchids, with fish pools and miniature rock mountains, stone seats, bamboos like fountains of springing green spray, and flowering trees for every season – magnolia, redbud, japonica, *kuei-hua*, crape-myrtle, pomegranate – and wisteria and grapevines trained upon arbours.

The rooms are furnished, in accordance with my uncle's eclectic tastes, in a mixture of old and new. In ancestral hall the tall carved chairs of a style used since the days of Confucius stand against the wall on either side, two and two, with a small stand between each pair. What generations of Chinese women have put up with the discomfort of these stiff chairs, so high that their tiny feet swing helplessly, unable to touch the ground! Even for men it is impossible to be at ease in these ceremonial seats. They must sit forward, rigidly erect, their long gowns flowing about them in stately folds. Third Uncle, with his instinct for comfort, has replaced these chairs elsewhere in the house with low upholstered sofas and arm-chairs of foreign style. Everywhere he has introduced innovations. There is a bathroom, though no plumbing, since our water system consists of a well with its ancient pulley and wooden buckets carried by the servants. There is a telephone which Third Uncle installed for his own convenience. No one else ever uses it. Grandmother disliked it and Third Aunt is afraid of it. She is panicky at the idea of receiving messages which issue from it in thin, unhuman sounds that to her are utterly unintelligible.

Once, Third Uncle in Kunming, after an excellent banquet where friends had congratulated him on his good fortune and happy family, felt so enlarged in spirit and filled with benevolence that he longed to talk with his dear absent wife. He got a trunk call through to Chengtu. Third Aunt, being alone in the house, perforce had to answer the insistent bell. But over the hundreds of miles of mountain wastes between, Third Uncle's voice came forth so faint, so ghost-like, that poor Aunt could not for the life of her tell who was talking or what he was saying. Wildly she kept crying into the transmitter, "*Wei! Wei! Lako?*" (Hullo! Hullo! Who?) That discouraged Third Uncle for ever, for trunk calls are costly, and he never again attempted to communicate with her by telephone.

Although the Big Family could no longer live all under the one roof, the four generations of my great-grandfather's descendants in Chengtu keep in close touch, paying courtesy calls back and forth and gathering at Third Uncle's house on all important occasions – anniversaries of births and deaths – on the average eight a month! – to venerate the ancestors and eat feasts together. I now set out upon a round of visits to meet these numerous relatives. Escorted by my uncle and two brothers, I went first to the house of Third Grandfather. He is the eldest surviving member of the family and therefore entitled to the most exalted respect.

It was a huge, sprawling aggregation of courtyards where Third Grandfather lived with his twelve sons, six of whom were married and had families, his seven unmarried daughters, his wife, his concubine, and a great many other relatives. It was quite five minutes' walk from the front gate to the *keh-tang* where Third Grandfather received us. He is a small, withered-up old man with a little wiry beard numbering about fifty hairs. Since few Chinese men are able to produce beards before the age of forty, these decorations are a much-prized distinction. Third Grandfather rose to greet Third Uncle. I was introduced. We sat upon tall, uncomfortable chairs and tea was brought in covered cups. Third Grandfather smoked his water pipe. It is an occupation. With small tweezers a little finely shredded tobacco is taken from the reservoir at the base and stuffed into the pipe tube. It is then lighted with a spill of rolled brown paper. In three breaths it is burnt out. The dottle is blown out, the pipe refilled, the spill blown to a flame again, and three more whiffs of water-cooled smoke are enjoyed. The cycle consumes several minutes and is repeated *ad infinitum*.

Third Grandmother entered. She is quite young, for Third Grandfather has been married three times. She has no children of her own, hence the concubine for her, a girl she personally selected who has provided several children. Immediately the room was full of people – cousins, aunts and uncles, babies in arms, shaven-headed schoolboys, small children with gaily embroidered caps and open-seated trousers – so convenient and saving of laundry – every one smiling, bowing, and calling me by name. After salutations and bows all round, we sat down again and sipped tea and ate sweets. Third Grandfather and Third Uncle conversed about the weather, the rising prices of commodities, and the health of their respective households. These were safe topics. For if, in Europe, conversation is made up of conflicting opinions, in China it is composed of similar opinions, endlessly repeated and expressed in well-chosen, hyperbolic phrases. It would not be courteous to disagree with the patriarch of the family, therefore all controversial subjects must be avoided. Third Grandfather is very conservative and disapproves of almost everything. He sat smoking his water pipe, gazing into space, and punctuating his sententious remarks with well-aimed shots at a shiny brass spittoon placed beside his chair,

Third Uncle made motions as if to depart, but all Third Grandfather's household pressed us to *shua* a little longer. *Shua* is a Szechwan institution. Strolling in the parks, ambling about the streets, flocking in crowds to temple fairs, going to theatres and cinemas, sitting for hours in the tea-shops, smoking tobacco, smoking opium – all is *shua*. Visiting is *shua*. If you have sat for half a day sipping tea, cracking melon seeds, and eating sweets, until all you have to say has been said many times over, yet you are entreated to *shua* a while longer. If you have stayed three months or more, you and all your family eating at your host's expense, he will gravely protest that it has been a few days only and beg you to *shua* for a few days more. *Shua* means to play, to linger, to idle, to neglect one's duty, to amuse oneself. It expresses that Chinese philosophy of leisure which in Szechwan is carried to the point of utter laziness. It is an attitude of mind remaining from the old days of indolence, when for those who had plenty of money, and for sages and poets to whom money was nothing, there was really nothing to do from morning to evening but gaze at the bamboos reflected in the tranquil river, smoke the water pipe, drink tea from covered teacups and wine from minute wine cups, and lie in the shade exchanging gossip and composing balanced couplets with one's friends.

Despite the chorused invitation to *shua* a while longer, Third Uncle rose and bowed, briskly explaining that we had a round of many calls to make today. Third Grandfather and Grandmother walked with us, and all the children and grandchildren trailed behind. At the second gate, with many bows, we persuaded the elders to go with us no farther. At the third gate, with more bows, we took leave of the younger adult relatives. The children and servants, with much laughing and chatter, accompanied us all the way to the street gate. That day we called upon all the uncles and aunts and brothers and sisters and cousins descended from my direct grandfather, and a busy day it was! The next two days we visited the indirect relatives. To this date there are many whose relationship to me I know only vaguely. Sometimes it takes ten minutes' recital of the family tree, up one branch and down another, to determine the exact degree of kinship.

At the house of Fourth Yima – Third Aunt's elder sister – mourning was in preparation for the concubine of her maternal uncle, who lay dying in an adjoining apartment. Robes of coarse unbleached material with unhemmed, ravelled edges were stacked between us on the table, where Fourth Yima, Third Aunt, and I sipped tea and nibbled sweetmeats. There were piles of white funeral candles; and "money" of coarse brown paper cut with the design of the old square-holed coins to be burned in sacrifice at the grave; and under the eaves of the courtyard the coffin of black-lacquered *lan-mu*, the wood that preserves the body imperishable, stood in readiness, all prepared for use whenever the death should occur. Fourth Yima called our attention to the details with pride and satisfaction. Already the old woman, whose relationship to me they defined as Great External Grandmother, had tasted no food for two days. The doctors had given her up. But she was a long time dying. She had been apprised of her approaching demise and consulted on the arrangements for her funeral. She knew that all the household were expecting her to die. Although she awaited the event half fretfully, half fearfully, with the trepidation which is in all of us, facing that ultimate lapse into unconsciousness, she took a lively interest in the ceremonies to be performed in her honour, asked the cost of the coffin which she could see from her window, and settled the final details of her funeral procession.

"We all hope she will die soon," Fourth Yima said. "Is is best. She has been ailing a long time." At the funeral they would weep; they would wail aloud and beat their breasts. On the announcement sent out they would be reported to have "shed tears of blood." This customary display of grief would not be entirely hypocrisy. They sincerely liked the old woman, and if they had thought Chinese medicine could prolong her life and relieve her of pain, they would have spared no expense. But everything had been tried, to no avail. She was old; the time had come for her to die. Everyone, including Great External Grandmother, accepted this. What need to keep up the pretence of wishing her to live longer?

The newspapers told of campaigns and victories and retreats. This side of Hankow the Japanese were pushing up the Yangtze. Shasi, half way to Ichang, was threatened. In the north-west they held the land as far as the Yellow River. When the river froze, they boasted, they would cross and march upon Sian. In the south-east they were spreading from Canton into Kwangsi. Shasi, Canton, Sian – these were names, printed characters upon a green and yellow and pink map. They were names in newspaper paragraphs, telling of attack and counter-attack. They were all far away from Chengtu, from Szechwan. Chengtu was almost unaware of war. Early in the winter Japanese planes had come over, two groups of nine, flying low under a cloudy sky. They had dropped bombs and made a few holes in the north air-field, and then they had gone away. Chengtu made ready for the New Year. No one gave thought to the war.

I felt myself slipping into this easy-going, day-to-day existence, hemmed in by the affairs of the Big Family. With my sisters I went strolling, shopping down the gay streets: the wide modern streets where plate-glass windows displayed clocks and cosmetics, lengths of bright silk, lamps and fountain-pens and coloured slippers; the narrow streets where seal carvers and jade cutters and silversmiths wrought their handicraft and there were offered for sale embroidered satin coverlets, bracelets, softly shining pewter vessels, brass basins, and copper jugs. Toy shops were stocked for the New Year with swords of silvered bamboo, tasselled spears, rabbit lanterns and lanterns in the shape of fish or cicadas or lotus flowers, bright red horses big enough to ride upon, little drum carts that beat a tattoo when pulled along the pavement, pink monkeys somersaulting, and trapezes, and huge lion masks with long beards of hemp and eyes of black and gold that moved. We would saunter on Big East Street in the late dusk, where the night market flickered with candlelights all along the streets and the pedlars spread their wares on mats at the kerb – woven bamboo baskets, chopsticks in bundles, antique bronzes, ink slabs, crockery, and everywhere oranges and tangerines in gorgeous piles, richly red and golden in the candlelight.

On each side of me, as we strolled, my sisters poured into my ears the gossip of the family. There was no malice in their chatter. It was a part of their acceptance of me that they made haste to inform me on all matters of current interest. One evening Fourth Sister, the daughter of Third Uncle, came into my room bringing Seventh Sister and Ninth Aunt. The girls entered with a conspiratorial air, glancing at each other, nudging, giggling, and hesitant. I bade them sit down, and we made a close circle about the charcoal brazier, for the night was frosty. The toes of our shoes at the edge of the brazier curled in the withering heat, but our breath was white in the chill air. I passed melon seeds round. For a time there was no sound but the cracking of the seeds.

At last Fourth Sister, urged by significant gestures from the others, brought forth – "We are going with Seventh Aunt to the cinema tomorrow and she wishes you to come also." Seventh Aunt was the daughter of Third Grandfather by his second marriage, a girl of my own age, unmarried, rather quiet and lacking in lustre. Though I had met her when I called upon the household I had little impression of her. Still, it was kind of her to invite me; I thanked Ninth Aunt, her sister, and accepted. Suddenly they were all talking at once.

"We are so glad you will come! For you are modern – you did not let anyone else choose a husband for you. Seventh Aunt asked especially for you. You see, it is because Third Grandfather is so out-of-date in his ideas! He thinks no modest and well-brought-up girl should presume to look at her fiancé before her marriage, but all should be arranged by the elders of the family. But where will you find educated young men these days who will agree to that? No cross-eyed or pockmarked brides for them – they insist on a pre-view. So there it stands, and how is Third Grandfather to find husbands for all his unmarried daughters? To be sure, there are cousins on the maternal side – two marriages already with them. But there is no boy cousin of an age suitable for Seventh Aunt."

I listened bewildered, unable to see any direction in this flood of information. "But the cinema?" I questioned.

"It is arranged for them to see each other at the cinema – oh, at a distance – Seventh Aunt and this brother of a friend. It is very daring and Third Grandfather would be furious if he knew. But Seventh Aunt has been looking about for herself, since she is past twenty-one and it is time she was married. And this school friend of hers has a brother who is thinking of marrying. So it is planned for Seventh Aunt to go with us to the cinema tomorrow, and this girl and her brother will be there. We shall know who he is, seeing him beside his sister. And she will point out Seventh Aunt to him. So they will have a chance to look, and if they are pleased with each other – who knows?"

Remembering the slowly maturing friendship between Pao and myself, the two of us alone in London, I was touched by this pitiful and inadequate stratagem that seemed to my sisters so daringly modern. All kinds of new and old ideas of marriage co-exist in this time of transition – everything from the most conservative, the young couple seeing each other for the first time when the groom lifts the bride's red veil at the conclusion of the ceremony, to the most free and modern, the young couple putting an announcement in the newspaper that they are living together as man and wife. Third Grandfather, clinging stubbornly to the old ways, even frowned upon the mildest infringement of convention in permitting the young man to see a photograph of the bride-to-be, and never could he have allowed a suitor to call upon one of his daughters in his own house for the purpose of acquaintance before marriage. In our family the change has come in the last decade. Ten years ago Third Grandfather would have had the final say in all decisions affecting his descendants, direct and indirect. Now the young men of the family listen to his opinions, outwardly respectful, but they do just as they please. And gradually the girls, also, begin to cast off his authority and the restrictions of convention.

Sixth Aunt, who is thirty-two, lives under the old dispensation and will never escape from it. Third Grandfather gave her in marriage at the age of sixteen to a cousin who had already died. She had been betrothed to this cousin since childhood, so they were never permitted to see each other. A little while before the date set for the marriage the "not-yet-wedded husband" died. This made no difference in the plans. Since he was the only son of his parents, they depended on him to provide descendants to worship at their graves, in order that their souls might have honour in the next world. So the wedding ceremony was carried out in every detail as it would have been had he lived, except that the bride wore ravelled white mourning instead of red satin and the bridegroom was represented by his sister, carrying his spirit tablet. In this way Sixth Aunt was married by proxy and entered the family of her dead husband and became his widow. She then adopted a son for him and taught the child to venerate the tablet engraved with his father's name. Sixth Aunt will never marry, but will live like a nun until she dies. Third Grandfather points to her as a model of virtue.

At the other extreme of the scale is Second Sister, whom I never met. She is the daughter of First Uncle. She is considered the black sheep of the family and is never mentioned by the elders. Only in bated whispers and in confidence was I told the scandal about her. Second Sister had run away to the northwest to join the Communists! "She's like a boy; in uniform you wouldn't know her for a girl," Fourth Sister said. "She went to school one day and never came home. She sent back a letter saying she was going to Yenan to join the Reds. Of course the uncles and Third Grandfather think she went off with a boy. A group of them went, both boys and girls. But I don't think she cared about that sort of thing. It was the adventure she loved." I should like to know her; she must be a girl of character and spirit.

Elder Sister, of the same household, has something of the same determination of will, though it is directed toward a different object. After many frustrations she has finally asserted herself. She is twenty-eight, born at the exact turn of the times, so that she narrowly missed having her feet bound. She is self-supporting, working as a book-keeper in the Chengtu branch of Third Uncle's bank. Here she had opportunities for meeting the opposite sex and twice she became interested in young men. But something was done about that. Neither of the youths would do; their social status was unsatisfactory. Third Grandfather and First Uncle intervened to put an end to these affairs. Elder Sister sulked and refused to have anything to do with the matches which the family proposed in consolation.

So some years passed and she was twenty-eight. Suddenly she, who had been quite prim in dress, began to wear gay gowns of chiffon and cut velvet, rather extreme in the shortness of sleeve and close-fitted at waist and hips; she used rouge and lipstick liberally and had her hair done in elaborate permanent curls like black-lacquered shavings. Occasionally the relatives would see her at the theatre or strolling along the street with a young man whom they recognized as an apprentice clerk at the bank, a boy who had far less education than she and earned only twenty dollars a month. A few years earlier there would have been prompt action; Elder Sister would have been disciplined and the young man dismissed. But all is changed. A great deal was said, but Elder Sister held her ground, defiant. Did not her younger sisters attend the university, where boy and girl students mingled freely? Had she not as good a right as they to choose her own friends? There were head-shakings, much muttered disapproval, but nothing was done. The authority of the old was broken.

And now Seventh Aunt, less assertive than Elder Sister and with fewer opportunities for choice, but bored with the wan inactivity of her existence at home, was making her bid for freedom. She called for us early; we were the first to arrive at the cinema. We sat alone in the empty building, a small group in the front row of the balcony. Seventh Aunt was pale with excitement; her eyes looked feverish. She was dressed plainly, but her hair on either side of her narrow white face was a mass of frizzy ringlets, stiff as wire, shining with oil. There is no regulation in the ancient prescribed observances of mourning concerning permanent waves. She was nervously vivacious, playing the hostess, passing pea-nuts and sweets, calling for tea, which was served us on the balcony rail, commenting on the people drifting in. The auditorium filled up. It was almost time for the picture. Seventh Aunt's sprightliness became a little distrait as she endeavoured to keep up the conversation and watch the people coming in. Suddenly she was silent, her hands clasped

166

in her lap. Fourth Sister touched my arm — "There he is!" — and pointed to a couple walking down the aisle to seats well forward. The top of a shiny black head and the shoulders of a brown, Western-style coat were all we could see of this young man who might marry Seventh Aunt. He and his sister settled themselves, then turned about in their seats, craning upward — the lights went out.

At the interval, when the lights came on, Seventh Aunt's cheeks were blazing with patches of pink, a little unevenly applied by touch. She sat like an idol with eyes downcast, but under her eyelids she stole swift glances at the young man. At that distance, and to my unbiased view, he was merely a somewhat chinless face with glasses. At the close of the picture we were stumbling toward the stairs before the last flicker of the film, to reach the lobby before he came out. He might — it was possible — he might ask for an introduction.... Past bobbing heads we had a closer glimpse of him, a side view as he passed, confirming my impression that he was chinless and quite undistinguished. He did not pause or look about. Seventh Aunt blinked rapidly. "The lights hurt one's eyes after the darkness in there...." We all began to talk about the picture.

After two or three days the young man's sister called. She talked of many things, but did not mention her brother. No one asked. Everybody understood. The look had been unfavourable. He was not interested further. When the friend had gone away, Seventh Aunt cried her eyes red, went to bed complaining of a "pain at the mouth of the heart," and had several doctors call to feel her pulses, right and left wrists, and prescribe remedies for her. Fourth Sister and I went to take her flowers. A little pot of dark brown medicine was stewing over a charcoal brazier and Seventh Aunt, with gloomy satisfaction, related her symptoms in an unscientific jargon borrowed from the Chinese doctors.

Eldest Sister's affair went more prosperously. Emboldened by my example in making my own match, she brought her friend to call upon the family. He was a gentle youth, six years her junior, with dreamy eyes and naturally wavy hair. She could not introduce him as her fiancé, since there had been no formal exchange of presents or betrothal ceremony. But her manner left no question. With a flushed face and aggressive voice, defiantly possessive, she presented her acquisition. When they had gone on to call upon others of the Big Family, Third Uncle returned to his practice of calligraphy, which their call had interrupted. After some moments he ceased, with brush poised, and pursed his lips judicially. He knew a business man; this young man was not one. Third Uncle said, "The Eldest Daughter should stand first, but with that one for a husband, she'll wag at the dragon's tail."

Thus, in the Big Family, no one was permitted to have a separate existence. Each of us was a fraction only; the unit was the family. Not realizing this at first, I supposed that there were matters between myself and Pao which were of no concern to anyone else. Every day I wrote Pao a letter and every day he wrote to me. This was our first long separation – months, it proved, instead of the weeks we had expected. I thought it was a natural thing that newly married husband and wife should write each other daily. But my sisters, who would find me at my desk filling pages and pages with the rapid brush writing called "grass characters," were astounded that we could find so much to tell each other. And by air mail! What was there of such urgency that we could not wait ten days for a reply?

The rumour of this almost indecent extravagance spread by word of mouth until every one in the family knew of it. In these pre-New Year days there were more callers than usual, come to *shua* the afternoon, sip tea, crack melon seeds, and smoke the water pipe. For some reason, the time of greatest concentration of the family in Third Uncle's *keh-tang* usually coincided with the postman's daily visit at five o'clock. The postman would unsling his big leather bag, extract a handful of letters, and in a loud voice read off the names. I was put to it to decide which was the lesser evil, to receive my letter in person, red with embarrassment under the eyes of the relatives, or to be absent, waiting for one of my sisters to bring it to me after the envelope had been passed round, handled, and commented on, the postage counted up. . . . Either way it was an ordeal. Usually my impatience prevailed; I would be there. In audible silence the relatives would gather round. Wonder, growing to unbelief and at last stupefaction, greeted the phenomenon. If ever a day passed that I did not have a letter, it would be because there was no plane and on the morrow I would have two. Flinging away good money sending by air mail at thirty-three cents, when five cents would pay for a letter twice as heavy by slow mail! The climax came when Pao wired me greetings at the New Year. The elders were scandalized! They discussed the whole matter quite impersonally, as though I were not present. These young people did not know what it was to eat bitterness; they did not know the uses of money. Third Grandfather, who was at our

168

house that day, ruminated at length, gazing into the air, expectorating aside into the spittoon, disapproving strongly of such a flagrant display of feelings, not customary or correct in our province and our family. I felt extremely guilty. I wrote Pao that he must not send me any more telegrams. Whereupon Pao grew furious and called me up by long-distance telephone at eleven o'clock at night – and *that* caused a real sensation.

When Pao left for the north-west it was impossible for letters to pass between us daily, since communications were less regular than between Chungking and Chengtu. We therefore wrote diary letters, each day adding instalments until the accumulation of pages could barely be forced into an envelope. My family, when they knew of Pao's transfer, all exerted themselves to relieve my melancholy, lest I should mope and go into a decline. They took me to mah-jongg parties, to feasts; they took me to walk about the streets, stopping at Wu Chao Shou for chicken *mien*, at Si Tang Yuan for sugar dumplings. I put on five pounds during the few weeks at Chengtu! They comforted me with gifts – New Year gifts, wedding gifts – thus setting their seal of approval on my unconventional marriage. I received boxes full of embroidered satin coverlets, small bowls and vases of silver, gay slippers embroidered on the toes, dress lengths of exquisite silks and fifty yards of pure white Kiating silk – surely enough to console any bride for the temporary absence of her husband! Fifth Grandmother sent me ear-rings of seed pearls and jewel jade in a little glass box, and assured me that she could tell, upon inspection of Pao's photograph, that we would have a great many children, at least six sons, and Pao would never take a concubine.

The last day of the old year, when the bright edge of the waning moon had thinned to vanishing in the morning sky, there was a bustle of coming and going – servants sent out laden with presents; servants coming in from the markets and shops with food enough for three days' feasting; visitors and messengers arriving with gifts of flowers, of cakes, of oranges, of toys for the children. Perfume of *mei-hua* and narcissus mingled with the rich flavours of frying fat, of boiling sugar, of wine being drawn from the cask for the evening's feast. It is the day when all the year's accounts are cleared, all debts paid. All friends must be greeted with suitable gifts, all quarrels settled and enemies reconciled. At midday the first of the relatives began to arrive, for on this day all members of the family greet one another and make obeisance to the ancestors. As one by one and in groups they drifted in, we saluted, bowed, and made them welcome. Fourth Sister and I assisting Third Aunt in her duties as hostess. The whole house was full of the Big Family: men smoking in Third Uncle's study, women chatting in the bedrooms, the elders seated in the *keh-tang*, the children romping in the gardens and courtyards, the smallest of them carried about by amahs and wet-nurses – everywhere a pleasant hum of expectation.

The sunlight was slanting toward evening. All were now assembled. In the courtyard the servants burned a quantity of silver-paper and gold-paper money for a sacrifice to the spirits of the dead. The *ching sen* ceremony of respect to the ancestors began. In the ancestral hall a row of cushions had been ranged before the altar. One after another, in the order of precedence, or a number of the same generation simultaneously, we knelt upon the brown cushions and bowed, each one fifteen times. The spirit tablets were too numerous to be saluted separately, so we made three bows collectively to each of the five generations represented there. Then we turned the kneeling cushions about and made one bow toward the courtyard, then rose and gave place to the next of the relatives. All through the late afternoon, as the smoke of incense drifted blue before the tablets and the sunlight dulled to night, the ancestors looked down upon us from their portraits, ever more sombrely as the shadows deepened, while the descendants knelt and bowed and rose, yielding place to those of the next degree. At the last, when it was already night and the mysterious diffused radiance of red candles on the altar was the only light, it came the turn of the youngest, the babies in their amahs' arms. Gay in padded silk garments and caps embroidered with gold thread and sewn with silver emblems of luck and long life, they were carried before the ancestors; their small fat hands were placed palm to palm, their heads gently pressed forward to make the requisite bows. The *ching sen* ceremony was ended.

The feast was ready. In the dining-hall, in the *keh-tang*, in my uncle's study, and in the open pavilion between the courtyards, tables were spread. The women ate separately from the men; the children had no fixed place, but ran about from table to table, eating a bite here, a bite there, collecting handfuls of pea-nuts or fried walnuts, tangerines, a piece of white steamed bread or the drumstick of a chicken to gnaw upon. We ate to repletion, for it was the first banquet of the New Year season and we were not yet sated with good things. Szechwan food is strange to the northern palate, accustomed to milder flavours, for almost everything is spiced with red pepper and ginger and a stinging spice called *hua-chiao* which leaves the tongue numbed. But the "crisp-skin fish", dressed with vinegar, soy sauce, chopped onion, celery, red pepper, and oil blended together, is unexcelled. And there is a sweet pork dish, thin slices with the rind on, stuffed with sugar and brown bean-meal and steamed over a mound of gluten rice; there is a soup of little meat balls and pea greens with a dash of *hua-chiao*; there is a mixture of white chicken meat and white of eggs beaten together smooth and poached in oil; there are "spring cakes", limp and thin as tissue paper, to be made into little packets wrapping up strips of carrot, ham, chicken, and leeks, to be eaten quickly before the rich sauce soaks through. . . . Szechwan cookery has its points.

It was late when the banquet was over, but no one thought of going to bed. The babies napped and nodded in their amahs' arms, undisturbed by the commotion about them. The older children were still alert, their eyes brilliant with excitement. We gathered again in the ancestral hall for the ceremony of greeting to the living. The elder generation took the place of greater honour at the left of the hall; the younger stood facing them at the right. We bowed, to the elders once, those later born – with the greater respect due – twice. Then there were individual greetings, beginning with Third Grandfather, to whom we all made reverence as the living ancestor. Following in the order of their standing in the Big Family, each was greeted with the appropriate degree of respect. The servants then entered; they stood upon the right in the place of lesser honour, while we of the younger generation joined the elders on the left. The servants knelt and kowtowed to the floor in loyalty. In return, the masters and all their children knelt to the servants and bowed, but less profoundly, in token of our obligation to these who are also considered of the family.

This concluded the ceremonies of the evening. There was a cheerful confusion of leave-taking and the relatives departed to their various households. We of the house of Third Uncle were left to continue our celebration of the turn of the year. It was the custom to watch the night out. In former times when our family were engaged in trade, the shops were open until very late and every one worked to wind up the year's business and clear the accounts. But now Third Uncle's bank was run by the

Western calendar; New Year was January the first. Nor did we observe the ceremony of changing the kitchen gods, which in many households is the feature of this night's celebration. Toward midnight of the old year the smoke-stained gods of the hearth and kitchen are taken down and burned, that they may carry their report to the spirit world, and new ones are put up in their places. But in our household this rite has been abandoned. First Grandfather had contended that all belief in fox fairies, spirits of wind and water, idols, gods, or devils was superstition. He believed and wrote many essays to prove that the only elevating form of reverence and the only rites conducive to stability of the family and state are those of veneration of the ancestors. No ancestor-worship, he insisted. There is a distinction – not a religion but respectful commemoration. Third Uncle holds the same views.

So when the large company of relatives had gone, we sat about in easy chairs and talked or told stories, played Chinese chess, mah-jongg, guessed riddles, and listened to Third Uncle's reminiscences of the good old days in Szechwan before downriver people flocked in to cause high prices, bad manners, and bombings. Toward midnight we were supposed to eat of a second feast, but this was quite beyond human powers. We could only view with apathy the steaming savoury dishes and wave them away untasted. About one o'clock Third Aunt began to yawn, her eyes disappearing into creases in her round face. She made no other sign of drowsiness, but sat primly erect, her tiny feet together, her hands folded in her lap, and her hair as neat and fragrant as when it was dressed sixteen hours ago. I lay back in my deep chair, half asleep, mournful – though not unpleasantly – with loneliness for Pao. Conversation flagged. At two o'clock Third Uncle, rousing from a momentary lapse of consciousness, gave up the intention of keeping the customary watch until dawn and sent everybody to bed.

Except for the intermittent sputter of fire-crackers which exorcise devils and malevolent ghosts, the first day of the New Year is strangely quiet. Morning shines down upon empty streets between boarded-up shop fronts, with none of the customary push and struggle of traffic, the heavy-laden two-wheeled carts pulled by men, carriers with buckets, carriers with baskets, people with packs and bundles, a two-way speeding of rickshaws. For this one day of all the year work ceases. Every one sleeps late after watching the New Year in. No broom is wielded,

172

lest the year's luck be inadvertently swept away; and no water is poured out on the ground for fear the year's wealth be poured out with it.

In the afternoon people walk about the streets for pleasure, pausing to call upon their friends. Tradesmen and workmen in long gowns of new blue cloth and little black satin caps stroll with their children. Women in new blue *shan*, circles of bright rouge on their cheeks, flowers in their hair, walk together in the cool, soft sunlight, carrying branches of *mei-hua* and camellias for gifts. Rickshaws are few; for this one day they rest. Under the eaves of the closed shops in the evening are hung lighted lanterns of red silk stretched upon carved wood frames. More bursts of fire-crackers flash in the dusk and there is the tang of gunpowder smoke in the air, innocent and festive. Children draw along the pavement gay rabbit lanterns on wheels. The hair-line curve of the new moon is silver sharp in the pale western sky.

New Year lasts fifteen days. That first day, rising late, we ate the traditional breakfast of wheat-flour noodles and went in the afternoon to burn incense at the various houses at one time or another occupied by our ancestors. Toward the end of the half month Third Aunt, with three of my sisters and a few brothers and cousins, took me to Pihsien, where the family owned fields, the estate of my great-grandfather, and where many of the ancestors are buried. None of the family lived there now. The land was let to tenants and the old house was empty. No one dreamed that within a few months it was to be crowded to the gates again with womenfolk and children taking refuge from air raids and alarms in Chengtu.

The road to Pihsien, on the frosty morning when we set out, was like a ploughed field, a morass of churned red mud. Our rickshaw pullers struggled, bent double between the shafts, to wrench the wheels out of the muck. In the biting wind they were stripped to the waist and streaming with sweat. On either side of the road lay the rich farm country of the Chengtu plain, kept unfailingly fertile and green by an irrigation system two thousand years old. Like islands in the level fields the farmsteads stood, their walls of packed red earth or whitewashed and gleaming, their tiled roofs or thatch glimpsed through densely clustering trees and bamboos. The winter crops made a variegated mosaic: the even, brilliant green of young wheat; the dark blue-green of stalk beans with small violet-grey blossoms

173

clinging like moths close to the stem; the rape from which *chin-yu* for lamps and for cooking is derived, coming into flower with clear yellow like cool fire over the green of the leaves; and among these, fallow rice fields with standing water which held the sky and passing clouds. We travelled toward the mountains which guard, invisible or shadow-grey, the Chengtu plain until on some morning after rain the constant haze clears and they stand out like crystal on the sky-line.

From the air, as one looks down, flying over, the little walled towns of the Chinese plains look like pies set down among the fields, neatly contained within their four-square bounds. With the pressure of growth, some have spilled out in four directions through their gates, or even hammered down their walls, to sprawl without pattern. But Pihsien keeps within its boundaries. The grey brick wall with its battlemented parapet fronts open country, but entering the narrow gate one is immediately in a street densely built up with shops and houses. In Pihsien, at the lintel of every doorway fluttered a row of red paper tabs with the character for joy in gold, and flags were hung out, the bright-sun flag of the republic, the whole length of the street. New door-gods were pasted upon the gates, warriors or bearded sages in bright, crude colours.

We walked through the town and out of the west gate, as narrow and deep as the east gate by which we had entered. A row of wheelbarrows waited, idle, the coolies loafing, smoking, sunning themselves against the city wall. At sight of our party the wheelbarrow men at once began to shout and beckon and talk prices. For a few minutes the storm of bargaining raged about us, then we set out in a single-file procession of wheelbarrows, zigzagging through the fields to my great-grandfather's house, the wheels all squeaking in every key for lack of oiling. I do not recommend the vehicle. One sits above the wheel in precarious balance, traversing paths so narrow that the least deviation would precipitate the passenger into a flooded rice field. The breath of the man pushing plays on the back of one's neck. The piercingly bright sun scorches one cheek while the freezing wind numbs the other. Every jolt is transmitted through the spine to the base of the skull; before we had covered the three li along the narrow, rutted footpaths, my head was almost shaken loose.

Nothing I can tell will adequately make known the charm of this house of my great-grandfather at Pihsien. When I saw it first, I caught my breath with delight. It was a house to be put

174

into some tranquil Chinese scroll painting, with its encircling stone wall, slim *lan-mu* trees, bamboos bowering its roofs and flowering *mei-hua* in its courtyard, streams and bright water fields around it, and beyond, the shadow of high, grey mountains in outline, hazy on the sky. Characteristically, the house was built by the compass, facing due south, indifferent to the web of paths among the fields. We crossed a bridge which was a single slab of stone, skirted the wall by a wide road under trees, and thus came to the open, meadowy space before the roofed gateway. Opposite were the family graves – clustered mounds with one great tomb of the Ching Dynasty in the centre – and behind them a screen of *lan-mu* trees, straight and tall, with laurel-like leaves, delicately swaying in the thin, uncertain wind.

At the right of the gate a little wooden shrine had been built against the wall, shielding from rain a faint, illegible writing and the dim mark of a red seal posted there. Despite the protection, the paper was almost worn away by time, as well it might be, for this was the Emperor's own hand and seal, appointing my grandfather magistrate in this district sixty years ago. Nothing was changed except by age. Then, as now, there was this space of close-cropped grass before the gateway, the fallow rice fields reflecting the grey silhouette of mountains. I could imagine that day – the imperial courier in rich, travel-stained attire, riding up to the gate; my grandfather hastily buttoning his satin robe of ceremony and coming forth to receive on his knees the Emperor's message. He would prostrate himself on a coir cushion, thoughtfully placed for him by a servant, just as it is done in the theatre, and the courier would kneel, too. The commission would be read aloud, then affixed to the wall – where its fragmentary trace remained still. . . . Nothing changed except by time – though in the world outside the Emperor and his dynasty and the very Empire were gone. Here still was the old house, touched lightly by the years. The wall with its stain of ancient writing was here, and Grandfather's grave with Grandmother's, two mounds before the curving line of *lan-mu,* and their spirit tablets which we had brought with us for the final ceremonies of the New Year.

The gate was open, for servants had gone before. They met us with hot water in basins and freshly infused tea. The children of the tenants ran crying the news, "The master's family have come!" The womenfolk came to bow and greet us and drink tea with us, as we sat in the great dim room, the High Hall facing the gateway, where the ancestral tablets we had brought were already placed above the altar.

When we had rested my aunt showed me about the house, the bare rooms furnished scantily with the big red lacquer cupboards and chests, tall formal chairs and huge canopied beds. I am not Spartan enough to prefer the chairs and beds of our ancestors to the comfort of upholstery and coil springs, but I would delight to inherit my aunt's cupboards with their fine plain surfaces and their brass handles and door plates. She opened the cupboards and showed me a hoard of old ceremonial robes and ornaments. There were official gowns embroidered all over with dragons, with the deep border of many colours representing light on sea waves. There were *putzu*, satin squares for the back and breast, with the insignia of the Manchu Dynasty done in gold and silver thread couched on with fine silk. There were skirts of heavy stiff satin with little flowers on all their pleats, and wide-sleeved, short coats with wide embroidered bands. No one would ever wear again these extravagantly beautiful things of an ancient style, nor would they be sold or given away. They would be placed in chests, kept, to be looked at now and again. They were a part of the family history.

I was examining a bridal head-dress of tarnished filigree and kingfisher-feather enamel, partly peeled away. Though the pearl tassels were gone, it might be the very one worn by my great-great-grandmother in her portrait that hung in the place of honour in the ancestral hall. Third Aunt took from another drawer a round fan. On the paper, toned to dark ivory by age, a skilful brush had traced a mountain scene – a precipice with one gaunt pine tree and a thread of waterfall dropping sheer into mists below. There was a scrawl of "grass writing", and a small red seal mark. Third Aunt said, "This was your grandmother's. It was painted by a very great artist forty years ago, given by him to your great-grandfather, who was his friend. It is for you. First Grandmother, when she died, thought of you and wished you to have it for a keepsake." I know there were tears in my eyes as I took the fan. It seemed to bring me very near to the shrewd and gracious lady whose eyes and brows and small, straight nose I have inherited.

The sun burned fiery at the edge of the mountains. I stood in the open grassy space before the graves, tearing apart the leaves of cash paper and dropping them one by one into the small bonfire. I had already lighted red candles and incense and stuck

176

them upright in the earth at the left and right before the new grey stone cut with my grandmother's name. I had knelt and bowed my head to the ground three times. Watching the cash paper blacken and curl in the little yellow flame, I reflected on the meaning of my obeisance. I was not worshipping First Grandmother's spirit. But standing there in the cool late afternoon, with the smell of rape flowers and bean flowers from the fields about me and the brink of sunlight along the mountain edge making a slanting light in the grass, I felt a kinship with her in this sure sense of aliveness which she also had possessed. I was grateful to her for this heritage and went through these forms of ceremonial in expression of that gratitude. It would have pleased her. It was what she would have wished.

All afternoon the tenants kept coming to pay their respects and offer presents. They brought us eggs, measures of their finest rice, live chickens, home-cured meats, and tender new peas which were just coming into season. We feasted on these good things for supper, and afterwards until a late hour the cook and two helpers were busy in the kitchen preparing the dough to make *tang-yuan* on the morrow.

Tang-yuan are a tradition. They are little sugar dumplings, made of fine rice flour with centres of brown sugar mixed with fat and walnuts or sesame seed, sometimes of minced meat or preserved fruit. They are dropped into boiling water, scooped up in two or three minutes, and served with a sprinkling of sugar and sesame oil. In the north we sometimes deep-fry them after boiling, to make a delicately crusty surface. Everybody eats them. Everybody delights in them. Even Pao, who eats nothing sweet, makes an exception of *tang-yuan*, and Sixth Brother, who is fourteen, holds the Chengtu record, having consumed at one sitting eighty of the largest. It would be almost treason not to like *tang-yuan* at New Year's time!

The fifteenth, the last day of New Year's, we walked in the sunlight. It was spring, early March. We walked into Pihsien along the narrow paths between the blossoming fields, sweet with the warm scent of spring, alive with the hum and traffic of bees. The low mists of the early morning had dispersed, leaving the day clear, not yet clouded over with the white dimness of afternoon that dissolves the mountains to air. And there in the west, as it is given to see only a few days in the year, the mountains were piled in dazzling beauty, in clean, flashing whiteness, cut crystal sharp in all their lines. Across a field of bright gold rape,

177

framed in by black-green cypresses, there loomed the mountains, the nearer ranges pure and aloof in winter snow, the highest peak of all, Minya Koncha, rivalling the tall Himalayas.

In Pihsien the shops were closed for the final festivities of New Year and the climax of all, the dragon procession. Through doorways, in the cave-like darkness of the houses, as we passed, we could see people busy rolling *tang-yuan* to eat that evening.

Down the street, when it was dusk, would come the dragon, carried high on pikes, its glittering head turning this way and that; and there would be bonfires, there would be fireworks, there would be drums and fifes and loud cymbals. Through the town and out of the gate and through the fields the dragon would go, to bring prosperity and good harvests. The moon would come up in the late dusk, the round full moon of the fifteenth of New Year, and the whole of Pihsien would cheer and jostle around the dancing dragon and eat *tang-yuan*, being filled with joy and hope for a new year of plenty. . . .

At the house of my Eighth External Grand-aunt we awaited the dragon. We sat on bamboo stools under the eaves by the kerb. At every doorway hung square lanterns of white paper with designs in red, lightening the darkness a little so that we could discern each other's faces. When the moon rose there would be more light. Far down the street there came a dim beat of drums and clashing of cymbals and a great murmur of many voices. From time to time there was a strange hissing sound, followed by a great shout. A pause, then "Hiss-ss-ss!" and the shout; a pause with only the monotone of the drum, then again the hiss and roar. It was almost frightening in the dark night before moonrise, with only the faint circles of lantern light to relieve the gloom.

Then from kerb to kerb the narrow street was filled with boys running, shouting, and capering with delight. Behind them, ten feet above the jostling shoulders of the accompanying crowd, the great horned head of the dragon towered and, segment by segment, its body writhed after. At least a hundred men, stripped to the waist, barelegged and sweating, were of the train of the dragon. Those who bore the sections of its body swung into a dance – five to the right, five to the left, reverse and repeat – while the beautiful, terrifying head, all scarlet, purple, green, and gold, dipped and reared among the torches to the mad rhythm of the drum and cymbals. At the moment of climax there was silence, as though every one at the same instant caught breath in expectancy. Then – "Hiss-ss-ss!" Jets of sparks flashed

178

from bamboo tubes of gunpowder in the hands of the torch-bearers, lashing about in comet tails of fire, playing over the bare backs and chests of the men who carried the dragon. The crowd fell back with a roar. The dragon writhed as its bearers leaped and twisted in the streams of sparks. It looked like torture, and indeed there are laws forbidding the dragon dance because of this feature. But the ancient custom holds. Actually, in their excitement the men feel nothing and seldom do they sustain burns of any severity, though accidents do occur. But there are never lacking young men eager to prove their fortitude, for car-riers of the dragon are said to be immune for a year from all illness and bodily harm, and by their deed prosperity is ensured for the town.

The dragon went on its way, with all its attendant clamour. The tall head stooped for the city gate. The procession passed on into the fields. We did not follow. We returned home in single file along the narrow paths, guided by a little white lan-tern. The enormous moon came up, sudden and silent on our right hand. Far across the fields came the distant din of the dragon dance, but less in sound than the murmur of water under the bridge as we approached home. The *lan-mu* traced their shadows on the wall; the grave mounds were silvered with moon-light.

The *tang-yuan* were ready. Plates piled high with the little white balls had been carried to all the tenants. Now Third Aunt took a dozen little silver bowls and in each put two *tang-yuan* and a little of the sweetened water, placing ivory chopsticks across each bowl. These were carried by the servants into the ancestral hall and set upon the altar before the tablets. Two were placed outside the gate on the stone paving before the great Ching Dynasty tomb. Then, having shared with the ancestors, we sat down in the courtyard to eat *tang-yuan* and admire the moon.

The night was spring, with a soft languor in its coolness, calm, with a gentle, indefinable sadness. I sat a little apart from the others, upon the gate step, letting my thoughts drift in vague memory and longing. There was too much of loveliness; I could not accept so much, and Pao not here to share it. There was no spring yet where he was, in the black loess hills of Shensi. In the courtyard the bare branches and little fine twigs of gingko and crape-myrtle made a web for the moon. Lamplight behind the windows was dull golden, crossed with the intricate pattern of lattice. Beyond the open gates all was mysterious in the sifted silver of moonlight – a thin mist lying level on the fields making a lake of reflected pallor; the *lan-mu* standing up tall and shadowy silver beyond the mounded graves; hedges, bamboos, the willows bordering the stream, all cloud-pale, and beyond them, nothingness . . . mist of silver without shape or substance.

Nothing is changed; time changes nothing. My great-grandfather looked out over these fields, saw that this was good land, and bought it for his children. Balanced panels at right and left of the gate are carved with his verses : –

In the evening mists, far removed from city clamour,
Under the bamboos of my planting, I play my lute.
In the quiet of life's ending, duty completed,
With my sons and sons' children, rest and make poems.

Deep under the surface wave of war is this unshakable peace of China. This heritage of tranquillity. . . . In me the thread of life, continuous. This will go on. . . .

CHAPTER ELEVEN

BURNING CITY – CHUNGKING

In the north we say *jeh-nao*. In Szechwan it is *nao-jeh*,
the syllables reversed, but the same meaning. Literally translated
it is "hot and loud." It means many people, a great deal of noise,
a joyous crowding, excitement, fire-crackers, bright red colour,
bright lights, everybody happy. I could never make the meaning
fully clear to my English friends. Americans, I think, might
understand. "A hot time" – they say that, also.

All through the New Year season it was *nao-jeh*, and when the
festival was over it continued *nao-jeh* in slightly lesser degree.
It could not be otherwise in the Big Family, there were so many
of us. We all lived together within sound of each other's voices,
coming and going through the courtyards under the watchful
windows of all the relatives. We had no private concerns; it was
taken for granted that everything should be known to all, discussed by all. Of course, this was intended for the best. The
family stood together for protection. Its life was based on
routine, ceremonial, continuity. Within its circle the younger
members were brought up in the tradition of simplicity and
the established middle-class virtues. They learned self-control,
good temper, courtesy, thrift. They were not spoiled with too
much money and too little restraint, for what wealth my family
possessed was not hereditary but earned in the last generation
or two.

It was my family's idea that I should remain with them in
Chengtu until Pao's return from the north-west. I had eaten too
much bitterness, they said. Now I must rest and *shua* and build
up my health. They would cherish me, entertain me, so that I
should never feel lonely or sad. They rallied to protect and sustain me. They never left me alone! Even though New Year was
ended, they kept up the programme of visits, cinema, mah-
jongg parties, excursions, always in groups, always joyous, surrounding me with animation and activity. They even made a
nao-jeh occasion of illness. If I had the toothache, no less than
four or five sisters and aunts went with me to the dentist's,
hovering about me solicitously. If I had a cold I was put to bed,
smothered under quilts and sympathy, visited, entertained, and

urged to try all kinds of Chinese herbal drugs said to be of miraculous efficacy.

Undoubtedly they did as they would be done by, but I was not accustomed to having so much attention. Well or ill, I dislike having a fuss made over me. I require long stretches of solitude. But this was a thing my family could not understand. They liked it *nao-jeh*! Solitude was all very well for hermits. Certain of the poets, who had odd ideas, surely, extolled the pleasures of lonely communion with nature. But who else in his right mind would not prefer to forgather with his own kind in genial social intercourse? It never entered their thoughts that mah-jongg today, mah-jongg tomorrow, might become monotonous; that an endless repetition of the limited round of amusement might stale. It never occurred to them that I might grow tired of this protected, wrapped-up, cotton-padded existence within the Big Family.

I was not unhappy in Chengtu, but neither was I happy. I was half asleep. I had no interests but tepid, superficial ones – clothes and food; no intellectual curiosity or delight in the realm of ideas. I felt cushioned against life. It seemed even my physical senses were dulled. I was less perceptive of stinging cold, sun, the scent and colour of flowers. I felt the ground under my feet less as I walked. That sharp awareness which to me had meant life was numb and dormant. I began to realize the cotton-wool effect of the family's kindness to me. And so I resolved to go away.

Third Uncle was flying to Chungking. His banking business demanded his return for a few weeks. I went with him to take charge of his household. For a long time it had troubled the Big Family that the house in Chungking was without a hostess. People came and went; it was a hostel rather than a home; there was no one in authority excepting Third Uncle himself, and he was very busy and often absent. Third Aunt had her hands full with business affairs; she could not move to Chungking, even if she had not preferred Chengtu as a place of residence. In China it is very much the custom with the middle class for women to handle property, investments, and savings. Only in the idler upper class, decadent with hereditary wealth, are the women treated like dolls. My aunt had charge of shop rents, farm rents, the repair and upkeep of various properties belonging to the family, in addition to her housekeeping, which was perfection. She could not leave Chengtu.

The best thing, the elders of the family declared, was for Third Uncle to take a concubine to manage his Chungking house. He did so. But the concubine proved to be a lazy, inefficient woman, quite incapable of filling the position. Making the best of a bad bargain, Third Uncle quietly provided her with a country house, and there she lived comfortably with a large number of her relatives, perfectly content with the very infrequent courtesy visits my uncle paid her. He was not interested in further experiments along that line.

March, April, the first of May.... Chungking in the spring gave hint of the coming summer. Far up the Kialing River in the morning the sun came up in a white glare. Blazing to noon, high overhead, it shone down into the well-like courtyards, unshaded by any tree. In the evening haze and smoke hung in the still air over roofs hot with the long hours of sun. Within the old city walls the rocky point of the peninsula afforded no roothold of moist earth for trees, bamboos, or grass. I used to look out over the ridge of the city from the roof garden of our house, to the rivers on both sides, and there were not a dozen trees to be counted. Roofs, confused geometrical pattern of roofs, greytiled, close-crowding, shelving downward to the river levels, eaves shadowing the narrow alleys, no street plan distinguishable in the packed density of houses. Eastward up the peninsula, all the way to Fu To Kuan, where twenty years ago stretched the largest graveyard in the world – acres and miles of grave mounds on the bare rolling hills, all cleared now – the city sprawled beyond its ancient bounds, and there were gardens and parks and a vast network of new roads graded for wheeled traffic.

Our house was on high land near the backbone of the city, on the Kialing side, by the Ling Kiang Men, the River Gate. Along the ridge extended Tu Yu Kai, the richest street, with its shops taller than the surrounding dwellings, leading down toward the point where buildings towered six and seven stories high, skyscrapers for Szechwan. Among them stood my uncle's bank, an imposing structure of green stone. From our roof garden I could look down to the Kialing, fuller now than in winter, and almost as muddy as the Yangtze, where the mat-roofed boats came down from Hochuan and Suining, sliding with the current, dark on its burnished sheen, the rowers singing to the stroke their old, rhythmic river chanties. Their song came faint through the clamour on the wide steps going down to the landing, and the strident, vigorous noise of life under the grey roofs on the slope between the cliffs and the shore. Across the Kialing I could look over to sand beaches, where soldiers drilled, and the old town of Kiangpeh with its stone walls winding up the hills. Upstream, downstream, the banks of both rivers were built up with houses, white plaster, grey brick, red stone, clustering thickly at wharves and landings, following in double file the course of roads, forming knots and concentrations at village business centres, or scattered out among fields and trees. Chungking. The first of May, 1939.

My duties as hostess in Third Uncle's house were unexacting. The servants knew far better than I could instruct them all the routine of the household. There were eight or ten servants; I never learned to know them all by name because they were constantly changing. The inner ring of three, however, was permanent. There was Lao Tseng, the steward, a thin, stooped, solemn man of middle age, silent and efficient. He hired and discharged the underservants, kept the accounts, and carried the keys. He knew everything he needed to know – where tickets could be bought, how to tie up intricate packages, where any of my uncle's business associates could be found at any hour of the day, which callers were to be admitted to the *keh-tang* immediately and which to detain at the gate pending inquiry; he knew when to send gifts and to whom; he knew at a glance whether Third Uncle's temper was good or bad and saw to it that every one in the household behaved accordingly. He was afraid of no one but the cook; when there was a squabble between them, Lao Tseng always gave in.

Lao Li was the cook and a good one, for the saying is that a greasy apron betokens culinary skill and all good cooks are fat. If he used lard and red pepper too lavishly for my taste, that was Szechwan custom. He was very jealous of his dignity. Once when I ventured the suggestion that he serve the noodles "white" – that is, unseasoned with red soy sauce, oil, and pepper, but plain as we eat them in the north – Lao Li gave me a pitying look, and addressing the kettle he muttered, "Boiled noodles and water! It must be they have no cooks at all in the north!" So, since his cuisine seemed to suit Third Uncle and his guests, I made no further suggestions.

The third of this inner ring of servants was Hong Sao, the amah. She had a husband somewhere at the front and an eight-month-old baby. She was a healthy young woman, but ill-tempered and domineering, so that the two maids who were under her orders seldom stayed more than a week or two, when Lao Tseng had to look for new ones. She carried the baby about everywhere, tied in a square of blue cloth on her back. Quite unhampered by the burden, she moved so energetically it seemed the child's head must surely snap and roll off. Yet the baby was well satisfied with the arrangement. It never cried, but slept quite happily with its head lolling and jerking about.

The one task the servants permitted me was the arrangement of flowers. Though we had no garden, since nothing would grow in our courtyards on the barren rock, all the flowers of Szechwan spring were for sale in the streets: feathery plum blossom; peach blossom, white or pink, double-flowered; wild orchids, their veined, translucent petals having the perfume of citrus fruits; roses; *chi-li-hsiang*, the "seven-mile-coloured; deep-tinted Japanese quince blossom; pale lavender-grey wild iris; creamy freesia – brought in from the country in wide flat baskets to be sold for a few cents. It was a delight to handle them, damp and fresh, to mass them in vases of blue or ox-blood glaze or in old bronze jars, to change them to fresh ones each day in the *keh-tang* and bedrooms.

It was a casual household. Third Uncle divided his time between Chungking and Chengtu. Second Brother lived here sometimes and sometimes at the bank, where he had a room. Week-ends and holidays the house would be full of young people, my sisters and brothers and cousins and their friends, who attended universities in or near Chungking. My uncle's business associates, all of them Szechwanese formerly connected with the various war lords of the province, were frequent visitors. I saw none of Pao's friends. I doubt if they knew I was in Chungking, or if they did, they probably considered it disrespectful to call upon me in my husband's absence.

If there was an undertone of uneasiness in Chungking that spring, we were scarcely aware of it. Within the secluded courts of our house the days were very quiet. A narrow passage led in from the street between the shops, high walls on either side. In the first courtyard lived the servants. My room was between the second and third courts. When Third Uncle and Second Brother were away, I was quite alone in the inner apartments. Here the city's constant voice was subdued to a vague murmur. I had the solitude I needed. I read, wrote letters to Pao, did a little translation work, wasted the time idly watching the goldfish in the green depths of the huge Soochow fish-bowls, or climbed to the roof garden to look at the boats on the Kialing and the high, dark hills on the south bank of the Yangtze. In the evening there would be guests for dinner, Third Uncle's friends and their wives. The massive banquet table in the *keh-tang* on the third courtyard would seat twenty; often it was filled. The conversation was of rising prices, of the never-ceasing flood of refugees crowding into Szechwan, of air raids. Yet no one was perturbed. The war was far away, down-river, beyond the mountains.

There had been air raids. Not many. A few planes came over and bombed occasionally, usually military objectives, but once, in January, within the city. The damage was not great. The government issued warnings and orders to evacuate the city. Few heeded. Szechwan had always been so remote, safe behind its mountain ranges. A habit of mind is not easily shaken. Chungking *felt* safe. Refugees told of their homes destroyed, cities on fire, fleeing crowds mowed down with machine-guns. That was at Nanking or Chapei or Wuchang, far from Szechwan. To the people of Chungking bombing was something that happened to other cities; they could not apprehend the threat to themselves.

Until the fear suddenly flashes real, a naked lightning thrust of revelation, each one feels himself the darling of fate. Whatever happens to others it will not – cannot – touch him. Because ... because he is utterly unable to believe in his own dissolution. Something of this immunity is conferred upon his environment. This house, this street, this quiet and well-known place where he goes to and fro every day – nothing can happen here. Against reason, in defiance of fact, each one is immortal in his own mind, and all his family and his goods safe with him until that lightning flash of living fear.

Underground shelters were being prepared. There was one at the head of our street, small and poorly constructed. They were too few in number for all the people and there was no system of assignment. People went where they pleased. Some shelters were overcrowded, others empty. There was so much confusion and excited clamour in the narrow streets during a raid alarm that many people preferred to remain quietly at home, trusting to luck that nothing would happen. We were of that number. Remembering the pontoon bridge at Kweilin and the contagion of panic, I would go to the innermost room of the house, the *keh-tang*, as far as possible from the shouting and excitement of the street, and there bury myself in a book. Third Uncle was always blandly optimistic. If he happened to be at home he would stay calmly at his desk, practising calligraphy with a big

186

brush. Any rigidity or quiver of the muscles would ruin the fine sweep of the strokes. The hand must be controlled free in order to form the beautiful proportions, the shaded lines, of Chinese characters. Third Uncle's imperturbability was evident in the unvarying excellence of the characters he wrote while the alarm was on.

When the all-clear was given he would go down to the bank to check up. Once I went with him, going in by the little side door, for the big iron gratings of the main entrance were closed until the bank opened for business, usually within half an hour after the all-clear. Inside it presented a scene quite unlike the orderly routine of business hours, yet there was order and system despite the apparent dislocation. Servants thronged the stairways carrying up from the vault bulky armfuls of bedding. Girl employees ran about with boxes and suitcases and wash-basins. The men were bringing up drawers of filing cases full of accounts and returning them to their places. A wet-nurse trudged past with a baby at her breast, dragging by the hand a three-year-old, and two amahs obstructed a doorway with an overflowing basket of laundry.

For the employees all lived at the bank, one big family, with cooks, water carriers, and wash-women provided, the sixty-odd men clerks living together in large dormitories, the thirteen girls in a smaller dormitory on the roof, and a few married couples with rooms to themselves. Every large organization, government or private, is run upon this system, partly co-operative, partly patriarchal. The employees elected from their number dormitory heads, appointed persons to supervise the kitchen, to keep accounts and purchase supplies. A doctor who had his office in the building was engaged to give medical care. Behind the correct and business-like front offices flourished this teeming communal life. One walked through lofty halls where business was methodically transacted, typewriters clicking, telephones ringing – and stepped through the back door into a commotion of family life on an extensive scale, with courtyards criss-crossed with clothes-lines, amahs quarrelling, children shouting and playing.

During an air-raid alarm all flocked down to the vault, taking with them their bedding and valuables. Second Brother was in charge of the vault, a position of great responsibility. Looking for him, Third Uncle and I went down to the basement. Second Brother was just locking up. Against the huge steel door of the vault (American make, cost – twenty thousand dollars, gold) he stood tiny and frail. He weighs rather less than one hundred pounds and stands five feet four. His hands and feet are small, like a girl's. His hair is very black and curly and his eyes lively. He is for ever dashing about, distributing keys, signing receipts, stamping papers, telephoning, shouting orders. Yet during a raid he is usually very cool. When all the others crowded down into the vault he would climb to the roof and search the sky with binoculars, trying to spot the Japanese planes and determine their objective.

March; April; the first week of May. Raid alarms were more frequent, the government more insistent, urging evacuation of the city. As in Kweilin, there was an alarm almost every sunny morning at about ten o'clock. A slight tension was perceptible. The underservants made one excuse and another to go away for a while – it was the time for transplanting rice; there was illness in the family, or a wedding. They asked leave and went away to the country. But the die-hard three, Lao Tseng, Lao Li, and Hong Sao, stayed on. They refused even to go to the public shelters during raid alarms. It was in part inertia, in part that feeling of responsibility so strong in Chinese servants. They must stay to look after the master's house and the master's things; thieves were active while the alarm was on. We did not demand it of them. On the contrary, we urged them to go, but they would not.

On the first of May, Third Uncle took the plane for Chengtu. I went to the air-field to see him off, not realizing how the sight of the great silver plane poised on the yellow sand would overwhelm me with the memory of that other day when I said good-bye to Pao. I was blinded, choked with unshed tears. Returning home, I plunged into a fury of activity to keep at bay this desperate loneliness and longing for Pao. Third Uncle had left all in my keeping; I decided to pack and store all the valuable things – books, paintings, furs, his collection of antiques – since he would be gone for some months. And at the back of my mind, half-acknowledged, there was the apprehension of air raids. I was not afraid, but it was only sensible to take precautions. Things would be safer at the bank. To be sure, the strong-rooms were already crammed, but we were privileged. They would make room for our things. I started packing the books.

Two days later there was a raid. I was alone with the servants. In accordance with our custom we did not leave the house. The planes came over; we heard their engines, directly overhead, droning dully. They were flying very high; they were passing.

. . . There were the crashes of explosions and our windows shivered violently. Bombs! And near by, inside the city! Hong Sao and I, on either side of a packing case, stared at each other unbelievingly. It could not be true. Some trick of the wind that magnified sounds, in reality distant. We waited in the tense stillness of the city bound to silence by the urgent alarm we felt, and with every minute the doubt grew. Surely the bombing was farther away than it had seemed; what objective was there near by?

A sharp whistle in the street. I ran with the servants to the gate, curious to know. A first-aid squad strode by with stretchers. All down the street people massed in the doorways and under the eaves, peering and questioning. "Where?" "Just over there in the next street." Back came the stretchers, loaded – a woman with blood-matted hair; a child dead, ripped by shrapnel; others . . . I had seen enough. I went back into the house. The telephone was shrilling. Second Brother at the bank had put through a call.

"Are you all right?"

"The next street to us –"

"So near! . . . They were flying too high for aim. I think it was meant for the air-field. There's no point bombing inside the city; what good would it do them to smash a lot of houses? It must have been a mistake. You're packing? I'll send men this afternoon to bring down the more important things. Send whatever you have ready. There might be more – accidents."

All afternoon, with the help of the servants, I packed, and we sent off several crates of my uncle's treasures. The *keh-tang* was stripped but a great deal remained – the winter clothes, the rugs, many more books, my own things and Pao's. The other rooms had scarcely been touched. But by evening I was exhausted with the heat, the oppressive, stifling heat of Chungking summer. The season was too far advanced for May. The land was parched, dusty, yet the air was dense with humidity. It pressed down into the narrow courtyards as though it were some heavy, unbreathable fluid. I climbed to the roof garden for escape, but even here the air was motionless, stagnant as in a windowless room. The sun had gone down, but there was an almost visible exhalation of heat from the vast expanse of grey roofs. The sky was coppery, like a close-fitting cover riveted down at the horizon all the way round. The moon hung low in the east, in a smoky violet haze, a heavy, mis-shapen moon three days short of completion.

Looking out over the city I could see little effect of the morning raid. From a greater height scattered gaps left by demolition bombs must have been evident, but seen from the slight elevation the roofs appeared continuous as before.

Lao Li stuck his head up from the stair well to announce, "The meal is opened." I went down to the *keh-tang*, where he had set out my supper on one corner of the huge bare banquet table. Although the room stood open to the inner courtyard there was no coolness or current of air. The naked dazzle of the unshaded electric bulb seemed to focus the heat. This room that had been so gracious and pleasant, with its fine scroll paintings and vases of fresh flowers, had an uninhabited look – the walls bare, chairs pushed together into a corner, a half-filled packing-case in the middle of the floor and strewn around it a litter of things to go with it. Most desolate of all, the massive bare table with one place set. . . .

In the morning, unrefreshed by a dull sleep, I got up early and packed a boxful of Pao's books, then later went with it to the bank. Flags were out. The day, May 4th, was a significant one for Chinese youth, commemorating the great resurgence of national consciousness when in 1919 students and schoolboys rose up in protest against the Twenty-One Demands, which would have delivered China, bound and gagged, into the hands of Japan. But for a few older men – writers, revolutionists – no one else was awake to this betrayal; only the young sprang to the defence of their birthright. Boycott, agitation, publicity – they used what weapons they had, and the whole people were roused to their support. More than ever now, in war-time, with our freedom again threatened, Youth Day had meaning.

There was a curious blend of excitement and indifference concerning the scattered bombings of yesterday. Plans for celebration of Youth Day went forward unchanged. There were assemblies and rallies of the various youth organizations. In the evening there would be parading with lanterns and torches. Shops were open, people went about their business as usual. On Tu Yu Kai the stores spread out their beautiful things for sale and their shelves were piled with merchandise. No apprehension here as in Kweilin. But at the gate opposite ours a motor-car was being filled with baggage, and rickshaws loaded with household goods were going out of the city. At the bank Second Brother helped me to store away the box of books. Second Brother, who was never afraid of air raids, frowned a little dubiously. "Of course it was an accident, not likely to be repeated, but . . . it might be advisable for you to move out to Ta Er Woh?"

Ta Er Woh was a little country place ten miles up the peninsula, beyond Fu To Kuan. The bank had storehouses there for the goods it bought on investment, and a little house for the man in charge. There would never be bombings there, it was so far from any centres of military activity – a fenced garden on a hill of pines, with rice fields in the valley below. It would be safe. Thus Second Brother in May 1939. . . . The fields around it now are pitted with bomb craters, a crater in the garden itself, the pines splintered and the buildings shaken awry. At the raid alarm everybody runs for the shelter. . . . I answered him I did not think it was necessary to leave the city yet. If things grew worse – but in Nanyu after the one bombing there were only false alarms. The planes never came again. And in Kweilin the same. I could wait.

When we came up from the vault they said there was a *ching-pao*, a raid alarm, on. It was about ten o'clock, the time when alarms were to be expected. I tarried at the bank; if there should be a raid it was a good place to be – seven stories overhead to stop a bomb before it reached the ground floor, and under that the vault, hollowed out of the solid rock that underlies Chungking. I had lunch with the bank employees. I waited around for hours.

The programme was not going according to schedule. Usually during a raid alarm, after the first siren, or *kung-hsi*, which meant that Japanese planes had entered the province, not more than an hour elapsed before the sirens went off again, either the urgent or the all-clear. But this day, after the preliminary *kung-hsi*, hour after hour went by and no further signal of any kind. At two in the afternoon everything seemed normal. People were walking up and down in the streets; the shops had re-opened. I thought of all that packing yet to do at home. There seemed no point in waiting longer.

The day was sultry, with a white, blinding sun. Passing motor-cars – not a few, and all loaded with baggage – stirred up clouds of thick dust. The street seemed quite as usual, plenty of people moving about. Yet there was a vague disquiet abroad. From time to time a kind of uneasy ripple ran among the people. I stopped at a shop to buy a cake of soap. "Is there or isn't there an alarm on?" I asked the clerk.

"Something has gone wrong with the siren machinery," he hazarded a guess. "Of course the alarm is off! When did it ever

191

run four hours? People are nervous after yesterday, that's all. Why, a little time ago a man started running, yelling "*Ching-pao!*" and all the street began to run. Frantic! No sense at all. In a minute they knew it was nothing and stopped. As a matter of fact, the planes have come and gone. Fighters, no bombers. There was a dog-fight with our planes over the hills on the south bank. It's all over for today, you may be sure."

It seemed the sensible thing to ignore it and go on with work in hand. At home I continued sorting and packing. Pao's winter overcoat smelled musty; I hung it over a chair in the courtyard to air. Shoes had mildewed a little in the damp heat; I rubbed them clean and set them out to dry. I packed away my wedding presents, the lovely embroidered coverlets and silks my family had given me. With every hour the heat grew more intense. About five o'clock I gave up and retired to my room for a siesta. Half an hour later I was roused a little by Hong Sao, snapping the switch of the electric light, flicking the button up and down without result.

"Bulb burned out," I suggested. Though why she should wish to turn on the light...it was broad daylight still....

"No, Third Mistress. I tried it in the bathroom and it's off there. All over the house...." She looked frightened.

I felt impatient with her fear, the more because it struck an answering spark in myself, that instant, unreasoning flash of physical terror in the moment before the mind assumes control. There were plenty of reasons why the electric current should be off; the most obvious at once presented itself. "They're repairing where the wires were damaged in the bombing yesterday. Of course that's it! We're on the same line as the next street, I suppose." Both of us forgot there had been lights on the night before. Satisfied with the explanation, Hong Sao left the room. It came to me afterwards that, for once, she had no baby on her back – too hot, perhaps.

I drowsed on in the heat. Ten minutes elapsed. Then, faint and very far away, a siren hooted – a single note, choked off abruptly. If I had not been unconsciously listening all day, something in me alert for this signal with a slight but unrelaxing attentiveness, I should not have heard it, so dim it was and far away. I held my breath – urgent or all-clear? Silence. One blast of the siren meant all clear. It was over! Lao Li came in, glad relief in his smile. "It's over! People are coming out of the shelter. I am going to serve supper, Third Mistress."

I stretched and sat up, pushed back my damp hair, thrust my

bare feet into strapless slippers, lazily slid off the bed, and saun-
tered toward the *keh-tang*. Late afternoon left half the courtyard
in shade; it was time to take in the things I had airing – Pao's
overcoat, the row of shoes. Even as I stooped to pick them up
there was a distant hum, a drone. . . . I stiffened erect. The sound
swelled to the heavy, dragging roar of a raced engine – a car
starting? Or . . . I turned about, meaning to go to the gate; I
would make sure. I reached the second courtyard. The roaring
had redoubled; the sky was all one thunderous vibration. I
looked up. . . .

One glance – planes! and the bombs already released, black
in the air, a little behind the planes, falling – and I went flying,
flying as I never ran before, through the rooms, through the third
courtyard, snatching up Pao's coat and throwing it over my head,
into the *keh-tang* and a dive under the table. There came a terrifying sibilant wail, splitting the roar, then a shattering, tearing
crash – earthquake – darkness. . . .

Out of that moment's chaos and dispersion I felt my senses
converge to a focus of pure rapture: "I'm alive! It's over and
I'm here! It has landed; it's over and I'm alive!" I think I said
it aloud – "It's over. I'm lucky. I'm not touched. I'm alive!" I
remember distinctly that at the moment of the explosion my
mouth was wide open – not because I had been warned of concussion; because I was too stunned to close it. I had been crouching, staring out between the legs of the table at the wood-
pannelled wall opposite. And suddenly – darkness. . . .

Then with the next instant fear came flooding over me, vast,
overwhelming fear. I was choking. I could not breathe. My mouth
and throat were full of dust. The house had collapsed. I was
buried under the table – buried alive! It was all dark. The
roof and walls had fallen. The house had fallen down upon
the table and around it; the table held and I was under it, walled
in. . . .

Holding my breathing, I flung myself against the wall of my
prison, pushing, thrusting at the splintered panels, the rubble.
The barrier gave. I put forth all my strength and broke through.
Stones rolled in upon me as I crawled out. Bits of tile rained
down. It was all a matter of seconds. Blindly, hands groping
before me, I ran, stumbling over heaped debris. I could see nothing; the air was dense black dust. Dust gritted under my eyelids;
thick dust choked my breathing. Coughing, half fainting, I ran
through the side passage to the second courtyard, felt my way
along the wall, instinctively avoiding the crater in the middle.

"Lao Tseng, Lao Li, Hong Sao!" I cried. "Are you there? Lao Li, Lao Tseng!"

In the black whirlwind an answering cry: "Third Mistress! This way – keep to the wall." Lao Li's voice. I stumbled toward it. His hand caught mine, guiding me. "Are you safe? Were you hurt? Lao Tseng and Hong Sao's baby are buried underneath. We have to get them out. Hong Sao and I were at the gate." Lao Li began to dig desperately. I fell on my knees beside him, clawing at the wreckage of the servants' quarters. Somewhere near by in the dust haze Hong Sao was shrieking, shrieking for her baby. We called Lao Tseng by name, over and over without answer. We dug frantically, hopelessly, knowing it was useless.

The dust thinned; we could see each other dimly. I glanced back over my shoulder, past the crater in the courtyard, toward the inner apartments. The blackness of slowly clearing dust behind us was laced with yellow, flickering fire. Incendiary bombs. Lao Li saw it. "Third Mistress, you go away," he urged. "We can't save Lao Tseng and the baby. They're dead." I shook my head and dug the more madly, tearing with both hands at the tangled debris.

"Look! At the gate!" The three-story flimsy wooden buildings hedging in our narrow passage to the street were towering beacons of flame. Hong Sao, with the glare of the fire in her face, flung up her arms and fled shrieking; we never saw her again. Lao Li called wildly once more to Lao Tseng. Then, despairingly – "He doesn't answer! It's no good trying more. Third Mistress, come!" We ran out through the gate. Tall flames arched over us as we leaped through to the street. There was a rending crash; the building on the right bent, swayed, and collapsed in blazing wreckage upon the gate we had passed the moment before. All that side of the street was one mass of fire. We stared, aghast. Then Lao Li ran one way, I another. I started toward the bank.

Fire all along the streets. Broken tile, rubble underfoot. Wires down, tangled and snarled. Telephone poles on fire, standing like burning crosses or fallen athwart the road. The increasing roar of flames. The diminishing drone of the planes, going away now their errand was done. I became aware of people about me. Hushed, stunned – no one spoke above a whisper. Little knots of people in doorways, silent, or crouched on the threshold, head in hands. People caught strolling on the streets, cowering back under the eaves of houses not on fire, their eyes empty as the eyes of the dead. At a street corner a small crowd staring up at the

194

blank sky. Policemen, revolver in hand, watching to prevent looting. They glanced at me, incurious. I must have looked like a ghost or a devil, grey dust in my hair and clothing, dishevelled, my face a grey, staring mask, the dirt blasted into the skin. No one spoke to me until some distance farther on a policeman directed me to detour – Tu Yu Kai was impassable, a furnace of flame.

It took me an hour to reach the bank, going out of my way through steep alleys and unfamiliar streets, half lost. The sun was down, the sky clear, opal-coloured. Everything was very still, except for the crackling, rushing sound of the flames on all sides. At the bank the garage and entrance were crammed with people, hundreds huddled together, talking in whispers, as though afraid their voices might call back the planes. The bank building, solid stone, almost fireproof, among the frail shops of wood and plaster, offered sanctuary. The policeman at the side gate knew me and led me in. We went through corridors and down stairways in utter darkness. My groping hand touched warm cloth, warm flesh; I could smell the close-crowded bodies. We pushed through the shifting crowd, their low, indistinct talk going on about us. In the vault there was a faint diffusion of daylight still. Folded quilts had been forced against the small, high, barred windows as defence against splinters, though any explosion near by would have blown them in with the concussion. But the stifling, re-breathed air was unendurable; here and there the quilts had been removed. Thronging heads were outlined in the dim light.

I called Second Brother by name, my voice startlingly loud in the whispering stillness. He came to me through the crowd and drew me toward a window. I caught his sleeve; I started to tell him and could not for the sudden rush of tears and the tight ache in my throat. I was crying hysterically in agonizing gasps, shivering, my heart beating wildly. I had not cried before, in the black whirling dust of the bombing, in our courtyard with fire behind and in front, or hurrying through the streets, death-still but for the rushing sound of flames. But now, with the reassuring touch of Second Brother's sleeve, the solid walls of the bank about me, I sobbed and could not stop. I said, "The house is gone. Lao Tseng was killed." We cried together, comforting each other.

Then I took a deep breath with almost a laugh, and called for tea to drink and had to sit down on some quilts on the floor. I was shaking with exhaustion. Between sips of the lukewarm tea

I told what had happened. People gathered around me, the employees of the bank, only the whites of their eyes visible in the gloom. I answered their questions – what it was like in the street, where there were fires. They had all been in the vault, where they could hear only the muffled report of the bombs and could see nothing. The bank had received a telephoned warning in tim for them to get down to the vault.

But the sirens? Some said there had been three or four alarms, on and off several times during the day. Others had not heard any. A breakdown in the mechanism, negligence on the part of men who should have been on duty – there were various conjectures. Without doubt, the one short blast we had heard about five-forty, which we took for the all-clear, was the beginning of a *ching-chi*, cut off at once because the planes were almost over head.

By now it was night. Moonlight made a grey-white blur against the barred windows. Here and there small *chin-yu* lamps were lighted. There was no electricity. The vault was suffocating. Surely the planes were gone, though there had been no all-clear signal. Bolder ones among us went out on the streets to scout. The telephone wires were down; we were cut off from all news. Second Brother and I followed a flickering *chin-yu* flame upstairs to the main office. We sat on a bench against the wall. The congestion here was less; many people had gone. The one tiny lamp set on a desk was the only light, the radius of its faint beam reaching scarcely five feet in the immensity of the room. I was extremely thirsty, with the dry taste of fear in my throat, and the dust. The water-mains were broken. The precious reserves of fluid left in tea-pots and thermos bottles were going fast. It was necessary to restrain oneself, pouring an ounce or two into the cup, sipping slowly, politely insisting, "It is enough, it is enough" – even while one longed to snatch back the tea-pot, gulp from its spout. . . .

Now there was a rush of people crowding in again. The planes! The planes were coming back! Winged with panic, I dashed down the stairs to the vault, flung myself down among quilts and burrowed under them, covered over completely. I cowered there, my heart beating so furiously I could hardly draw breath, until the stifling heat under the quilts became intolerable. I crawled out then, wiped the sweat from my face with the skirt of my *shan*, and looked about and asked questions. No one had heard the planes. It was a wild rumour born of uneasiness and dread, one of the many wild rumours of that night.

About ten o'clock Second Brother and I climbed the seven flights of stairs to the roof, from which high point we could look out over all Chungking. It was a scene of appalling beauty. Fire streamed up in long pennons and banners, bending a little in the slight draft of night breeze. Flames whipped from their roots, soaring into the whirling columns of smoke like flapping wings. We looked toward Ling Kiang Men where our house had been. There stretched a lake of fire, its troubled surface flinging up a fiery surf. On the Yangtze side, farther away, from a petrol depot shot up leaping bright yellow flames, higher than the hills across the river. In every direction fires. We could hear the dull, distant roar. The air smelled of smoke; cinders and ash rained upon us.

In safety – for me fires were near enough to threaten the bank building – high above the burning city, we looked down upon its splendour of destruction. Overhead, remote in the milky sky, floated the high, white moon, almost rounded to the full. I was exhausted of all emotion, incapable of feeling pity or terror for those trapped in the blazing streets below. Afterward, when I heard the stories of that night's many tragedies, when I saw people digging in the ruins, caught phrases from their lips – "My wife was killed" – "My children" – "My husband" – and knew that even while I was gazing down on the sea of fire hundreds had been burning to death, their cries drowned in the roar of the fire, I could not conceive of my own dull indifference.

I could feel nothing. All emotion was swallowed up in a vast physical weariness. I came down the stairs, flight after flight, my right hand slipping along the rail to catch and check myself from falling, when I became aware of an accustomed weight on my left arm, something heavy and hot I had been carrying a long time. It was Pao's overcoat. . . . Hours ago – years ago – I had caught it up as I shot through the courtyard and unconsciously I had clung to it ever since. "Pao. . . ." I framed the word automatically. It was a name; it did not mean anything. I was so utterly tired. I lay down on a hard wooden bench to sleep, bunching up the coat for a pillow. The rough wool was harsh under my cheek. I twisted a button in my fingers and tried to call to mind Pao's eyes, his mouth, his voice. But under my closed eyelids a pattern of leaping, coiling flames obliterated memory of him. I cried a little, weakly, because he was gone and I could not bring him clearly to mind.

In the big office there was a constant drifting of people – coming in from the streets, going up to the roof to look, coming down again. I was not asleep, but lay in a trance of fatigue, conscious

197

of the passage of time, each minute, each second, drawn out to
nightmare slowness. I heard them talking. "The full moon is
bad ... night raids ... the fires will guide the planes. ..." Suddenly there were many more people, and every one crying
"There's going to be a raid! Planes again!" Second Brother was
shaking me – "Planes! We're going down to the vault." But even
fear was no longer real to me. I would not go.

The room was very quiet for a time, empty and dark, for at
the report of a raid they had blown out the *chin-yu* lamps. Perhaps I slept a little then. About two in the morning I was awakened by one of the girl employees. "We are going away. The
Japanese planes are coming back at dawn, and this time they will
entirely destroy the city. Hundreds of planes. They say it was
on the Tokio broadcast – they're going to bomb Chungking until
not one stone is left upon another. Every one's going."

"Where?"

"Ta Er Woh. We have talked it over and it's been decided."

I was reluctant. "Surely the vault will be safe enough."

"But not one stone. ..."

The employees gathered in the hall. They had their valuables
in small bundles; some carried blankets and quilts. Second
Brother said, "I have locked up the vault. Get up and come with
us." If every one went away, I could not stay. So I picked up
Pao's overcoat and went with the others into the street. The doors
were locked behind us.

The bank was abandoned by all its employees. If the policeman at the gate and two or three servants stayed, it was their own
choice; nobody gave them orders. It may sound mad, this un-
premeditated sudden flight of every one in responsible posi-
tions. It was mad. But all were convinced Chungking would be
demolished before sunrise – not a building left standing, not a
human being left alive. They fled from certain doom. Now after
many months, after tons and tons of explosives have been sown
upon Chungking, so that this narrow, rocky peninsula has received more bombs per acre than any other spot in the world,
we are less credulous. We smile to remember that we ever believed Chungking could be wiped out in one night.

The street, one half in moonlight, one half in shadow, was a
moving current of people between the dark houses. They came
bowed under loads or clutching bundles, carrying quilts, swinging baskets at the two ends of a shoulder-pole. They came with
babies slung in a cloth on their backs, babies in their arms. Families, strings of young children holding hands to keep together.

Old, old women with sticks, hobbling along on tiny bound feet. Young women, many of them big with child. Boys, young men running, threading swift passage through the slower-paced crowd. The blind, dragged by the hand. All moving with the same urgency, with the stamp of the same fear on their faces – knotted brows and lips parted by their panting breath.

A lurid ruddiness in the sky stained the white moonlight. At cross streets one looked down into seething flame. Faces, turning all one way, staring in horror, fright, fascination, were lit by the red glare of fires. The flood of people swelled, like a river fed by tributaries. There were a few rickshaws. Occasionally motor-cars with headlights dimmed bored through the dense crowd, horns blaring. But most were on foot, burdened with bundles, clinging together, calling to each other hoarsely yet barely above a whisper. The soft, infinite rustle of footsteps made a sound like distant rain. Dust swirled up, suspended like mist in the moonlight. All Chungking seemed to be running away.

We came out on the high road above the Yangtze. Here the road had been cut into the hillside. On the left the cliff dropped sheer; on the right was the cut face of the hill, steep as a wall. The road was a narrow shelf above the river. Below us now we saw the white shining plain of the air-field, lapped by a ripple of moonlight and silver. Of a sudden the dim murmur of the crowd burst into screams and cries of terror – *"Ching-pao!* The planes are coming!" Madness came upon them, caught between the cliffs and the high bank. *"Ching-pao!"* every one yelled. People flung down their bundles and packs upon the roads and ran. Men were like animals, like stampeded cattle driven with a whip of fear. Poor little elderly women, stumbling on bound feet, were flung roughly aside. Lost children howled for their mothers and women shrieked for their children. There was no control, no discipline. Trucks and motor-cars drove headlong into the frenzied mob, lurching over the cast-away baggage – perhaps over bodies fallen in their path. I was torn from Second Brother. I was alone in a human hurricane, tossed and jostled, hurled forward on the wave of advance. I was not afraid of the rumour of a raid; I was afraid of the madness of terror about me. The slippers fell off my feet – I dared not stoop for them. I went on, barefoot. It was a thousand times worse than the bridge at Kweilin – fear at a higher pitch and Pao not with me to help me. I cried out, "Second Brother! Where are you?" but I could not find him in the press and uproar. I went onwards; there was no stopping. *"Ching-pao!"* The rumour goaded us on. If there had been a siren or the drone of bombers we should hardly have heard the sound in that pandemonium.

A mile beyond where the road curved away from the river among low slopes Second Brother stood waiting for me. We caught hands and ran, leaving the highway for little footpaths over the hills. Trees made velvet patches of darkness. The moon guided us. I walked in the close-cropped grass at the side of the path; it felt cool and my bruised feet were grateful. For a long time we climbed toward the higher land. Near Fu To Kuan, where the peninsula narrows between the rivers, we sat down on a hill-top to rest. Chungking was a red bonfire in the distance. Eastward the sky paled with the faintly unpleasant iridescence of a fish belly. I sat rubbing my feet and trying to think. Some anxiety, some vaguely disquieting thought, floated half submerged in my mind and I tried vainly to grasp it.

It was seven o'clock, full daylight, and another hot day, when we reached the small village of Ta Er Woh. There was a teashop open, doing a flourishing business. Scalding water arched from the tea-kettle spout into our cups. I drank it off without waiting for the leaves to infuse, so hot it burned all the way down my throat, and called for more and more again. My whole body was thirsty. I could not remember what it was not to be thirsty, not to be tired.

We climbed another hill and came to the place owned by the bank. Besides the godowns where goods were stored, there was a small brick house in part occupied by the caretaker's family. We were fourteen girls and thirty-nine men, when all our group had arrived. The rest of the bank employees had scattered to their own homes or the homes of relatives. There was one spare bed in a small bare room upstairs. The girls were assigned to this room. The caretaker's wife brought us a little warm water. I took my turn, washing my face in a scant two inches of water, then wiping my swollen, bleeding feet. Then we lay down to sleep, seven on the bed, the rest of us in a row on the floor. I curled one arm around Pao's overcoat, burrowed my head into its rough folds, and slept like the dead on the unyielding plank floor.

The sun beat down upon the valley where the high road wound between the hills. I sat listless on the veranda step, watching the road. Two hours' sleep had dulled the edge of my weariness without satisfying it, but the blaze of heat on the tiles had driven me from the crowded, airless room. The road below was a crawling ribbon of dark-clothed people. It was like a migration of ants, steady, purposeful, unswerving. Where the road curved into sight through a gap in the hills they came in an endless stream. There they were, as I had seen them so often, the familiar current of refugees – the women carrying and leading children, the bundles, the shoulder-poles, the backs bent under loads. "Roads of China!" I said in my heart. "Will you always be worn to dust by the feet of the fleeing, the driven, the weak, the terrorized? Roads unpitiful in the hard sun. . . ."

Pao's overcoat lay beside me on the step. My hand stroked it aimlessly. And suddenly Pao was with me – clear, vivid to my mind. I could hear his voice; I could see his lips move. Pao was real to me again. "Suyin!" I could hear him saying my name. With that, something ripped through my apathy. The vague anxiety which had hovered just beyond my reach flashed into recognition. Pao will have news of this! He will hear of the Chungking bombing; he will be beside himself with fear for me. I must get word to him. He will try to telephone to the house – and the house is gone. He will telephone the bank – the bell ringing and ringing in the locked, empty office, no one there to answer it. I must reach him with the assurance that I am safe. No one else, none of Pao's friends, knows where I am. If he has no word from me, if he hears that the house was destroyed by a direct hit, he will think. . . . He will do something rash! My mind flickered over that thought – Pao at the front, flinging away his command, regardless of discipline, spurred by desperate dread, abandoning everything to come to Chungking to find me. . . . Pao hearing nothing from me; days passing; Pao believing I am dead. . . . "With or without leave, he will come to find me, or giving up hope he will . . ."

I sprang to my feet. I must return to Chungking and send him a telegram. Immediately! I looked for Second Brother and found him sitting in the shade of a tree, half asleep, scratching his arms and slapping at gnats. I told him I was going back to the city. There was no telegraph office nearer and no telephone.

"But all Chungking is in flames!" he protested, astounded at my plan. "Probably the telegraph office is gone. The wires will be down!"

"There's wireless," I answered.

"But how will you go? There are no buses. And you will not be able to get a rickshaw. They are all coming this way."

"I'll walk!"

"It's thirty li!"

"I can walk it."

"There will be no one on duty when you get there. Everybody

201

will be gone. The planes are coming back. With the sky cloudless and a full moon at night the planes will come in hundreds. They will come in waves, night and day, until Chungking is bombed to the ground, every building levelled and no one left alive. You'll walk right into it."

"I have to send a telegram," I persisted. "Pao will already have heard about the raid. I must let him know I am alive."

Second Brother argued, entreated, and finally grew quite annoyed at my stubborness. "What good will it do to get killed telegraphing Pao you are alive?" But at last, unable to shake my resolve, Second Brother gave me his only spare pair of shoes (tied on at the ankles they were a fairly good fit), forty dollars in cash, and the key to the side door of the bank. When I had drunk tea and eaten a bowl of rice I set out. All sought to dissuade me, shaking their heads sorrowfully over my obstinacy as I went down the hill in the hot blaze of the sun.

All the way to the city I went against the current. No one else, it seemed, was going toward Chungking. People stared at me curiously as I passed, Pao's overcoat on my arm, returning to the doomed city. I grew a little doubtful and began to wonder if, as Second Brother had said, I should find everything entirely deserted. I grew a little afraid, but for sheer stubbornness would not turn back. At one place, rounding a turn, I saw the road stretching before me bare and white, and people clustering under trees, apparehensively peering up through the branches. They beckoned me into hiding. "Raid!" they whispered. I listened but could hear no engines. "There's a raid on now at the city." Where we were, in a hollow of the hills, sight and sound from that direction were cut off. I waited for a time, then as there was no further sign and people were moving again, I went on. Somewhere I took a wrong turn and came out on the Kialing side of the peninsula. The city came into view, overhung with a pall of smoke. I kept on. It was afternoon; with each hour the heat and dust grew worse. I was very thirsty. Presently in the outskirts I began to see ruins where high explosive and incendiary bombs had fallen. The wreckage caused by a demolition bomb is like a carelessly built crow's nest – shattered timbers scattered crisscross about a cup-shaped crater. Where fires started by incendiary bombs have swept whole blocks, great bare walls tower dangerously, their bricks calcined and crumbling, above heaped broken tile and charred debris.

I went on and on. About three in the afternoon I came to the Y.W.C.A., where friends of mine lived. The gate swung open.

I walked in and down the flight of steps from the street level to the garden. The whole place was deserted. The door yielded when I turned the kob. In the hallway I called, but no one answered. I roamed through the rooms and found a cupful of water in a thermos bottle, which I drank. My thirst was unsatisfied. In a lavatory I found a pitcher with a little water, unfit for drinking, since it had not been boiled, and I washed my face clean of the sweat and caked dust. There was nothing to eat, though I searched everywhere. On my way out I encountered a sleepy, surly gatekeeper, who emerged from his room to eye me suspiciously. I asked him for something to drink, but he jerked his head moodily and did not answer.

I went on. I had been hours on the way. Pao's overcoat became very heavy; my arms ached with the weight of it, though I shifted it from one arm to the other. My throat was raw with the rasping irritation of smoke, cinders, and dust in the air, and my eyes stung. Fires were still burning. I made a detour around them. The water-mains were wrecked; firemen were fighting the blaze with bucketfuls of water carried up the hundreds of steps from the rivers. I met rescue squads, white aprons over their khaki uniforms, masks of surgical gauze covering their mouths and noses. Electricians in blue overalls were busy untangling the snarl of wires in the streets. I stepped over wreckage of telephone poles, crunched through a litter of broken tiles, walked through silent streets of barred and boarded-up shops, unbombed but deserted, and came at last to the bank, where I let myself in with Second Brother's pass-key.

Inside it was cooler; the motionless air smelled of night, shut in by closed doors and windows. The main office was vast and empty. I tip-toed on the polished marble floor, half afraid of the sound of my own footsteps. Nobody. I was the first to return. I wandered about the offices looking for water. In a private bathroom adjoining the magnificent office of the director I found a jug half full. Boiled or not, I drank it. Then I discovered there was water still in the pipes; the tap ran when I turned it on! Forthwith I stripped and washed myself from head to foot. It was marvellous! I had known nothing so wonderful since the stolen bath on the train journey to Kweilin. I shook the loose dust from my *shan*. I put my underclothes in the basin and scrubbed them, wrung them out, waved them in the air half dry, and put them on. When I had dressed and combed my hair I felt refreshed and ready to start out again upon my errand.

The telegraph office was two blocks away. It had not been

bombed. But it was impossible to get to the door for the people gathered before it, clamouring to send messages to relatives and friends. I waited on the fringes of the crowd for some time; it would be hours before all would be attended to. It was already dusk. Presently a notice was posted in the window: "No more telegrams accepted today. Come tomorrow morning to Huang Chia Ya Kou. The office is being moved." One learns fatalism.

The crowd melted away and suddenly I was alone again, in a twilight tinged with a smoky, smouldering glow. I hurried home to the bank through the unlighted streets. I thought of supper, but there was no eating place open. It did not matter, for I was not really hungry. But I wavered as I walked, drunk with weariness, unable to hold my course straight. Food might clear this dizzy faintness. I thought I was having hallucinations when, approaching the bank, I saw a small wandering glimmer behind the windows, but when I went in I found the policeman had come back and one or two servants. It was their *chin-yu* lamp I had seen. They had eaten their supper; there was nothing left for me, but they brought me a pot of tea. They spread their quilts in the main office. I groped my way to the reception-room, where I established myself on the huge, plush-covered couch. It was very soft and very wide, but unfortunately infested with bedbugs. However, by the time I discovered this it was too late to do anything about it. I was too far spent to look for another place to sleep.

I spread Pao's overcoat for a cover. It smelled of dust and faintly of camphor, but it kept a slight, indefinable scent of Pao. I sniffed it as a dog would, and it was good. I rubbed my hand over the rough wool; it was like touching Pao a little, and I fell to sobbing. I had saved nothing else but the coat. I cried when I thought of our marriage certificates burned, and the watch Pao had given me, the little Bible with my name and the date of my wedding written on the flyleaf ... then I caught myself between one sob and the next, decided I was foolish to weep over anything since I was so supremely lucky to be alive, and so fell asleep.

In the morning hunger woke me early. The bank servants still slept in their quilts; the policeman was gone. It was too early for the telegraph office to be open in its new quarters, but I started out on foot, intending to pick up a breakfast on the way. There were workmen busy clearing wreckage, but no one else was abroad in the streets. No shops were open. I climbed over heaps of rubble, skirted bomb craters and slowly eddying pools where the water-mains had burst. The bloated bodies of drowned rats drifted and circled in the pools.

In a street of closed and eyeless houses stretching in an unbroken succession of tightly boarded fronts I came upon an old man sitting on the pavement at a trestle table, such as is used to display small wares for sale in front of shops of the poorer sort. He was smoking a slim bamboo pipe about three feet long, sipping tea and eating *ko-kuei* – round cakes of unleavened bread baked on a griddle. Behind him, one or two boards of the shop front had been taken down, and through this cleft emerged two younger men and several children, with more tea and *ko-kuei*. They sat down and began to eat their breakfast. I paused and smiled. "Could you spare me a little tea and something to eat? I cannot find a shop open."

The old man was on his feet at once, bowing, smiling. "Of course, of course!" They brought out a little wooden stool for me. The old man rinsed a cup and filled it, offering it to me with both hands, ceremoniously. A woman came from the house with more cakes. The *ko-kuei* were warm and crusty, though tough; I ate two and drank the tea. They asked no questions; they accepted me as their guest, pressing me to eat more, to have another cup of tea, to take one or two cakes with me. There was no talk of payment. They shared with me what they had with gentleness and courtesy, and when I thanked them and went away, we bowed to each other many times. They were of the coolie class, the men naked to the waist, with faded cotton drawers girded about their loins, their feet bare in straw sandals. But their hospitality was princely.

Huang Chia Ya Kou was a long distance away and I was still very tired. When I had covered a third of the distance I squandered six dollars on a sedan chair to take me there. Fares were exorbitant and there was no bargaining, transportation was so scarce. There was a crowd of people ahead of me at the telegraph office. I waited there three hours to send two messages, one to Third Uncle in Chengtu, telling him that Second Brother and I were safe but the house was burned down, and one to Pao: "Safe. Unhurt. Going to Chengtu. Don't worry. Suyin." I sighed with relief as I handed in the telegram and paid for it. That would set at rest Pao's anxiety for me. I thought of the words flashing along the wires. By tonight, at the latest, he would know. . . . It was twenty-seven days later that my telegram was delivered to Pao. . . .

On my return I found that Second Brother and two or three other employees of the bank were back. A truck was to take them out to Tar Er Woh about seven o'clock in the evening. Every one was very apprehensive of night raids during the season of the full moon. They urged me to go with them, but I preferred the lofty lonely halls of the bank to the clatter and congestion at Ta Er Woh. By evening a few eating places were open, lighted like the shops of a village with little *chin-yu* lamps and white paper lanterns. Boiling water and tea were available, and pedlars with portable charcoal stoves went about, rattling spoon and bowl together in token of *mien* for sale. In the hour before moonrise we went out for supper, carrying torches of twisted bamboo withes, yard-long pieces of old boat-towing rope, which burn with a clear, bright flame.

When the others had left for Ta Er Woh I drained the last of the water from the taps in the director's private bathroom and bathed, then in the darkness sought the reception-room and my velvet couch. But as I sat down upon it there was a muffled grunt, an explosion of profanity, and something heaved under me. I leaped up, startled at the contact with bare, sweaty flesh, and fled without a word. Evidently the night watchman responsible for the bed-bugs in the couch had come back to his accustomed lordly comfort. I did not argue the rights of occupation with him. I climbed to the girl employees' dormitory, which was a penthouse on the roof. Second Brother had left keys with me. I entered and by the beams of the new-risen moon through the windows looked about for a place to sleep. Most of the beds of woven coir rope were bare, but I found one covered with a mat and took it. It was less luxurious than the velvet couch with its deep springs, but it proved to be free of vermin.

It was the fifteenth of May. Over the stricken city, unlighted except for the dull redness of a few fires still smouldering, the full moon swung low, round and perfect as a pearl. In villages and little market towns all over Free China people would be rejoicing in the spring moonlight, resting in the cool of evening at their thresholds, lighting a few sticks of incense and two red candles at each door. They had not learned to dread the full moon. . . .

There came a far-off, insistent, confused clamour, as of gongs and rattles. I sprang up – *ching-pao*? If the sirens were out of order, any inexplicable sound might be a raid warning. I went out on the roof to see, to listen. The dim rumour of drums and gongs came from every direction, intermittent, receding, then nearer and then more distant. Looking up I saw that the round mirror of the moon was cut by a notch, a clean curved bite at one edge – eclipse. The dog in the sky was nibbling at the moon and everywhere people beat upon wash-basins and kettles and made a *click-clack* with wooden sticks to frighten him away. I watched the shadow slide across the moon's rim, until the silver disk was restored and the city lay silent in its white radiance. The moon was saved. If all threat from the sky were so easily dispersed!

Next day Second Brother and I went to the place where our house had been. The whole district was devastated, entirely destroyed by fire, a wilderness of dust and debris, oven-hot, with here and there a smouldering of fire and smoke, or a thread of steam curling into the air where broken water-mains leaked among the scorching stones and brick. Streets still blocked with wreckage were hot under our feet. Clean-up squads of soldiers and Red Cross men and Boy Scouts were at work, their feet bound in straw for protection, their mouths masked with gauze, prising up the stones, pouring water upon the embers, extracting "things" from under the ruins. I call them "things" for they were not like anything that once had life and human form. Shrunken to half normal size, stiff, dark red-brown or black, limbs reduced to charred bone, they were laid out in a row on the pavement. Foreign newspapermen were climbing over the hot ruins in their good leather boots.

Our own house was identifiable only by location and ground plan. The courtyards, the squared pattern of foundation stones that marked the rooms, all looked strangely small in the bright sunlight. A twisted jumble of iron rods was all that was left of my uncle's fine foreign spring bed, and a fused greenish lump of glass stuck with cinders all that remained of his glass-topped desk. Miraculously, the two big Soochow fish-bowls in the upper court were without a crack; the fish in them must have been boiled alive. In a litter of broken tile where Third Uncle's study had been, a row of books stood, seemingly intact – but at a touch they fell into impalpable ash and blew away in a whiff of warm breeze. Protected by the heavy bookcase, they must have burned last, after the whole house had collapsed about them. In the servants' court where Lao Li and I had dug among the crashed timbers there was nothing but a scattering of broken tile. The fire had burned it clean.

And now on the third day a wonderful thing happened – Chungking began to live again. This resurrection of a city was an amazing thing to witness. Suddenly the hush of stunned horror was broken; voices quickened, sounding clear and cheerful in the streets; there was laughter again. Shops reopened with flaunting signs: "Business as usual"; "Resist to the last!"; "The more we are bombed, the more we are strong to endure"; "Fresh eggs, direct from Tokyo" – this last with a crude sketch of a plane shedding bombs, for by a play on the word, *tan* may mean either eggs or bombs in my province. People came back. The bank employees returned and decided to open for business from seven to ten in the morning, leaving for Ta Er Woh by truck around the *ching-pao* hour and continuing the routine bookkeeping there. By the time the bank director arrived to take charge (he had been out of the city the day of the bombing) everything had been settled.

About four in the afternoon that day the street resounded with the cries of newsboys, running excitedly to distribute a one-sheet tabloid, almost all headlines. It was the first issue of Chungking's composite newspaper, produced by an amalgamation of four or five leading dailies whose offices had been bombed out of existence. They had pooled what could be salvaged of type and presses and brought out this single sheet. The newsboys thrust it into the hands of passers-by and ran on shouting, scarcely pausing for payment, so eager were they to make known the miracle of the rebirth of a newspaper.

Evacuation was in full swing, not the unconsidered, precipitate flight of that first night, but a steady exodus of thousands of families. The government had urged it for months, against a wall of indifference. Now, to speed removal to the country, it commandeered trucks and buses and private cars and put them at the disposal of the poor and those who had lost everything. The Generalissimo's own car made many trips a day, filled with ragged, destitute refugees. Relief stations were established where the victims of disaster might receive food. Plans were being made for rebuilding, with wide fire lanes left open to limit the extent of incendiary fires. In every mind was the thought, "Next time." There was no more false security, but a sober preparation for things to come.

That night Second Brother and several others of the men employees had volunteered to remain on duty at the bank, but all the girls had gone to Ta Er Woh. I was alone in the penthouse. I looked out over the city, all silent and dark. Occasionally someone passed in the street, carrying a blazing torch. The moon rose, so huge, so white, so brilliantly revealing, to light Japanese planes over the mountains into Szechwan. Between the pale moonlit rivers Chungking was a skeleton city with all fires burnt out, a clearly marked, dark target. I looked at the moon and hated it, that unwavering, white, betraying floodlight. I could believe, then, it was a barren fragment flung off into space, without life, without light of its own, mechanically reflecting the sun. All that poets and lovers had seen in it was illusion. It was no longer the moon I had loved, the golden moon of Nanyu, the silver, misty moon of Pihsien. . . .

It was that night we had our first night *ching-pao*. We had both first and second alarms, though the planes must have turned aside at the last moment, for they did not bomb the city. The sound of the sirens by night is of a strange quality; the alarm by day is a matter-of-fact thing in comparison. Sometime past midnight I awoke out of sleep suddenly, rigid, my whole body tense and listening. An ominous crescendo – the alarm! My heart throbbing wildly, I sprang up from bed. While I dressed I told myself, "It's only the *kung-hsi*. There's plenty of time. If the planes do come, it's half an hour – an hour yet. Even after the *ching-chi* there's time." But my hands trembled, my heart drummed in my chest, and my mouth was dry with unreasoning fear. Not fear of the planes coming, but, like the fear of thunder, an instinctive reaction to the sound itself. This sound was like a palpable substance; it had weight and pressure; I breathed it in with my breath. Pervasive, it came from every point of the compass at once. Higher, shriller, an aching intensity of panic. Then a growing murmur – voices, cries – footsteps and voices in the streets – haste, fear – all blending to the roar of rushing water – and above the torrent the sirens like great fountains, still spouting frenzy toward the indifferent moon. . . . When I went down I found the stairways, the halls, packed solid with people thronged in from the streets. . . .

Chungking was still a city of tragedy, though no longer bound in an enchantment of despair. Excavation continued. In the clean-up more and more dead came to light. The whole city smelled of burning and ashes and, mixed with that, the sour, penetrating reek of decay. Where demolition bombs alone had fallen, the bodies of those killed by blast and falling walls, buried for days in the wreckage, were horribly decomposed when unconvered and smelled far worse than those who had been burned to death. On the pavement in front of the bank, one morning, we found nine of them laid out in a row, rolled in padded quilts and giving off a sickening stench. A truck came for them presently. It was loaded high with rough board coffins, some empty, others – for we could see – already filled. The covers were not nailed down; some had slipped half off. The bodies on the pavement were picked up and crammed into the coffins. The truck drove away, the coffins bouncing up and down and clanking against each other.

The official estimate of deaths was placed between six and eight thousand. No one knew, actually, how many died. Constantly one hears in conversation still, "My mother – my child – my wife – lost in the May fourth bombing." Families separated at the time of the raid or in the panic afterwards were seeking for each other. Communications were destroyed. Those who had fled the city were afraid to venture back because of the rumours of further bombing. Everywhere questionings: "Were they killed? Are they alive? Have you seen them?" The newspaper carried lists of the missing. Where brick walls were left standing in streets of ruins, people gathered to read the names posted, dead or missing. Street-criers were paid to go about beating upon gongs and calling the names of lost children: "Fu Tseng-pao, three years old, answers to his name; Liu Mai-mai, two years old, wears silver locket and chain with name. . . ." I suppose few of these children were ever found – tiny, unidentifiable bodies dumped into a common grave, or not even that much left. Demolition bombs making a direct hit leave nothing to bury. The parents waiting day after day, hope ebbing. . . .

One week . . . seven days which shaped a new pattern of life. I could hardly remember any other existence. Or I could remember it only as a book I had read, telling of customs and scenes remote from my own experience. So when I came back to Chengtu, one week after the bombing, it was less a return than it was arrival at some strange and foreign place. It required days to tie together the broken thread of continuity, to place in perspective the events of that wild interlude. Riding through the streets of Chengtu in a rickshaw, I could have cried with happiness to see a city so beautifully *whole*! The shops which lined the broad streets were so decently roofed, so neat with walls and windows. And the streets themselves so clean of rubble, unbroken by craters. A city bombed is untidy, with its littered wreckage; a house half shattered is like a mutilated body, pitiful and almost obscene in its revealing disarrangement. There is the greater tragedy of death and suffering, but for myself – perhaps because I am a woman – the filthy disorder of war's destruction, only a little less than its cruelty, arraigns it.

210

At home Third Aunt welcomed me with tears and questioned me and wept again at each new detail of my story, though I think it was in sympathy and joy, not in regret for any loss of possessions. Third Uncle laughed when I told them everything and said, "Well, I always declared that was a fine table! You don't get such wood these days." He was quite indifferent to the loss of his house, making an outward gesture of the hands as though tossing away a thing of no value and saying, "*Suan-la!*" which means "That's that!" But he was troubled over Lao Tseng's death. Lao Tseng had been a servant in the household many years; he was one of the family. Third Uncle decided to have Second Brother burn candles and brown-paper money at the site to comfort his spirit. He also planned to make provision for his family.

No letter yet from Pao. . . . Surely he had received my message and the several letters I had written to him afterward, telling more fully of my escape. If I had guessed or even faintly imagined that Pao had heard nothing from me I could not have slept for anxiety, knowing his intense and impetuous temperament.

Pao at the north-west front had heard the first news a day or two after cables had carried it to Europe and America. Word-of-mouth rumour – "There's been a bad bombing of Chungking." No details. The dissemination of news in China, even in peacetime, is attended with inconceivable difficulties. Reports are distorted by all kinds of rumour. In war-time, there in the front lines, the troops lived a daily routine preoccupied with immediate danger. What went on in another province did not concern them. Someone had seen military dispatches or a bulletin and idly passed the word along – "There's been a bad bombing at Chungking."

Well, there were bombings reported every few days. Slight, severe – the degree was as report might make it. At first Pao thought little of it. Then details began to filter through: the city was in flames; whole sections were levelled to the ground. Immediately Pao tried to put through a long-distance call from the nearest town that evening when he went off duty. Telephone service to Chungking was interrupted, they told him. He then sent me a wire; of course I never received it.

Further particulars, more disquieting, were coming in. Pao learned that the number of dead ran into thousands. In the day since the bombing he had had no word from me. With growing apprehension he wired to the General Staff to send someone to my uncle's house to investigate. Military dispatches had right of way over private messages on the slender line of communications. The wire went through promptly and a brother officer was sent to the address Pao gave. He found the place in the midst of acres of ruins. He found a bomb crater within the outline of the walls of our house. What was he to think but that I was dead? He made inquiries and people told him of the death of a young woman named Chen (and my uncle's name was Chen), the wife of an army doctor who was at the front. She and her new-born child had been burned to death in the house next door to ours; the bodies were recovered and buried. As he got the story, garbled in the telling, Pao's friend supposed it was I who had been killed. He returned to headquarters with the report of my death and wired Pao: "In May fourth bombing your house demolished and burned. Direct hit. No trace of your wife. Making further investigations."

There was only one thing Pao could think when he received that message, reading between the tactfully phrased lines, as it was intended he should. I was dead. "Direct hit. No trace. . . ." Only if they believed me dead would they dare to send such a telegram to him. Dazed, Pao stared at the pencilled scrawl of characters on the telegraph form. Thinking nothing, feeling nothing for the moment . . . just reading the words over, shaping them with his lips . . . waiting for the rush of pain which, when it came, would storm the very centres of reason. . . .

This is the supposedly impassive and unemotional Chinese. Pao made a resolve, the one firm thing in all the whirling chaos of agony in his mind. He would go to Chungking and find me – find my body, find where I was buried. After he had found me he would kill himself. He made this bargain with fate, that he would not kill himself until he had made certain of my death. But when he had seen for himself and there was no doubt or hope left, then he would refuse to live. . . .

He went to his superior officers and demanded leave. If they had not granted it he would have gone without leave. They were stern men, their minds bounded by duty and discipline. They may have thought it weakness in Pao that he showed his feelings for me so frankly. But they let him go, for he was nearly insane.

He reached Sian, but there was no transportation farther. There were no planes, no buses. He learned of an army truck leaving for Chungking in two days – perhaps three days. It was the earliest chance. For those two days Pao roamed Sian in a torment of restlessness. Nothing that had gone before could equal the agony of that delay. The anaesthetic of the first shock had worn off. He was awake, conscious of each moment's suffering under the torture of his vivid imagination. The uncertainty – not to know! Almost he could have borne it better if he had final proof that I was dead.

He wired my uncle in Chengtu for more news, for proof – a telegram which we received twenty-three days later. Military headquarters in Sian had a second message sent for him through official channels, asking the General Staff to make further search for me. He paced the streets, he neither ate nor slept. Pao, the agnostic, who dimisses all talk of god as idle conjecture – Pao went from temple to church, praying at every shrine one prayer: "Let her be still alive! Or let me only know!" He lit white tapers before the Virgin Mary; he burned red incense before Kuanyin, the benign, the goddess of mercy. He paid the grey-robed Buddhist priests to perform the divination of the rods cast down before the lotus throne, and when they gave him a happy augury pressed more money upon them and went away with the same hot burning of fear in his breast, knowing the rite as superstition. He knelt in a little white-washed Protestant chapel and read from a scroll there – "Deliver us from evil," and added – "Deliver her. . . ."

And for a week and more I had been in Chengtu. Safe. . . . It was 20th May – sixteen days since the bombing. Almost to the hour. I was at the far end of the garden, sitting with my hands in my lap, looking up at the translucence of bamboo leaves in the yellow evening sunlight. I heard the distant, sharp, repeated. "*Zing-ng-ng!*" of the telephone bell, and knowing Third Aunt was alone in the house I went to the rescue. She had taken down the receiver and, looking very frightened as usual, was shrieking, "*Wei! Wei!* Who? Yes, she is here. *Wei!*" I took the receiver from her hand. There was a crackle as of static in my ear, then Pao's voice – very excited, angry, berating the telephone operator for cutting the connection.

"*Pao! Pao!*" I gasped.

"*Suyin!*" – and I knew his face was tense as I had never seen it, his voice was so choked, his words such a torrent, half incoherent. "It's you! Your voice – you! Suyin, I'm leaving Sian tomorrow morning – I have a place on a truck. I'm throwing up this job – resigning my commission. I won't be away from you. We belong together! Suyin – we'll go away, quietly, to the country, to the mountains, some place where there's no bombing. We'll be happy –"

But I couldn't let him say this; it was as if I put a finger on

213

his lips. "Pao — wait. I'm safe; I'm quite all right. Why, it was nothing — nothing at all. I was safe at the bank. All the time you've been worrying, I was at the bank, or here in Chengtu. Safe. . . . And I wired you the next day —"

I could not let him forswear his loyalty. It was his agony speaking, I knew, the week of terrible uncertainty he had been through, not Pao's self. After a few days, if he remembered what he had said in this wild outburst, he would retract his words. For, first of all, Pao is a soldier and it is necessary for him to do the things a soldier does. He would not be happy otherwise, for his dream is yet young and he needs to feel he is doing what is right, giving himself in this war of resistance. It was for this he was shaped and trained. Not that he would be blamed or censured if he gave up. He could quietly resign; my uncle would find him a job and nobody would think the worse of him. Gentlemen and the sons of gentlemen in China are not expected to risk their lives in war. They are too valuable. That kind of coarse work is better done by the humbler sort. And so the sturdy peasants march away to die, while the sons of moneyed families attend the university, idle in pleasant gardens, read books, and prepare for careers in finance, medicine, law. . . .

No, we should not be criticized if Pao left the army, if we went away together to happiness and safety. But our own judgment would condemn us. There is a debt we more fortunate ones owe to the vast, uncomplaining, sustaining masses of China, who die for us. In payment of that debt I am the servant of any coolie woman in childbirth. And Pao, in recognition of that debt, must go back to the lines, to join the peasant soldiers, to be one with them.

I had no words to tell Pao my meaning. "You must go back," I said. "Now that you know I am safe, it will disgrace you with your superior officers if you do not return to the front. I have faced it for you that I must let you go into danger, to risk your life. You must face the possibility for me. Duty . . . honour . . obedience. . . ." All the timeless arguments.

I may have thought once of the word "heroism" and the word "sacrifice" and thrilled to them. But now I think only of endurance. One must live through it all — bombing, sickness, hunger and thirst, babies, anxiety, discomfort. With life there can be no bargaining, only acceptance. And so I must let Pao, with his honesty and cleanness as a shield protecting him, go from me again when I might have held him. Knowing that all war is hateful, stupid, wasteful, and ugly, detesting the violence, the pitiful, unnecessary bloodshed, I cannot but accept that Pao should have a part in it. In ten, in fifteen years, I think, he will find another way of service, upbuilding, productive. But now there is no choice.

It is deep evening now, almost two years since that evening I sent Pao back to his work. Our poets have said: "Today passes and although there is another day, it is not today. Next year is no longer this year. Our days are daily shortened." Pao and I, who are so keenly aware of the onward rushing of life into the abyss of nothingness, the cataract of time – we flung away one year of beauty and youth and love together. We might have had that year and all the future, too. There was no command upon us we could not have refused; only this inner compulsion, this sense of debt. We might have had the year together, but we did not. I do not think we were wrong.

CHAPTER TWELVE

CHUNGKING SUMMER

And the year was past.... In the early summer of 1940 Pao was transferred back to staff duty in Chungking. I had hoped to join him in the north-west, that stern land of new opportunity, that ancient desert home of our race. When Pao wrote of it, I could see and feel it, and longed to know it with him. He told of riding the roads which wound among eroded loess hills, cones of dust springing from under his horse's hoofs to spin along with animate, malignant existence of their own; whirling up into his face; subsiding into nothingness again. He told of lonely desert towns, half buried among the sand drifts, their massive ramparts carved by time and the wind. He wrote of hospitals and industries and a military academy of ten thousand cadets, evacuated from occupied territory to Shensi and housed in communities in caves dug into the hillsides. He wrote of the bitter northern winter and the Japanese troops camped on the far side of the Yellow River, waiting for ice to bridge it for them. Bearded, stocky, brown-faced men; through his binoculars he could see them clearly.

He told of a night of intense white moonlight at the foot of a range of mountains when he was wakened by a purring and snarling as of an enormous demon cat in the sky, leaping above the barren hills. "I went out to look. I saw them, black crosses on the fierce white moonlight, moving in regular formation, going north-westwards. I counted them. A hundred. Three hours later they passed over again, returning, their motors growling under the moon as though still unsatisfied. Next day I heard Lanchow had been bombed."

He wrote again: "Come to me here, Suyin! You will love this country. We shall wear furs, sleep on stone *kangs,* ride the stubborn-muzzled Mongol ponies. We shall know breathless horizons. Here in the heart of Asia, sand and wind will forge our spirits. This is the land of youth, where we can work and see our work grow...."

For the whole north-west, the Kuomintang area where Pao was, as well as the Communist region around Yenan, was awake with new life. Here, as in Kwangsi, there was a contagion of democracy and progress. Perhaps that is the most important function of the Communists – to stir up other more conservative organizations to vigorous reforms and new projects. Pao wrote of a public-health service newly launched in Lanchow, and promised he could find work for me there. If his transfer had not come just then, I should have gone.

For a little while after my return to Chengtu the pampering kindness of the Big Family, the amusements, the idleness, were exactly what I needed. But in a short time, as before, this purposeless existence palled. When Third Aunt and most of the household moved to Pihsien in anticipation of bombings in Chengtu, I did not go with them. I took up work in a maternity clinic of the public-health service. There is a kind of compensation, when so much killing is going on, in helping to bring life into being.

Many times we performed deliveries in homes little better than the shed at Santang where I had my first case in China. But our equipment was better. We carried with us everything needed to make a little island of white cleanliness in the midst of squalor and filth. Many nights we watched in dark hovels by the minute quarter-candle-power glimmer of a pith-wick lamp, bitten by fleas, mosquitoes, and worse. Fortunately there is no bubonic plague in Szechwan, but I never climbed on to a verminous bed to administer an anaesthetic but that I wondered about body lice and typhus.

Obstetrics is ninety per cent waiting and ten per cent tumultuous drama. Waiting hour after hour, squatting on a low bamboo chair with my arms folded on my knees and my forehead resting on my arms, half asleep, half conscious of the intermittent, subdued moaning of my patient, the rustling of rats, the snores of the men of the household on the other side of a mat partition. Then – action! My assistant flames the basins, standing like the priestess of some occult rite, turning and turning in her hands the vessel of blue alcohol flames. Boiling water and harsh scrubbing brushes and the strong smell of lysol. Extra candles are lighted and the women of the household pressed into service as light bearers to bring the illumination where I need it. To them I must seem very strange and rather frightening in my close white cap and long sterilized white gown, gauze masking the lower part of my face, my hands grotesquely unnatural in brown rubber gloves.

There is, after all, little one does in a normal case but help to ease the pain a little, preserve cleanliness, protect against serious lacerations and infection. For the rest we merely encourage the suffering woman to put forth her strength. "Once more! A deep

217

breath. A little more and the baby will be here." Chinese women almost never scream in labour; it would be unseemly. So there is no sound but a grinding groan of supreme effort, a panting of exhaustion. And suddenly it is over. Triumphantly I hold up the child by its feet, clean its throat with a gloved finger and pat it on the back until the little red face wrinkles, the tiny hands clutch wildly, and the small chest expands to release a healthy bawl of protest. Every one laughs, the mother as well. "Is it a boy or girl? . . . Well, a girl's all right, too."

Sudden emergencies arose. There is nothing more terrifying, nothing more satisfying when the crisis is safely past and one knows beyond doubt that a life is saved that would have been lost. Stemming the furious flow of a post-partum haemorrhage, resuscitating a stillborn baby – these things a midwife must know how to do, for there is no time to call a doctor. I do not think I could have endured the year apart from Pao if it had not been for the absorbing interest, the deep reward, of my work.

The long year was past. Pao and I had been apart from each other for so long, life together seemed a distant hope, almost impossible of achievement. Then, suddenly, Pao's transfer to Chungking brought that hope within reach. As soon as he found lodgings I was to join him. I resigned my job and put in my application for a place on a plane – the earliest date two weeks to wait. But it would take as long as that to find a house.

Chungking was being bombed almost daily. Chungking was destroyed and rebuilt, smashed and the fragments put together again repeatedly in those months, with equal stubbornness on both sides. The Japanese returned to the attack persistently; they seemed to have an obsession in regard to Chungking; it was as though the continued existence of life upon that rocky spur between the rivers was an insult to their might. And for their part, the people of Chungking developed a routine of endurance. Five hundred thousand lived there still, though the city had been reduced to a quarter of its boom population. Air raids were an accepted element of their life; they stoically adapted themselves to the terror and discomfort and refused to abandon their city. If it was the intention of the Japanese to break their spirit with terrorism, their non-success was complete. With each new bombing the people set themselves the more stubbornly to resist to the last.

"But it is unchanged!" I said, unbelievingly, at first sight of Chungking from the approaching plane. There it stood as I had seen it first, brick walls and towering buildings, tier upon tier, rising above the rivers, where wide sand beaches were left bare by low water. It was only as we circled to a landing, coming low over the city, that the ravages of fire and of explosive bombs could be seen – the gaps in continuity, the roofless walls with empty window holes, standing like stage scenery, giving the illusion of solidity.

We swooped down upon the air-field. As we landed with a light jolt and then rolled to a stop I pressed both hands against the window-pane and searched with my eyes among the small crowd of people waiting to greet the passengers. Pao was not there. . . . No slender figure in khaki, taut with impatience. I had telegraphed him, but he was not there. I was crushed with misery. It felt as though a heavy hand pressed down upon my heart. We alighted from the plane and crossed the sand to the inspection shed, where our baggage was to be examined. Though it was only nine o'clock in the morning, the sun blazed down upon the shadowless sand with the ardour of noon; the heat and brilliance made a shimmering vibration in the air. The sand burned through the thin soles of my slippers. For the dazzle and my own unhappiness, I could not lift my eyes to look up at the cliffs of Chungking.

As they examined our luggage the inspectors would glance up occasionally at the fiercely blue-white sky and mutter, "There's going to be a *ching-pao*." And they would look about at the hill-tops, anxiously. For the *kung-hsi* siren was no longer the first signal. It was too startling, coming suddenly out of silence, unexpected. So poles had been erected on the hill-tops, and at the first intimation of a raid big red balls were hoisted into sight for a preliminary warning. When I had waited half an hour, hoping Pao might come, there was a sudden outburst of voices, almost with an accent of relief. "The red balls are up!" It was no use waiting longer. Perhaps Pao had never received my telegram. I bargained for a *hua-kan* and started for the house.

Scarcely were we up the cliff when the *kung-hsi* sounded. My bearers quickened their pace, almost galloping with me through the crowds. But the distance was too far. We could not make it. The house Pao had found for us was beyond the walls of the old city, up the peninsula on the Kialing side. "We'll have to take shelter in a public shelter," the carriers said. "After the *ching-chi* the police allow nobody on the streets."

In Chungking the public shelters are all at the foot of the hills; they consist of ramifying tunnels, seven or eight feet wide, wet, dark, and suffocating. The walls drip moisture; the floor is mud underfoot; there are no seats. People stand hour after hour, packed together; a few bring stools or folding chairs. After half an hour the stench is fearful. The only conveniences provided are one or two open buckets outside the entrance for the men. The children relieve themselves like little animals. It was in such a shelter I spent that first day from ten in the morning to four in the afternoon – six hours.

The carriers put down the *hau-kan* at the base of a forty-foot ridge, and we pushed into the mouth of the cave. At this outlet the crowd was most dense; striving for fresh air themselves, they cut off air for those within, except for an inadequate supply drawn through ventilating chimneys by hand-power revolving fans. Jostled about, I maintained my place as near the outlet as possible. Few women made the effort. Around me were coolies, most of them stripped to the waist and sweating in the stagnant heat. At best I shrink from physical contact – it is one of the reasons I avoid crowds. At this forced and intimate contact with bare, wet flesh, with rank-smelling bodies – their sweat-soaked clothing – I felt nauseated and faint. It did not help to reflect upon my democratic principles.

We heard the drone of planes and distant detonations. Between relays of the attack we ventured out for a breath of air, or for other purposes. The sun overhead was merciless. There was just one small tree within our range, and its meagre shade was full of coolies, fanning and smoking, cheerfully inured to the daily ordeal. "Just *shua* a while; it will soon be over," I heard one say. I risked sunstroke on the bare hillside. If I had stayed inside the shelter I should have fainted. At last the siren sounded the all-clear and people streamed out of the shelter. My carriers, rested – actually rested! – by the long hours of inactivity, picked up the *hua-kan* and with loud whoops of joy carried me to my destination. I lay back exhausted and admired their high spirits.

The house which was to be my home was in a district half country, where streets straggled out among fields and wound among hills, at whose bases gaped the dark mouths of shelters. My carriers left the paved high road, went down many steps, then climbed a small pyramidal hill, on the exact summit of which stood my house. It was a battered two-story building, painted soot-black, as are so many houses in Chungking, with some idea of invisibility. But this, situated on the point of the hill, with cornfields all around it and no trees for shelter, could hardly have been more conspicuous. My carriers set me down at the gate. I pushed it open and stepped into a narrow courtyard littered with broken tiles and debris. An amah came out on the upper veranda and poured an apronful of plaster bits and rubbish into the court. I jumped back under the gate roof to escape the shower. She leaned over the rail and asked, "Were you looking for someone?"

"My name is Tang," I said. "I think I live here."

A thin, friendly woman in black, with a child hanging at her breast, came to the railing. "Do come up, Tang Tai-tai. You live upstairs with us. Our name is Wen. We were expecting you, but did not know which day. Excuse the litter; we were bombed today and aren't cleaned up yet. It was quite a small bomb, so there is still most of the house left. But the kitchen is smashed, as well as your back room."

I climbed the rickety stairs to the veranda. Wen Tai-tai met me, smiling graciously, and led me to my rooms. Downstairs the house was locked and shuttered. The absentee landlord, who had moved to the country with his family, reserved those apartments – illegally, for the government had decreed that all unoccupied premises must be made available to tenants, the housing shortage was so acute. Upstairs there were three rooms on either side of a roofed open space. The two rear rooms on the left were ours. In the front room slept four of the Wen children. On the opposite side lived Wen Tai-tai with her husband and four more children and another family of five. The servants slept on the veranda and in the courtyard below.

Plaster was still falling from the ceilings; doors hung askew, wrenched from their hinges. The windows were blank holes framing the landscape; the glass and woodwork had long since disappeared. The rooms were very small and hot. To reach our apartment one went through the front room, occupied by the Wen children. In our back room two walls were gone and a large part of the ceiling. The tiles were blown off and one looked through to the sky. In our good room there were a table, a stool, a broken chair, and a cheap, narrow bed. The sheet was rumpled and not very clean; the mosquito net hung awry. On the table, strewn in the disarray typical of a man living alone, there were paper, shoes, a wash-basin, a pair of socks, a greasy lamp stuck with dead moths, a glass and toothbrush, and two soiled shirts. The place was eloquent of Pao's loneliness.

In a passion of pity and tenderness I fell to cleaning the room. Everything was covered with dust, broken tile, bits of plaster. I knelt and swept the rubbish together with my hands, gathering it into the skirt of my *shan* and carrying it out to the veranda to dump into the courtyard. I dusted, carried water, and washed the dirty clothes, rehung the mosquito net trimly, spread clean sheets on the bed, smooth and neat. Darkness came and I lit the *chin-yu* lamp, which I had wiped clean with an old newspaper. All the electric wires in the neighbourhood were down. I washed in a little basinful of water and changed my clothes, then took my lamp and went out on the veranda in quest of coolness. There was not the slightest breath of air. The night was as warm and stifling as the day: the lamp flame erect and unquivering in the stillness.

On the veranda Wen Tai-tai, unbuttoned, and her breasts bounteously distributed to two of the smallest children, was feeding a third with rice porridge. Cordially she beckoned me to share the simple supper of rice and one vegetable. "My husband does not come home until late. He is off duty at eight o'clock. Captain Tang should be here about the same time. I am sure he did not know you were arriving today."

The lights of Kiangpeh across the river glittered bravely; the north bank had not been bombed today. Stars were small and dull and few in the heat haze. Presently the gate creaked and Pao came into the courtyard below. The year was over. . . . I could see only a vague, dark figure, but I knew his step. I did not call to him. He came up the stairs and saw me. He paused in the darkness at the stairhead. Then he said, "Oh, hullo, there you are. . . I was expecting you any time now. . . . No, didn't get your telegram. . . . Sorry I didn't get off to meet you at the air-field." He came into the circle of light – Pao, thinner than I remembered him, his hair damp with sweat, his shirt wet and sticking to his lean body, his voice casual but his eyes blazing with suppressed excitement.

We paused a few moments for courtesy, then excused ourselves. I took up the lamp and we went into our room and shut the door. Pao and I were then in each other's arms, our happiness almost unbearable in its intensity. "Oh, Suyin!" Pao whispered. "To see you again! It's been so long – a year – more than a year without you. I could never go through it again. I've been only half alive, I've needed you so!"

And it was like discovering we had been doing without breathing for a long time, each to the other as necessary as air. . . . I wanted to *do* something for him! I ran and brought him warm water and fresh towels to wash away the heat and dust of the day. I got tea for him. "You've cleaned the house!" Pao said admiringly. I was so happy he had noticed. We sat side by side on the edge of the narrow bed and sipped tea. It was then the ceiling came down.

In our other room what remained of the ceiling, weighted down with tiles which had fallen through on to the thin laths, gave way of a sudden, and fell with a crash. Immediately the plaster partition between the two rooms buckled, cracked, and collapsed on to our table. The ceiling in this room then sagged down about a foot at one corner, separating from the walls, and through this gap poured in a cascade of tiles, dust, stones, and broken plaster. At the first ominous crack, Pao and I had jumped up and retreated to the door. We watched anxiously the swaying ceiling; in another moment we would have the sky for roof. But three corners held; the rumblings ceased, the dust settled.

The whole household – amahs, children, Wen Tai-tai and her husband, the other family on their side of the house – rushed in to see and exclaim. With the help of the resourceful Wen Hsien-sen, whom I admired at once and have never ceased to respect, a plan was made to support the ceiling. A detached door was found; since the house barely held together, such repair material was readily available. With four bamboo poles it was raised as a kind of platform or canopy in contact with the pendent part of the ceiling, thus pushing it up into place. When it was done, and everybody had been thanked and sundry bits of plaster removed from the eyes of helpers and onlookers, it was past ten o'clock. We bowed the last of our guests out of the room. The floor, table, and bed were still inches deep in debris. But we were too tired to attack it. We simply picked up the top sheet and slid it off to the floor and lay down to sleep. But there was no sleep that night. The temperature was well over ninety. We dozed restlessly, wet with perspiration, until in the hour after dawn there came a hint of freshness, a faint breeze blowing through the gaping holes in our rear walls. Then the sun rose and it was hot again.

Chungking summer.... In the early morning the sun comes over the horizon, glowing with baleful intensity, and heat gathers heavy in the air. The faint freshness of dawn stales and withers. Dust rises in the streets, already thronged with traffic. Banks are open, food shops crowded with people eating their "before-the-raid meal." People hasten to transact business before the alarm comes. They pause to look up at the surrounding hilltops, squinting against the unbearable light and shading their eyes. No red ball yet. But every one knows there will be a raid. Every one is waiting for the signal and the expectancy is almost worse than the moment when the whole city seems to shake with a shout – *"Ching-pao!"* The red ball is up.

Immediately there is orderly pandemonium. Noises are louder. Cars and buses, overloaded, shrieking their horns, rush toward the country. Private rickshaws clanging their gongs and handcarts piled with the scanty stocks of goods kept in the city mingle with the hordes of people on foot, burdened with their bundles, bound for the shelters. There is haste but no confusion. It is like an exciting play which has been performed so often it has lost meaning for the actors, though they go through their parts with the same motions each time. There is, of course, always the possibility that this time the play may have a different ending. . . .

The hours pass. We sit in the stifling damp, drenched with sweat, fanning, stirring up the foul air to no purpose. In the dim cave light faces are white, glistening with sweat. Babies lie in stupor in their mothers' arms, dead still as though anaesthetized. Listless, the older children sit hunched on the benches, drugged with exhaustion. Between attacks a few of us shake off the lethargy to go outside for air. Boys of the Three Principles Youth Corps and agents of the women's relief organizations go in and out, passing out aspirin for headaches, doling out a little lukewarm drinking water, encouraging the children with sweets, and bringing news – "Only three more batches of planes – the first twenty-seven the second fifty, the third . . ." They go from one shelter to another with news, medicine, sweets, and smiles.

Three o'clock. The last wave of the attack has come and gone. People come out of the shelters and stand around the entrances, waiting for the all-clear. Far off, a single siren shrills faintly; the sound is taken up by nearer sirens in chorus, and voices join in with loud shouts of relief, and the black mouths of the shelters disgorge surging crowds.

The shelter where I took refuge was a little better than the public caves. Admission was by ticket. It accommodated about two hundred. At the last moment twenty or thirty extra would rush in, for it was the law that after the *ching-chi* had sounded no one was to be refused. There were four rows of backless benches and the walls were panelled with wood planks against the dampness. There are a great many semi-private shelters of this type, owned by banks, institutions, companies, or the bureau of public safety. Some are better, some worse.

There is an extensive and well-equipped shelter of many corridors for the highest military officers and their attendant staffs. Here the Generalissimo retires during raids. He works at his desk until the planes are almost within hearing. Then, reluctantly, he lays down his papers and goes. At the far end of a corridor is a small room reserved for the highest-ranking generals. Here the Minister of War, in tightly buttoned uniform and very shiny boots, paces up and down restlessly. Other generals converse in low tones or look over papers. The Generalissimo sits erect and stiff on a hard wooden chair, his arms folded, his back six inches from the back of the chair. He is resting. He is never seen to relax, to slouch or cross his legs; not a muscle moves. Overhead, bombs crash. Others in the shelter start, glance upward. They open their mouths and some stop their ears. Not Chiang Kai-shek. His face wears an expression of curbed annoyance, as though he were trying not to listen to a boring speech. Staring straight before him, he sits motionless – resting.

Labour gangs in blue and khaki-clad conscript troops march past with picks and shovels and buckets. Fires are quickly brought under control if the water-mains in the region are still intact; not so quickly when there are only bucket lines to fight the blaze. Everything is organized. Shell-holes in the street are filled up within an hour. Rescue squads are at work amid the wreckage of demolition bombs, taking out the dead and injured; there are always a few who did not go to the caves. Sometimes shelters collapse under the shock of a direct hit and people are crushed or suffocated; then the labour gangs dig them out. Blue-overalled electrical repair men clear the tangle of wires, erect poles again. People return to their homes. Everything may be untouched, or there may be nothing left.

Shops reopen. Motor-cars return. Cheerful, unconcerned crowds throng the streets. Restaurants are full of people eating their "after-the-raid meal." It is dusk. No lights. People bring out the *chin-yu* lamps. Up on the poles, silhouetted against the amethyst evening sky, electricians work feverishly, twisting and splicing the wires, cutting out the bombed areas, connecting up the circuit. And suddenly the miracle happens – all the lights of the city go on together. "Ah-h-h!" from the crowds. It is like the sigh of a long wave of the surf, breaking on the coast and running down again into the sea. The city stands proudly above the rivers, like a ship majestic with all its lights ablaze, riding the ocean.

We adapt ourselves; perhaps we grow a little callous. After the hours underground we emerge avid for lights and pleasures.

In one street newly bombed that day the rescue squads will be removing corpses, and in the next street a well-dressed crowd, gay and eager, will be waiting for the opening of the cinema and admiring the posters advertising the more-than-life-size embraces of a pair of Hollywood lovers.

So from the lowest to the highest we lived two lives this second summer of bombing – one the dark underground existence of the shelters, the other life hasty and interrupted, fitted into the irregular schedule of raids. Before and after the almost daily retreat to the shelter I did the housework. Pao was gone from seven in the morning until eight at night. He took two meals at the office. I hardly knew whether I ate or not; it did not seem to matter, the weather was so hot. In the evening I cooked a supper which Pao dutifully ate. I had never cooked before. We both lost weight. It made Pao very unhappy for me to carry water and scrub floors, so I did the heavy work while he was not at home. We could not afford an amah.

In the stress of adaptation to the difficulties of life in Chungking I could not but admire the frictionless, easy ways of our neighbours, the Wen family. They never spoke about money in that household. They just lived, cheerfully, unconcernedly, and all the world was welcome to share what they had. I have seen Wen Hsien-sen take up the big crock of rice which Wen Tai-tai had just cooked for their supper and carry it down the hill to the conscript camp, to distribute it as far as it would go among those hungry men who were given only two meals of thin gruel a day. When he took it, Wen Tai-tai said nothing. She made no protest, but looked at him with her eyes strangely like his own, and went to cook another kettleful for her children.

Wen Hsien-sen was a short, bow-legged man, with a large head and bulging brow. But one quickly forgot the element of the grotesque in his appearance, there was such warmth of strength and kindness in his face. His eyes were remarkable – brown, not black; the thoughtful eyes of an idealist; dreamy yet penetrating. His voice was gentle and all his movements measured and a little tired. I never heard him angry; even in reproof he was quiet and kind. One of the little boys broke the half-gallon thermos jug. It was irreplaceable, for the prices of manufactured goods had gone up more than twenty times, beyond the reach of modest incomes. Wen Hsien-sen did not scold; he and the little boy looked at each other with tears in their eyes and he said, "Son, because you were careless, now twelve people will go without water at the shelter."

Some years ago Wen Hsien-sen, with his wife and the nine children they had then, went to the north-west to take part in the new Communist regime. Only after four of the children had died of the privations of that life did he give up and return to the south. Now a minor official in the government, he believed firmly in the Three Principles and retained all his socialistic ideals, and practised them. I have seen him, after a spill from a rickshaw on a steep curve, pick himself up and, without regard for his own bruises, help the coolie to his feet, help him to right the rickshaw, and let him rest before going on – whereas any other passenger would have berated the man for the wreck. He had none of the contempt for manual labour at one time prevalent among the educated class. He would carry water and chop wood with the servants; he would go up on the roof and straighten the tiles after a bombing. He made a garden, digging and planting himself, and all the older children with him. They were the nicest children I ever knew, well-behaved but unrepressed, always helpful toward each other.

Housekeeping in Chungking is contingent upon keeping the house. If the bombs sounded near, on emerging from the shelter I always sought anxiously to see whether we still had a place to live. The house was in such extreme dilapidation, it shook at the lightest step. Above our precarious ceiling there was no adequate roof, though Wen Hsien-sen and the coolie had gone up on top and tried to arrange the remaining tiles so that they would overlap a little. With the first heavy rain the apartment almost disintegrated.

Weeks of hot weather – temperature one hundred by day, eighty to ninety at night – broke in a storm. Cumulus clouds mounded up into the sky, rumbling with thunder. The air was almost unbreathable. Then the smell of rain and the sound of rain and a grey veil of rain advancing over the hills, and the first heavy drops splashing as big as silver dollars. The children laughed and ran out in the rain naked, their hair streaming, tossing their arms, trampling in puddles and shrieking with joy to stand under the pouring eaves. In our room the ceiling began to leak. Pao and I dragged the bed into the one dry corner and set basins, jugs, and kettles about the floor to catch the drip. The numerous receptacles gave forth a varied tinkling, each with its own note, a light *obbligato* to the roar of the rain and thunder. Presently above the bed the rain began to come through. With strings we rigged two umbrellas over it, and lying one at the foot, one at the head, we slept, quite dry though somewhat cramped.

In the morning the floor was swimming with water. We knelt on the bed, shipwrecked in this flood. The ceiling was soaked and bending dangerously under the weight of fallen tiles. It was a marvel it had held up all night. We hastily moved out to the veranda and conferred with the other tenants, whose rooms were in little better condition than ours. It was unsafe to live upstairs any longer, so we decided to break the padlocks of the landlord's rooms and occupy them. We wrote him a letter advising him of what we were doing, and all of us moved downstairs.

Whatever objection the landlord might have made was forestalled by fate. Two days later the sun came out; there was a *ching-pao* and we retired to the shelter at the foot of the hill. When we came back our house was gone —one big crater on the top of the hill and the house strewn around it in pieces. Wen Tai-tai and I looked at each other and laughed. It was so startling it was funny. The whole raid seemed to have been concentrated on the one object of demolishing our house, for the open cornfields round about were pitted with shell-holes.

After that Pao went to live at his office and I moved to the bank until we could find another apartment. The girls' dormitory at the bank had been demolished by a bomb which went through three stories, but rooms were allotted elsewhere in the building. I had taken with me to the shelter a couple of changes of clothing and a few toilet articles, so I did not need to borrow anything. After ten days we found rooms at a rental more than we could afford and again had a home of our own.

The landlady, a plump but hypochondriac widow with hard eyes, let us have the rooms only after she was completely assured that we had no children and no immediate prospects of any. She refused to let to any family with children. The noise was bad for her health. So in all the lonely house there was only one child, her adopted son Maomao, a little boy of four with a thin, rachitic body and the face of a skinned rabbit and a mischievous grin. She had no affection for him. She must have adopted him for the sake of her dead husband, and now, bored with the role of faithful widow, she was tired of the child also.

My heart went out to the poor little waif. He had no toys and the big house was gloomy. He was always slipping out to play with other children, a thing his mother did not allow because he got his clothes dirty. She would beat him and he would cry. In a little while he would forget and run away again. Many times a day I heard him being whipped. But wherever he was, when the *ching-pao* sounded he would run home as fast as his short bow-legs would carry him. He would put on his enormous straw hat which was as big as an umbrella, pick up his little bundle, and trudge behind his mother to their shelter. It was a stiff climb up two hundred steps. Often he would whimper, his face quite pale and drawn with fatigue, and sit down on a step until his mother hurried him on with impatient words. Then, uncomplaining, he would get to his feet again and climb on in the hot sun.

The landlady soon raised our rent. We were at her mercy. We had to pay or get out; there were plenty clamouring for our rooms. Every day there were fewer and fewer houses available in Chungking, as more and more houses were destroyed. The poor left for the country or went into refugee camps or built their own rude shelters of mats. The better class searched everywhere for rooms. Often, in the midst of preparing a meal, I would be interrupted by an invasion of people coming in uninvited, looking for a place to stay. They came in families, thrusting in without knocking, the woman usually in the fore, a baby in her arms, behind her trailing a procession of children, and the husband, somewhat sheepish, smiling placatingly, hovering in the background. The tale was always the same: "We have been bombed out. We have no house. Please take us in with you for a few days!" What could one say? But the "few days" would mean all the summer, all the year.

They would pry and inspect our rooms. One, the bedroom, was very small, not much more than a closet. "Why ... two rooms! And only yourself and your husband? Why, ten people could live in here and three in there, and we are only nine. ... I can cook. ... We would share the rent, the food. ... A few days only – until we can find a house. ..."

I could almost have blessed our acidulous landlady then. For, hearing the commotion, the high-pitched voices of the children, she would issue from her rooms across the hall. "Excuse me, it is my house. I am very ill. Tang Tai-tai always has a great many guests" – this with a reproachful glance in my direction. "She could not accommodate you. Excuse me, I cannot stand children. ... My own child, Maomao, would not be good company for your children; he is very wicked. We have no room for you here. You see how it is." All the time herding them toward the door, sweeping them out with the torrent of her explanations.

One who knocked at our door was a slim young soldier in shabby, ill-fitting uniform, whose tanned, high-cheeked face seemed vaguely familiar. "Please come in," I said, trying to remember who he was. At my bewilderment the visitor laughed – a girl's laugh! – and called me by name. Then I knew her – Lin Shing-ru, whom I had seen last on the lawn of our university in Peking! She had slipped out of Peking one dark night, through all the circles of Japanese guards, and crossed into guerilla territory. She had been with the guerilla forces for months. She had learned how to handle a gun; she was a good fighter, she said, with a flash of her beautiful white teeth in a smile. She was on her way to the armies in Kwangsi.

I remembered her in our student days, a good athlete, a slim figure in shorts, her long bare arms and legs well-muscled, her hair cut in a straight bob with curls on the forehead. Now she wore her hair short but not shaved. One lock fell forward over her brow; she had a trick of flinging it back with a spirited toss of the head. She told of Peking under Japanese control. "They have cut out of the books the whole of our history since 1911. The children are not permitted to learn of Sun Yat-sen and the revolution. And they must parade with flags – the five-striped flag of occupied China and the red sun flag of Japan – to celebrate 'deliverance' on the anniversary days of the fall of Shanghai and of Nanking." There was bitterness in her voice. But when she spoke of herself, her voice was level and unemotional. She had been married. She had a baby somewhere in the north, left with her parents. Her husband had been killed three months after their marriage.

Lin Shing-ru stayed with us a few days. We made up a bed for her on the couch in our big room. When she left, climbing up the staircase street above our house, turning every few steps to wave and smile, looking like a young boy soldier, not a university graduate, and the mother of a baby, I wanted to run after her, hold her back, beg her not to go. But what life was better than the one she had chosen for herself? My own? And so she went, and though she promised to write, I have not heard from her since.

We were seldom without guests. One evening Pao brought home with him Ho Ensui, a brother graduate of the Central Military Academy. Ensui stayed two months. We gave him the couch in the living-room. Then the Y.W.C.A. was bombed and they sent me two of their lodgers. We moved the bed into the larger room and the two girls and I bunked there, while Pao and Ensui slept on the floor in the bedroom.

Ho Ensui was tall for a Chinese, with a square, serious face, very pink and brown. He was on sick leave from the north-west front, where he had been wounded. Though he still carried his arm in a sling, his fine physique made nothing of the injury. He was polite, honest, clean, and very, very sincere, entirely without a sense of humour. He and Pao are representative of that group of young officers, patriotic with a focused intensity which leaves scant margin for tolerance of any dissenting viewpoint, centring their loyalty upon Chiang Kai-shek, who is to them the man who can fuse all China by sheer strength of his conviction. He is to them the only hope of unity, the one man able to bring together all the diverse factions into national accord for a concerted effort of resistance and final victory.

Of our two girls guests, one was Chen Kefan, who had been doing Christian social work among the poorest of the country people, the last few months in a hill district where conditions were most primitive and there was not food enough to eat. In order to understand their problems, she entered into the life of the peasants completely, lodging with them in their crowded, dark, filthy hovels, sharing their inadequate diet, pointing out to them here and there a better way of living, but for the most part baffled by their desperate poverty and ignorance. She had striven against illiteracy and had started a vaccination campaign. She had broken through the reserve and suspicion which mark the attitude of the peasants toward an outsider. They liked and trusted her. "The groundwork is done, now," she said. "We can go ahead." But after some months she had collapsed under the strain. She was badly run down and anaemic and had contracted trachoma from poor food and lack of sanitation.

She brought with her only a little bundle of clothing and an old quilt with the caked grey cotton showing through a rent in the cover. She was always dressed in grey, always prim. I did not know her very well and she made little conversation. But she would sweep the floor and help with the cooking, and she was gentle and wise with Maomao, who adored her. Oddly enough, she had a thick, heavy body and deeply tanned face, which gave the illusion of health. But she tired easily. Her expression was stolid, belying her keen mind. When she smiled, however, one's first judgment of her was reversed.

There could hardly have been a greater contrast that Li Lisan, as unlike Kefan as possible. She stood in the doorway as though doubtful of welcome, holding out to me the note of introduction from the Y.W.C.A. She had a small, pale face and straight black hair, swinging to her shoulders. Her eyes darted nervously, with

231

a frightened, sad look. She wore a flowered *shan*, so beautifully cut and fitted that it could have been tailored only in Shanghai or Hong-Kong. She was perhaps nineteen.

The note gave me information about her. She had been a problem child at the Y.W.C.A. hostel, for she was so outspokenly Communist in her beliefs there it was embarrassing for them. She was of a well-to-do family in Shanghai. Her parents were divorced. She had been in a very good boarding-school, and spoke English fluently. But she could not remain in that "paradise in hell", as she called it. (The letter of introduction stated only the bare facts. I learned much from Lisan afterward to supplement it.) On fire with eagerness to do something for her country, she came to Chungking – by steamer to Hong-Kong, thence by plane, for she had plenty of money. It was her plan to go to the north-west, to the loess caves of Yenan, where the Communists have their domain, to wear a soldier's uniform, cut off her hair, eat millet twice a day, and suffer all their hardships. At Sian she was not allowed to proceed. She stayed for a time with the American missionaries there, but they did not like her ideas. So here she was back again in Chungking, but she was restless and constantly talking of another escape to the north-west. Meanwhile she earned good money, giving lessons to foreigners in the Chinese language. The Y.W.C.A. had helped her to the job, hoping it would steady her.

As far as I was concerned, she could be as communistic as she pleased; I didn't mind. But with Pao and Ensui, two Kuomintang men, in the house, I foresaw clashes. At our first meal together she told all her history and plans. She would tell anyone without discretion. She was always full of beautiful theories and noble ideas. When she talked of them, her great dark eyes glowed and she flushed prettily. Ensui slightly rose and bowed to her gravely. "I admire your patriotism," he said. "You have been willing to give up an easy life to come thousands of miles into the interior, and you choose the hardest of all, the north-west. This is really worthy of much praise."

Lisan looked startled. She had expected argument. For a moment she hesitated, suspicious of mockery. But Ensui's eyes were sincere. She turned on him the full dazzle of her smile. She leaned toward him, talking earnestly of capitalistic exploitation, but Ensui was looking at her eyes and her bright painted lips, on his own lips a dreamy smile. Lisan, vivid with righteous indignation, was really very attractive.

Lisan and I shared the narrow bed at night; Kefan had the

couch. Lisan kept me awake late, whispering questions about Ensui. "It is a pity he is not a Communist," she sighed, at length. "I shall teach him." Next morning, when Lisan had gone to her work, Ensui said to me, "She is very young. . . . I am going to convert her." I groaned inwardly. "Trouble!" I thought.

After some days we arranged with the landlady to let us have a room for Lisan, a tiny closet space where firewood had been stored. In the house next door we found a place for Kefan, in the loft under the sloping roof. We cleared a space wide enough to set up a bed. Pao and I had our bedroom again and Ensui returned to the couch in the living-room. We shared meals. It was the only way to cut down expenses to the dimensions of our income. Pooling our resources, we were able to have an amah to do the cooking, though Kefan and I helped.

Pao understood nothing of the problem of the budget. Once on the first of the month he generously turned over his entire month's pay to a friend in the office who had just had his house bombed. It was ostensibly a loan, but such friendship loans are tantamount to gifts. The best we could hope for in return was to be invited to a fine feast in gratitude, sometime when Pao's friend was in funds. We solved the problem by writing an article for the newspapers concerning the war in Europe. Pao has a keen mind for military strategy, and with his first-hand knowledge of European conditions just before the war he was able to make a clear analysis. He wanted to do the article for prestige only, but I showed him our lone five-dollar bill and persuaded him this was not the time for such gestures. For once he drove a good bargain. It brought us through the crisis without borrowing money.

The amah did not stay long with us. Lisan, for all her high-minded principles of equality, in her attitude toward servants and inferiors was like any other spoiled young lady of a rich family. She showed no consideration; she treated them as though they were not human beings. She was often lavish with tips, but was impatient with mistakes and furious on slight provocation. She accused the amah of stealing, but this was not proved. Lisan never knew how much money she had. Bills were thrust loose into drawers, left lying on the table, blown to the floor by the wind. Her door was never locked.

So the amah left and Kefan and I did all the work. After two weeks we found a woman servant to do the cleaning, but she could not cook, so we still prepared the meals. Ensui and Pao ate our cooking without comment. It was not good. We boiled or fried the food and served it. It was not raw; that was as much as could be said for it. Lisan detested it. Our dishes were not good enough to tempt her capricious appetite and not bad enough to exalt her with a sense of self-sacrifice. When we had gone a number of days without meat, which was expensive and hard to get, and the meal came on the table – beans and boiled turnips again! – it would be too much for her. She would send the amah out to the restaurant for some chicken or fish to add to our menu. Though she did not help with the work, she was free with money and shared with us all these sudden extravagances.

Water supply was our greatest problem, a recurrent crisis all summer long. The house was not piped; only the very richest homes in Chungking have plumbing. There was an outlet of the city water-mains about two hundred steps up the hill, and we paid forty cents a load – two bucketfuls – to have it delivered. But bombings, which continued unabated, frequently disrupted the mains or damaged the pumps. Then our water-carrier would bring up a scanty supply from a shallow well in the fields below. In two or three days the well would go dry, so many households were depending on it. Then it would be necessary to bring water from the river, much farther away, so that it took much longer for each round trip and the quantity delivered was proportionately diminished. The river water was a rich golden-brown colour, thick with silt, and it cost three, four, five dollars a pailful. The carriers reaped a rich harvest and grew arrogant; we were on our knees to them. Often in the early morning I would go into the street to intercept a carrier and beg him with smiles and polite words to bring us a little – half a pailful, even – so that we could wash our faces.

But in accordance with the law of supply and demand, the worse the water was and the more expensive, the more difficult it was to get any at all. The carriers were earning more in half a day than they had made in a whole day. Why work full time? When our big earthenware storage jar was empty we had to buy water by the kettleful from the tea-shop, enough for drinking and cooking purposes. Only two or three cupfuls could be allowed for a complete sponge bath, and afterward the same water was used to wipe the floor. We could scarcely afford to wash the dishes. Piles of unwashed clothing, rank with sweat, awaited the end of the water famine. Then when the city water flowed again, and our regular carrier came in, smiling and reasonable, with pails brim full of clear water from the mains, what delight! We would plunge our arms into the water, splash it into our hot faces, lift it in our cupped hands, and let it run back again in a bright stream. I never realized before how precious water is.

Maomao was ill. First he had measles; then he had bronchopneumonia. I saw the whole bungling business from beginning to end, standing by helpless, for his mother would not let me take him to a hospital. Her husband had died in a hospital. She tried, one after another, various Chinese doctors, who prescribed dark brown messes which the child promptly vomited. The sickroom was a hubbub of relatives, all proffering advice. They gave him water to drink in which gold ear-rings had been boiled – harmless enough. He had convulsions and they called in a Taoist beggar priest to make spells over him. He had more convulsions and they burned four little spots on his abdomen with a hot iron.

Then they called in a very renowned Chinese doctor from down-river, distinguished for two things: he saw patients only at night and he smoked opium. The government had tried to cut off his opium, but he said, "How then can I cure people? No opium, no strength. And so no cures." And as he had cured many important officials of many extraordinary complaints, he was allowed to continue smoking opium. According to his custom, he came at night. He looked at Maomao and felt the pulses of both wrists and in the hollows of both elbows. Then he wrote his findings on a paper – the measles had gone into the heart. He prescribed a potion to drive the measles out of the heart, collected a fabulous fee, and departed. The medicine did not cure Maomao, for he was unconscious, and when they tried to pour it down his throat he choked and became quite grey and the precious liquid trickled from his mouth and was wasted.

At the last, when each breath was a struggle, the mother let me call in a foreign doctor, who went over the child's chest with a stethoscope, shrugged his shoulders, and said, "It's too late." He gave a hypodermic of some stimulant, and for an hour or two Maomao's colour was a little better. But it was too late. When Maomao died, the mother wept loudly as was expected of her. In all, she had spent over twelve hundred dollars. The relatives all consoled her, saying, "It could not be helped. It was his time to die. You did your best and did not stint money to give him every care. It was fated." I wanted to scream, "You fools! Between you, you have killed him!"

The death of Maomao passed almost unnoticed. So many

235

deaths.... The servant washed all his little clothes and hung them in the sun to dry. She washed the floor and aired the bedding and put away the little paper packets of unused drugs and poured out the scummed potions brewed for him. There was no funeral. In China when children die there is little ceremony. The small coffin was carried away to be buried in the common grave. Even that cost four hundred and twenty dollars.

There was a full moon then, and for eight nights we had the *ching-pao*. One day ran on into the next without demarcation. and all sense of time was blurred. Yesterday morning, seen through the haze of endless, monotonous hours since, seemed aeons ago. We went about in a somnambulant daze. Sleep we snatched when we could and the borderline between dream and waking was indistinct. Nerves were frayed and unsteady.

Lisan and Ensui quarrelled. They were so alike, so opposite, both so young and passionately sure in their convictions. They were drawn together by the very qualities which made it inevitable that they must clash. They would walk together to the shelter, deep in argument, and sit together on one bench, spellbound in continuous, low-voiced debate. But after a week of day-and-night raids, when we had returned in the dawn to our apartment and I had dropped asleep instantly, I was wakened by their angry voices in the living-room.

"You are a Communist!" Ensui was saying scornfully. "You came from Shanghai here, and all the way luxuriously by ship and plane! You talk of going to Yenan to join the Reds – you talk but never go!"

"It's you – your Kuomintang – that will not let me go!" Lisan flashed in answer.

I stood in the doorway but neither heeded me. On either side of a table, they stood and glared at each other.

"You do not know what hardship is," persisted Ensui. "You cannot eat plain, common Chinese food – in the north-west you would starve to death. When our dinners are not good enough for you, you send out to the restaurant for something better. You get money tutoring foreign capitalists and you buy new dresses –"

Lisan sparkled with anger. "What do you understand! To you a Communist must be in rags and always throwing bombs!"

"No, but my best friend was a Communist," said Ensui – "a real one! He was of good family, but he gave up everything and went to the Reds. He was with them on the Long March –"

"If you admire them so much, why aren't you one?" Lisan demanded. "Because you care more for a flag and a name on a map than you do for the people. You like shouting and waving, and you condemn to death those who love China in a better way than you do —"

White with fury Ensui strode from the room. Lisan crumpled up in tears. "Oh," she moaned, "I hate him! I hate him!" She fled to her room.

When Ensui returned, looking very much like another Pao, with a *hsiung* young face, hurt and refusing to show it, I said to him, "Ensui, do not be too angry. She cares for you too."

"Sister-in-law," he said, "I love her. But I cannot change my beliefs for her. Truth is precious and more precious than love, sister-in-law."

"There are many truths," I said. "Truth is not the same for all, Ensui. She also believes, though she does not always live up to her convictions."

"Sister-in-law, I cannot change my allegiance or shirk my duty for a woman. The wife must follow the husband," he said.

I sighed. For each one, truth is self-fulfilment. Because of this, a year ago I had sent Pao back to the lines; I had given him back to his duty, perhaps to death. If I had held him from it, we should have grown to hate each other. For the greatest death is the betrayal of a man's self-fulfilment. . . . Yet it is constantly asked of women, and thought their natural duty.

September, October. . . . Raids are fewer now. Often it rains. Our house has escaped bombing. Even the glass in the windows I have saved unbroken, for I keep the casements open during raids. Pao and Ensui have freshened the stained plaster walls with whitewash. There is a wine-red rug on the floor. There are books in a little bamboo rack of shelves, some linen in the cupboard, curtains at the windows. A big blue bowl holds pale green autumn orchids and porcelain-pink begonias. I take pride in these possessions. They are worth nothing; they are junk — but all through the summer I have collected them and cleaned them and worked with them, making the setting of a home, until they have become mine and most valuable. Each time I leave for the shelter I open the casements; I look around once in good-bye. When I come back and everything is there as I left it, it is all given to me again, new. It is more dear and lovely for the threat of loss.

By the end of summer Chungking looks like Pompeii. Not a

Pompeii coloured pink and golden, all tragedy blurred and dulled by the passage of centuries; but a grey, unkempt, and dusty Pompeii of gaunt ruins, smelling of ashes and of death. But already wide streets are being cleared and everywhere spring up new shops, one-storey flimsy buildings of lath-and-plaster, painted bright blue and red and green; new restaurants, new bazaars. People are coming back from the hills, from the country. The theatres and cinemas are full.

In the morning the dew stays wet longer on the grass. Daylight comes later, and often with a fog as dense and white as bean milk. Slowly, as the fog thins, we discern grey outlines of houses, the curve of a hill-top, then trees blue-green in the haze and the golden sand and gold-brown water of the river and the faint blue outline of more distant mountains. The summer is past. In the newspapers the headlines are of the bombing of London. In smaller type it is mentioned elsewhere that the outskirts of Chungking were bombed again today. Grey rain dims the high ranges of the south bank. Grey cloud makes a low ceiling. The city hums with noise and work and hope. This is Chungking, not dead Pompeii – five hundred thousand Chinese with a will to withstand, to endure and build again. Next year, next spring, the planes will lay it waste again. Next autumn we shall be building. . . .

CHAPTER THIRTEEN

COMING OF AGE IN CHINA

The fifteenth of October, the Moon Feast. Autumn. The end of the second summer of bombing. The days will grow shorter; the mists will shelter Chungking. The low grey skies of winter will hide us. There will be cloudy nights and mornings of dull fog. We shall sleep. . . .

But tonight the sky is crystal, delicately luminous, curving to a horizon of dark, irregular hills, grey on the pale gold of evening. The full moon clears the world's edge, writes its scribble of silver and gold in the moving water of the river. We have forgiven the moon. Even though the planes come, it is beautiful. Even if at midnight the red lanterns are hung out on every hilltop and the sirens hoot for a *ching-chi* and we must snatch up our bundles and run to the shelter, we will enjoy this hour unshadowed. We will rejoice in the moon's beauty in the mellow autumn dusk.

We had invited guests for the evening – Kefan, the Wen family, Ensui and Lisan. To be in the tradition, we should have bought yellow wine and pea-nuts and salted meat and white moon-cakes, spreading a feast out of doors, that we might eat and drink and watch the moon's gradual ascent. But instead we had bought melons, huge red *hsiang-shan* melons and yellow sweet melons. They were spread out upon the table on the terrace and Lisan and I cut them up and Kefan poured out tea to cool it a little.

The silver night concealed the broken, scarred, patched ugliness of Chungking about us. But we were more conscious of it than in the frank daylight. We were so accustomed by now to ruin and wreckage that for days we did not think of it, but picked our path over rubble heaps and around bomb craters with utter unconcern. Then a night like this would stir memories of undisturbed loveliness and order – O moon on the Peihai Lakes, moon over the fields of Pihsien! – and we would pause and wonder, "What are we doing here on this dump-heap of Chungking? Why are we here? Why?" From the conscript camp, down by the river, weary bugles strove in hopeless uncertainty for one sure note in unison. Their unhappy disonance wavered questioningly and never came to rest.

We talked of other times, other places. Pao said: "A year ago when I was in the north-west, a night like this with an immense moon to eastward, I went up on the walls of the little town where we were garrisoned. The moon is even whiter there, more intense, and the hills naked and white as winter in the bleaching light. I heard singing, the *Song of the Exiles* – Pao hummed that haunting minor melody that has trailed across China with the exiles from Manchuria:

> My home is in the north-east, on the Pine Flower River,
> Where else can there be,
> Deep forests above, coal below,
> Mountains and plains covered with kaoliang,
> There are my brothers, my old father and mother.
> For many long years now I have wandered,
> Drifting along the floating wave of life.
> Oh, when shall I be back on the Pine Flower River,
> Among the man-high kaoliang of my home. . . .

"Three soldiers of the old north-eastern army were sitting on the parapet, looking toward the moon, toward Manchuria. For almost ten years they had been wandering, ever since Japan took their land from them. We talked. They told me they were unhappy. Years in the bleak north-west and never any hope of seeing their homes and families again. Fighting the Communists; afterward, with better spirit, fighting the Japanese. Fighting, marching, and no prospect but death at the last, as so many of their comrades had died. I gave them money, all I had with me – they got only eight dollars a month – and they accepted it with dignity. But it seemed to mean more to them to hear again the northern tongue and to talk freely with no barrier of rank between us. 'If all our officers were like you,' they said, 'we would follow them to the death.' "

"If we win this war –" Ensui said. He spoke quietly and his voice dispelled the bombastic oratory of a hudred patriotic speeches. "If we are to win, it will not be with driven armies but with led armies. Your old-time war lords, when they levied troops for civil wars, snatched coolies off the street, tied them neck to neck with ropes, imprisoned them in barracks, marched them into battle under guard, and put them in the front lines to be killed off first."

Lisan nodded. "Down there" – she gestured toward the river-bank – "the conscripts are dying of hunger typhus – on two bowls of watery gruel a day."

Ensui said, "That is a thing which is changing. For centuries in China official corruption has been almost taken for granted. But now we are ending all that."

"You will need to change more than that," answered Wen Hsien-sen. "For the war will not be won by armies. Generals think in terms of military moves, using bodies of troops as though they were chess pieces. Such a victory of technique is not possible. The army is drawn from the people. It is a living thing and its spirit is the spirit of the people. And sometimes the people have not had enough rice to eat. That breaks morale. The price of rice –"

Every one broke in. For if there is one absorbing question in China, it is the price of rice. All else – wages, costs, the sound-ness of currency – everything is based upon that standard. For months now the price of rice had risen in a steepening curve, until it had reached a point beyond famine prices. Why? Every-where people asked, "Why?" The season had been dry, the crop less than normal; that we could understand. Blockade, the dis-location of communications, the influx of thirty million refugees, the depreciation of Chinese currency in terms of foreign ex-change – there were other complex factors which always in war-time increase the cost of living. But all these facts together did not explain the dizzy advance of prices to ten and twenty times their standard a year ago, with rice in the lead.

"Mountains of rice in the granaries and none to be bought in the markets for food," said Kefan. "Speculators holding for a top price, holding it back for days, and the people unfed."

Lisan, her eyes enormous in her narrow white face, said: "How long will the people continue to make the sacrifices demanded of them? Their sons are sent off to the front. Profiteers keep theirs at home. There is not petrol enough to train pilots for the air force, yet every time there is a raid alarm the rich men's concu-bines go off in motor-cars fifty li into the country and back. Trucks are insufficient for bringing in munitions, yet there are companies with influence importing luxury goods, illegally, at exorbitant profit. Why should the people go on making sacrifices to win the war? The victory is being thrown away."

Pao said quietly: "You are quite unfair."

"These things happen! They have been proved!" Lisan flung back.

241

"That may be true. Isolated instances. No war in any country has been without its profiteers. Some officials are corrupt. In some divisions, especially those still under the control of former war lords, conditions are as you say. But you make a statement and it seems to cover all China. China is very big. Szechwan alone is larger than all Britain. You accuse and it is easy to accuse, for you are the opposition and you do not have the test of putting your theories into effect. We also see that these things are wrong and that they exist. But we must move slowly or we shall have disorder and anarchy."

"If you would move at all!" Lisan exclaimed impatiently.

"Less than ten years ago in Szechwan," said Pao, "the war lords did as they pleased. Opium was their chief source of revenue. Opium lands were more extensive than wheat lands. They collected taxes thirty years in advance. These abuses have gone. You say there has been no advance?"

"What other country," Ensui demanded, "at grips with a ruthless enemy, has done what China has done? We have built roads and kept up production. Our factories have been dismantled and the machinery carried inland on the backs of coolies. Our universities have fled to Free China, their students following often for a thousand miles on foot. Do you call this nothing?"

"This is what we are doing?" Pao said proudly. "We have our own social plan, slower but no less effective. One thing is to be remembered. What we have accomplished is proved by this: the Chinese have stood up to three years of war and through it all have stood as one people, together."

"The whole meaning of this war," said Wen Hsien-sen thoughtfully, "lies in the Three Principles of Sun Yat-sen. Sovereignty of the people – nationalism. The people's rights – democracy. The people's livelihood – perhaps the foundation stone of all – their food, their work. Victory must assure these. Only in this hope will the people fight. In this lies the strength of our resistance. Men will not fight for a nation unless it is *their* nation. The leaders seek to arouse them to fight for a name, for a label upon a map, for high-sounding words, for a flag, but how long will they continue to do so unless these are symbols of a life and a hope worth defending?"

The bugles had ceased. A noisy insect known as a *chiao-ku-ku* made a clattering in the grass like the machinery of some cheap mechanical toy. Another sound, a rhythmic, muffled yowling, intruded on my consciousness, and I realized it had been going on for half an hour or more. The landlady beckoned to me from the door. I went into the house. She wrung her hands in distress. "Tang Tai-tai, what shall I do? There's a mewing in the drain-pipe."

"Mewing?" I repeated.

"Yes. I believe the cat fell in. Would one of the gentlemen climb on the roof and see if he can get it out?"

"No," I said, "don't interrupt them; they are trying to think. I'll attend to it."

The drain-pipe was of tile, plastered over, descending from a gutter along the edge of the roof. I climbed out of the attic window with a flash-light in my hand, gingerly scrambled down the slope, silver-tiled in the moonlight, and reached the gutter. From the terrace below the voices of our friends rose clear, and a new voice, a large, pompous voice I knew at once, though I peered over the edge of the eaves for verification.

I do not like stout, middle-aged men in uniform, straining the buttons of their tunics. This man was an officer Pao had to be polite to. Wide jowls and narrow, low forehead, making a trapezoidal face wider at the bottom than at the top, shaven scalp, a roll of fat over the collar behind. No serious thought ever creased his brow. His features habitually wore an expression of bland serenity, disturbed only when something interfered with his meals or when someone contradicted him. The hours in his office were from seven in the morning to seven at night, and this official's cap was always well in evidence during the appointed hours; his bodyguard would hang it up for him outside his door. He was good for shouting slogans and making patriotic speeches, wherein he exhorted everybody to make sacrifices and die for the nation and work twelve hours a day. He always perspired a great deal and gestured with a clenched fist for emphasis, so that he would descend from the platform streaming wet and so exhausted he had to go home to rest. He had fought in one minor engagement eight years ago in the campaign against the Communists, and he was very proud of his military record. Many people suspected him of hoarding rice.

Everybody was standing up in respectful greeting and there was a buzz of polite welcome. I decided to remain on the roof. I crawled along the gutter to the drain-pipe and flashed a beam into its dark hole. Yes, there was the cat, its eyes round and golden, staring at me. It gave a piteous yowl. I stretched down the full length of my arm, but could not reach it. To the landlady, watching at the attic window, I said, "Get me the kitchen tongs."

I craned over the edge of the roof. The fat official had accepted the best arm-chair and was helping himself to three dollars' worth of melon. (They cost a dollar and a half a pound, fifteen times the cost of a year ago.) His mouth full, he said, "I don't know what we are coming to. I never saw such rude people as the lower classes in Szechwan. The rickshaw puller just made a row over the fare. Said the distance was more than bargained for and living was so expensive these days. And when I kicked him he laid hold of me and made such an outcry a lot of people gathered round. I was finally extricated by a policeman. But the policeman refused to arrest the rickshaw puller, even when I told him who I was. Merely slapped him and told him to go his way – and then he told me to go my way, too! Nowadays coolies think they are as good as anybody else!"

I heard Lisan's voice, metallic-sharp. "Do you blame this coolie for being conscious that he is a man, not a beast of burden to be beaten and kicked at will?"

"The young lady is very democratic, very!" I could see the disagreeable smile with which he turned to look at Lisan. "But these people" – with a wave of the plump hand – "my dear young lady, they were not worth your consideration! Foreigners judge China by these swarms of dirty fellows, with their puny bodies and dull faces, and for that reason they despise us as a 'nation of coolies.'"

"Go and get the axe!" I said, with more vehemence than necessary. "The cat has slipped down so far I can't reach it at all. We'll have to smash a hole in the drain-pipe."

"But my drain-pipe!" wailed the landlady. "It cost more than the cat. Oh, let the wretched beast go! It will die in a day or two and then we can shove it down through with a bamboo."

"I'll pay for the repair of the drain-pipe." I said. "Get me the axe."

On the terrace below the conversation continued, no one heeding our colloquy on the roof.

"Perhaps nutrition has something to do with the difference in physique," suggested Kefan.

"And are you forgetting," Wen urged, "that Chinese history is crowded with the names of sages and great scholars and statesmen who have come of peasant forbears? In China we have never maintained caste distinctions."

244

And Kefan added, "I am afraid you do not know them. I have lived with them."

"And I," said Ensui, "at the front. I have fought beside them, these 'inferiors', made only to obey and to die. They fight well. They have courage. We shared danger and hardship. When I left them they wept and from their meagre pay contributed money to buy me a beautiful, useless present, which one of them walked fifty li to the nearest town and back to buy for me. Coolie soldiers."

Wen leaned forward, fixing the official with his gaze. "You have probably heard and resented Hitler's gibe at our 'coolie armies.' For my part, I never felt prouder of our Chinese troops. Yes! Coolie armies! Armies of load carriers, boat pullers, peasants, armies of the underfed and overworked – those coolie armies standing against the mechanized forces of one of the world's Great Powers. Since then I glory in the word 'coolie'. One day the coolie of China shall be recognized a man, a citizen, in dignity before the world."

"They shall have rights that none but the Communists give them today!" cried Lisan.

The official looked from Lisan to Wen Hsien-sen in some amazement, then ponderously turned his back on them and addressed himself solely to Pao and Ensui. "This is very radical doctrine; I need not say, dangerous as well. I do not believe in Communism and neither do you, I know. The Communists traffic with the Japanese; they do not fight; their generals are no better than bandits –"

"We have not heard of any Wang Ching-wei among them," said Lisan smoothly. "And the accusation that Communist forces are not fighting in this war is slander. It is well known that in one year the High Command sent fifty-two congratulatory telegrams to the Eighth Army for its successes."

The official, determined to ignore Lisan, continued to Pao and Ensui, "They seduce the youth. They do not practise the Confucian virtues. They believe in free love; woman's chastity is violated –"

"A favourite accusation!" sneered Lisan. "You would keep woman's chastity sacred by holding her a slave, to be bought and sold, with a certain market value for virginity as for the lack of it. In Communist areas there is no prostitution and no concubinage. Men and women are equal and free. Among them there are true marriages, not contracts for transfer of property."

"The young lady seems to know a great deal about free love," the official said, looking now at Lisan.

She sprang up; her voice shook with anger. "Insult me! That is all you can do because you cannot answer me! Reactionary!" She spat the word, the strongest epithet in her vocabulary. She was crying now. She swung round upon Ensui. "And that – *that* is what you are fighting *for*. That represents your party, your Confucian virtues, that fat –!" Sobbing, she rushed into the house.

As I climbed the roof to the attic window, tiles crackling a little under me, I could hear Pao making apologies for her. "She's only a neighbour, a rather excitable schoolgirl. Don't worry about her; she really does no harm. Yes, I'll watch her."

I went down one flight of stairs to the second-story veranda, where I tapped up and down the drain-pipe to discover where the cat might be lodged. The landlady handed me the axe and I hacked into the plaster. The official's voice came up to me between blows: "Ah, yes. These young people. Must have discipline, control. They must not be allowed to run wild. They must be taught the Confucian virtues – ah – Propriety, Uprightness, Integrity, Self-respect." In Chinese it is *Li, I, Lien, Chi*. He rattled off the monosyllables with the glib meaninglessness of constant misuse. "Hope she's not a friend of your wife's. Your wife – fine woman, by the way – I haven't seen her this evening."

"She's cooking," Pao said. He always says that when he does not know where I am. It makes a good impression with such visitors as this, whose idea of woman's sphere, is "bed, board, and baby."

"Yes, yes, fine woman. Unspoiled by education, no crazy ideas."

The drain-pipe tile cracked into a hole. I enlarged it. A long furry black tail whipped out. I seized it and pulled. There was an ear-splitting yowl. I pulled harder; it was coming. Just as the rump appeared, instinctively I slipped a hand under the cat's belly and eased it through the hole. With a last howl the cat came free, clawed my hand deeply, leaped from my arms, and streaked through the door. The fiendish noise had arrested the attention of every one below on the terrace. They were all staring upward, but the shadow of a pillar partly hid me. I made a motion to the landlady to be silent and backed out of sight against the wall, shaken with laughter. "Just a cat fight," said Wen Hsien-sen, who, I think, had seen and recognized me.

The official made his farewells. I lurked within the hallway waiting for him to go. At Lisan's door I paused, but did not knock or enter. I could hear her stifled sobs. When the official was gone I unobtrusively joined the group on the terrace.

"Where have you been?" Kefan asked.

"Doing some obstetrics – Caesarean section on a drain-pipe and breech extraction of a cat," I said.

Wen Hsien-sen tilted back his chair, his high, bulging forehead white in the moonlight, his eyes musing. Out of the silence, seemingly apropos of nothing, he remarked, "Mencius said, 'Who cultivates his greater self becomes a great man. Who cultivates his lesser self becomes a small man.' "

Pao said: "You know he is not representative. He will be demoted one day, and we shall have our turn. We are young. In China youth is still a fault. Our time will come."

"Keep young," cried Wen. "The tragedy and failure is that men grow old. They acquire wealth, they become reactionary and cautious because they have so high a stake in stability. Youth dares, because it has nothing to lose but life. Even Wang Ching-wei had his heroic youth. And when I say 'youth' I am thinking of a quality of spirit. There are those who are born old, or who become old by choice. The sons of rich men, wanting security, comfort, coldly calculating the money reward, looking for advantage; the proud officials who feel themselves superior, for whom the Old Hundred Names ought to slave –"

"Who cultivates his small self becomes a small man," repeated Kefan. "This is very close to Christian belief – he that saveth his life shall lose it."

Lisan came out of the house, a coat over her arm. She came slowly down the steps, as though making a stage entrance. She paused for the exact moment of suspense, then said, "I am going away."

"Where will you go?" I asked.

"To – friends. . . ." Her face quivered.

"You have nothing to fear, Lisan. It is quite unnecessary for you to go."

She shook her head. It was for her a great dramatic moment. She would be able to say afterward, "I could not stay. After I had defied a high official – told him the truth – I would have been arrested. I left that night – alone – on foot. . . ."

We stood up stiffly, making an awkward leave-taking. Lisan and Ensui avoided each other's eyes; there was no reconciliation there. She tilted her chin stubbornly. "I shall find a way yet to go to Yenan. If they turn me back, if they arrest me, I shall make the attempt again. They cannot stop me unless they shoot me!" This for Ensui's hearing, bravado to his taunts.

Kefan and I walked with her to the gate. At the last moment Lisan flung aside the veil of restraint between us with an impulsive gesture. "Why do you not come with me? You cannot be happy here, repressed and hedged about by this kind of life."

Kefan smiled at her. "My work is here."

I said, "I have always wanted to go to the north-west. But it would be flight. Here we stand against the drift, our efforts often cancelled by reaction. We make little advance, but we stand. Someone must. We still believe the future belongs to us."

She looked at me with incomprehension and shook her head. "Well ... good-bye ... I shall send someone for my things. I don't think I am coming back." Looking very small and lost, Lisan walked away. We did not go with her farther; we understood she had a longing to go away from us.

Then Ensui said under his breath: "I suppose she will tramp all the way to Yenan in those thin-soled slippers, and wearing silk and her lips reddened!"

Wen answered: "Even if she flames up in false heroics, there is a core of sincerity in her. She is unhappy. She is seeking for something, for truth and meaning."

"We are all looking for that," I said, "that our lives may not be wasted and valueless, like water poured out on the sand. We want to give ourselves to something beyond and greater than ourselves."

"There is no need for them to go so far. For me the code of my ancestors, the Confucian ethic, the party principles are enough," Pao said firmly.

Wen shook his head. "There is no efficacy in moral codes in a society where man is coerced and enslaved, his labour bought and sold as a cheap commodity. You would uplift the people by teaching them the Confucian virtues. But Mencius, who was much bolder than Confucius, said: 'Feed the people and they will be virtuous.' So simple and radical a teaching. It is what Sun Yat-sen meant when he spoke of the people's livelihood. Confucius addressed himself to the superior man, but Mencius believed in the goodness of plain, common man. I have wondered sometimes what Chinese history might have been if Mencius and not Confucius had been accepted as our guide.

"Mencius said: 'Whom the court favourites call wise, do not select him for office. Whom the nobles applaud, do not choose

248

him.' But if the people have faith in a certain one and say he is wise, take him and test him, he is like to prove wise indeed. Use him! He also spoke of the right of revolution. Small wonder the Ming emperor commanded that Mencius be cast out of the Hall of Philosophers."

"The greatest of the world's thinkers are misunderstood or rejected," said Kefan. "See what codes and theologies and systems of religion have been built up around the teachings of Jesus, until humanity refuses to recognize Jesus the Socialist, who would be their comrade in the struggle for justice."

"Jesus, ah yes, a most extraordinary man," murmured Wen. "Yes, I have read His sayings. He and Mencius would have understood each other."

The hour was late. Our guests rose. Wen stood at the edge of the terrace. "Some believe in codes and discipline and organization. Some want the violence of class struggle to set the world right. Others believe that only the spirit can save man. But all of you want the same thing: to remake the world in the image of your truth – to find your own selves, to find yourselves in others." He lingered before he spoke again, a little solemnly.

"We all want the same thing, only our words are in conflict. Words, slogans, we have been taught. We are trained on words, they become a substitute for thought. Hatred is propagated through them. Think through them to the reality beyond, and determine if it be good or evil. The only thing worth fighting for is life, a shared fullness of life for all the people. Let us not give our youth to any lesser cause. . . ."

Toward morning I was awake and restless with thought. Quietly I slipped from bed. Pao's rhythmic breathing of sleep continued without break. I leaned from the window. The moon was past the zenith, stooping toward the west. Along the eastern horizon, dark, with no colour of dawn yet visible, stars marched in file. . . .

I saw again Pao and Ensui, their young faces drawn hard and stern, a little tragic in their grim earnestness; Lisan, burning too bright and fiery for a steadfast purpose, unequal to her passionate convictions; Kefan, perhaps the best revolutionist of us all, with her prim mouth and her hands at rest in her lap. . . . And beyond them I saw youth marching. . . .

As I had seen them marching. In the Forum of Mussolini, their heels ringing on the tessellated pavement with its myriad-times repeated pattern of *Dux, Dux* – black-shirted lads of twelve and fourteen, flinging up their arms in the Fascist salute. Refugee Catalan children in camps of exile, marshalled in line, singing, in rags, their legs blue with cold in the keen wind of this northern land, but singing the remembered, splendid songs of Spain. Steel-faced youths at Nuremberg, steel helmets low on their brows, uniformed thousands in step; one power, one purpose, one shout – Germany awake! Straw-shod Chinese students followed on foot a dream of freedom half way across a continent. Coolie armies, young men with the callouses of the shoulder-pole in their necks, young boys with the round cheeks and slender arms of childhood, grey and khaki-clad armies. Youth conferences I had attended – I could see again the eager, merry faces of my friends, the proud heads, tawny and russet and black, the boy and girl students of Europe, Asia, and America, coming together to plan a world without war; how many of them have died in wars since? Files of young coolies, the load grooving deep the flesh of the shoulder, the strain of tense muscles to an effort too much to be required of them.... Youth marching, like the stars along the horizon, and no pallor of dawn yet....

Everywhere, all our generation, and Pao and I with them, caught in the whirlpool of war. Some plunging into the current, joyous, eager for the testing, shouting of flag and country and cause, dying for symbols. Others, as young but unillusioned, seeing clearly the wasted sacrifice of life and the greater death in the hardening of spirit to hatred, lying, and killing. We are all swirled into the current, rushed into experiences of terror and exaltation. But what it does to us – that we determined for ourselves. There is no true adventure save within oneself. No experience has significance until one has received it and made it a part of oneself in thought.

So, as from a hill-top looking back over the long road traversed, I saw the direction and distance I had come since my twenty-first birthday in Hong-Kong, two years ago. I had a sense of maturity, a true coming-of-age. And what I had seen as a war of resistance only – China defending her freedom against Japan's aggression – I knew now for a single motif of great intricacy in a pattern involving all countries. What we thought was a war like other wars, simple in aims and dimensions, we know now for a change of world, a new age.

I seldom pray, for I do not think it right or profitable to demand of God that He rearrange the universe for me. But what I did then, in the hour before the first daylight, amounted to prayer. For it was an asking of life; it was a pledge to that awareness in me that reaches beyond flesh and space and time to the universal, which is God.

"I know You," I said, "to the extent that I know myself this moment. You are that spark in me, in Pao, in all of us, that will lay down life for an ideal; that knowledge within us that there is no fulfilment but in giving. It is what Wen Hsien-sen calls being young, what Mencius calls being a prince, what Jesus calls being the Son of Man. May we keep this, Pao and I. On this earth, this infinitesimal grain of dust whirling among the stars, the only value, the only reality, is Man. Make us great enough in spirit to compass the whole world of Man within our love. Let us never be warped to the purposes of leaders who would make us hate each other blindly. Let us possess our own souls, unswayed by the shouts of the crowd. Let us keep our ideals quietly and hand them on to others."

The dawn comes, misty. The road past the gate, narrow between walls, is a bridge between vague infinities of mist. Figures are born out of the whiteness, materializing to my sight; they cross the few rods of visibility to fade, ghost-like, into the pale fog. Coolies, the first of the day-long procession, climbing up and going down the steps with their loads. Some in their strength, swinging the balanced weights easily at the two ends of a shoulder-pole, calling to each other loud greetings, cheerful because it is morning. Some with muscles like taut cords, their faces strained with cumulative exhaustion, driven each day beyond their capacity. Coolies. The man-power of China.

I do not use the term as generals use it, pointing to this inexhaustible source of armies and more armies. Rather, I think of the words separately, "power" and "man". These are builders and carriers, the peasant farmers, the workers of China. They built the palaces of Peking and the Burma Road. They made the Great Wall and the shelters of Chungking. They keep traffic moving, carrying loads, pulling carts and rickshaws, towing boats. They keep life going; they dig in the fields, they plant and harvest. Everything in China depends upon them. Coolies. I would make the word "coolie" a name of honour before the world!

They go by as in a slow dream and they seem uncounted millions, coming out of the mist and going into the mist again. One of them stops. Slowly, with a grunt, he eases his load to the ground and stands panting. Then he crosses the road. There is

251

a newspaper posted on the wall. He pauses before it. His hand is raised. With his finger he follows the columns of characters, his lips shaping the words. Slowly, painfully, he reads....

We are not the important ones in China, we who ride in sedan chairs, while you bend to lift, to carry us. The officials, the bureaucrats, the would-be intellectuals – without you we are nothing. We are sterile and without power to create the future. The important one is you, coolie. You do not know how important you are, you who toil and fight and die dumbly, scarcely asking to know why. The significance of your gesture, coolie, when you raise your finger to trace the words on the wall ... it shows me that something curious is awake in you, is beginning to ask questions. It is a gesture of profound meaning, and I who watch am suddenly happy and confident of the future, because I see you, in the mist of dawn, lift your finger to read....